Capital Investment in the Middle East

Ragaei El Mallakh
Mihssen Kadhim
Barry Poulson

with assistance from
Fred R. Glahe
Carl McGuire

The Praeger Special Studies program—
utilizing the most modern and efficient book
production techniques and a selective
worldwide distribution network—makes
available to the academic, government, and
business communities significant, timely
research in U.S. and international economic, social, and political development.

Capital Investment in the Middle East

The Use of Surplus Funds for Regional Development

Praeger Publishers   New York   London

Library of Congress Cataloging in Publication Data

El Mallakh, Ragaei, 1925–
    Capital investment in the Middle East.

    (Praeger special studies in international economics
and development)
    1. Capital investments--Arab countries. 2. Arab
countries--Economic conditions. 3. Arab countries--
Economic integration. I. Kadhim, Mihssen, 1941–
joint author. II. Poulson, Barry Warren, 1937–
joint author. III. Title.
HG5816.A3E4   332'.0414'09174927   77-8026
ISBN 0-03-021986-8

PRAEGER SPECIAL STUDIES
200 Park Avenue, New York, N.Y., 10017, U.S.A.

Published in the United States of America in 1977
by Praeger Publishers,
A Division of Holt, Rinehart and Winston, CBS, Inc.

789   038   987654321

Printed in the United States of America

To our wives, with gratitude

This volume addresses a major and relatively new element in the fields of economic development and international finance—the phenomenon of surplus capital funds accruing to a few members of the Third World. With the drastic rise in crude oil prices in 1973-74, the massive inflow of so-called petrodollars to the major petroleum-exporting countries has given rise to claims that the rich, industrialized nations are now markedly less rich, the poor countries of the world are much poorer, and in the Middle East itself, the gap between rich and poor has widened so greatly that in no other region can such a vast disparity be seen. There, countries boasting among the highest per capita incomes globally, and significantly above those of the United States, are neighbors of nations whose annual per capita incomes hover near or below $500.

From this situation, which is reshaping the world economy and investment—what some would term the New Economic Order (NEO)—a set of problems emerges. These seem derived from a number of apparently contradictory factors: (a) while affluent, the economies of the oil exporters remain firmly in the developing stage; (b) their absorptive capacity for capital is, in most cases, severely limited; (c) the manner, direction, and degree of utilization of surplus funds could be a critical influence on economic and political stability or lack of such stability internationally; and (d) the level of petroleum output and its availability to the consuming nations are directly related to the ability of the producers to invest their capital productively both domestically and abroad. In this last factor, regionalism will likely play an increasing role.

This study has four distinctive characteristics. First, it concentrates on the place of economic factors rather than sociopolitical elements in bringing about any form of regionalism, however loose, among the Arab countries. Political inputs, nonetheless, are not disregarded, particularly where they have a direct relation to and impact on the economic considerations. For example, the volume deals with the interaction of political and economic variables in such situations as the crucial policy of rapprochement between Iran and Egypt, the two population axes of the Middle East. Such a policy is leading to Iranian investment in Egypt, for example, in the Suez Canal area. Again, the post-Nasser Egyptian open-door policy with reference to investment and encouragement of private enterprise is having repercussions throughout the region in an improved climate for capital mobility. This has played no small part in the establishment of the Gulf Authority, an institution financed by Saudi Arabia, Kuwait, Qatar, and the United Arab Emirates to channel economic assistance to Egypt. Yet another case has involved the recent diminution of friction between Syria and Egypt and its replacement by a level of coordination unexpected by many. The economic liberalization initiated in Egypt has been adopted, to a lesser extent, by Syria and even Iraq. The analysis used in the following pages is an economic approach to the investigation of determinants, implications, and possible evolution of the economic relationship between the Arab world and the West.

The second characteristic marking this volume is the projectional tenor. Maximum use has been made of the most current data available, and an inventory of existing financial and other regional institutions and their operations has been provided. This information has been employed to explore the potential for regional cooperation and to forecast its likely development. The scenarios presented, their likelihood and implications, should be of considerable benefit in formulating U.S. policy in the Middle East.

Third, the book provides information concerning regional developments in the Middle East which, being scattered in numerous reports, position papers, and memos in Arabic, is not readily available and/or is generally inaccessible. Specifically, the study possesses an all-important dimension represented by information pertaining to policy alternatives, objectives, motivation, direction of future change, and, in particular, perception of the issues by the policy makers in the Middle East. This information was obtained directly through interviews and discussions with high-ranking officials, business leaders, and economists in the Arab world over a number of years. Such background knowledge and interpretation are unequivocally of prime value in understanding the thinking of Arab economic policy makers and thus should serve well in fashioning U.S. policy, as well as that of other industrialized nations, toward the Middle East.

Finally, the volume is distinguished by the raising, outlining, and preliminary analysis of many related questions and issues and by the suggestion of avenues for further research. It shows the potential for regional cooperation in the Middle East, but does not neglect to emphasize the limitations and obstacles facing regionalism. In this sense, the study offers a clearer perspective with regard to the tensions between obstacles and opportunities.

The authors wish to acknowledge the assistance of the National Science Foundation in funding a part of the research project's costs, and the support of the International Research Center for Energy and Economic Development. The persons to whom our appreciation is due are numerous, indeed. Our colleagues in the Department of Economics—Professors Kenneth Boulding, Malcolm Dowling, Morris Garnsey, Charles Howe, Dwight Lee, Robert McNown, John P. Powelson, Lawrence Senesh, Larry Singell, and George Zinke—were unfailing sounding boards for theories and methodology. For their encouragement and suggestions, the authors wish to thank Professors Bent Hansen (University of California, Berkeley) and Charles Issawi (Princeton), Dr. Robert Mabro (Oxford), Dr. Herbert E. Hansen (Gulf Energy and Minerals Company-International), and Dr. C. A. Gebelein (Shell Oil Company).

Among our graduate students at the University of Colorado, mention should be made of Kathy Adams and Myles Wallace, and of the valuable resource offered by our foreign students and graduates, particularly those from the Middle East region: from Algeria, Abdel Kader Akacem; from Egypt, Dr. Hassan Selim (now director of economic research, Abu Dhabi Fund for Arab Economic

Development) and Dr. Faika R. Selim (presently director of economic research, United Arab Emirates Currency Board); from Kuwait, His Excellency Abdul Muttaleb Al-Kazemi (minister of oil), Dr. Muhammad Nasseer (undersecretary for economic affairs, Ministry of Oil), Dr. Yousef Al-Awadi (Gulf Bank), Dr. Faisal Al-Kazmi (deputy managing director, Kuwait Foreign Contracting, Trading, and Investment Company), and Taleb Ali (University of Kuwait); from Iran, Dr. Ahmad Shahshahani (University of Tehran) and Mohammed Fardenesh;from Saudi Arabia, Zain Barry and Abdullah Yamani; from Morocco, Dr. Abdulhaque Belkora (now with UNCTAD); from Libya, Dr. Taher El Jehaimi and Dr. M. El-Hassia (both with the University of Benghazi) and Ali Elhoudieri, from Iraq, Ismail Hummadi (Ministry of Planning); from Yemen (Saana), His Excellency Abdul Aziz Adbul Ghani (prime minister).

A number of government officials from the United States and from other countries have been generous with their time and expertise in supplying data and giving interviews. These include: Robert Blake, Frederick Levy, Gerald Newman, Peter Tosini, Di Pak Roy, Thomas D. Willett, John Bushnell, and Bernard Zinman, all with the Department of the Treasury; Howard Steinberger and Lawrence Dash with the Department of State and the Agency for International Development, respectively; George T. Beck of the Department of Commerce; Larry Rosenberg and F. Thomas Sparrow of the National Science Foundation. Among those in the Middle East, our appreciation is extended to Dr. Ali Attiga (secretary-general of the Organization of the Arab Petroleum Exporting Countries), Dr. Mahmoud Riyadh (secretary-general of the League of Arab States), Dr. Jaeb Jaroudi (president, Arab Fund for Economic and Social Development), His Excellency Ahmed Zaki Yamani (minister of pertroleum and mineral resources, Saudi Arabia), His Excellency Dr. Mana Saeed Al-Otaiba (minister of petroleum, United Arab Emirates), Dr. Mansour Al Turki (deputy minister of finance, Saudi Arabia), Dr. Hasham Jewad (Ministry of Planning, Iraq), Dr. Khodadad Farmanfarmaian (chairman of the board, Bank Sanaye Iran), His Excellency Dr. Hamad El Sayeh (minister of economy and economic cooperation, Egypt), Dr. Abdelhafez El Rifai (Ministry of Finance, Sudan), Dr. M.A. Hassanain (head of the Economics Department, Organization of the Petroleum Exporting Countries), Abdellatif Al Hamad (director-general, Kuwait Fund for Arab Economic Development), Dr. Akeel Al-Sadi (World Bank), and Dr. Mohamed Finaish (alternate director, International Monetary Fund).

Finally, constructive suggestions and contribution have been made by Dr. Dorothea El Mallakh, Nancy Glahe, Dr. Sieglinde Kadhim, Esther McGuire, and Karen Poulson. Although this has been a rather lengthy listing, the depth and scope of this volume have benefited from contacts with many others who gave freely of their time and knowledge.

Ragaei El Mallakh
Director, International Research Center for
  Energy and Economic Development, and
Professor of Economics
University of Colorado
Boulder, Colorado

December 1976

CONTENTS

LIST OF TABLES

LIST OF FIGURES

LIST OF ACRONYMS

ADFAED	Abu Dhabi Fund for Arab Economic Development
AFESD	Arab Fund for Economic and Social Development
AIIAD	Arab Institute for Investment in Agricultural Development
AMPTC	Arab Maritime Petroleum Transport Company
AOPEC	refers to the Arab oil-exporting countries and Iran
APIC	Arab Petroleum Investments Company
APSC	Arab Petroleum Services Company
ASRY	Arab Shipbuilding and Repair Yard Company
ECWA	United Nations Economic Commission for West Asia
EEC	European Economic Community (the Common Market)
GDP	gross domestic product
GNP	gross national product
GVA	gross value added
IBRD	International Bank for Reconstruction and Development, also called the World Bank
IFED	Iraq Fund for External Development
IMF	International Monetary Fund (Washington, D.C.)
KFAED	Kuwait Fund for Arab Economic Development
LNG	liquefied natural gas
LPG	liquefied petroleum gas
NEO	New Economic Order
NNP	net national product
OAPEC	Organization of the Arab Petroleum Exporting Countries
OECD	Organization for Economic Cooperation and Development
OLS	ordinary least squares regression analysis
OPEC	Organization of the Petroleum Exporting Countries
SDF	Saudi Development Fund
UAE	United Arab Emirates
UNCTAD	United Nations Conference on Trade and Development

Capital Investment in the Middle East

The Use of Surplus Funds for Regional Development

Of the many dreams of the Arab world since World War I, one dream seems today to stand a good chance of being translated into reality. The dream is Arab economic integration and the catalyst for its possible realization is the late dramatic surge in oil revenues. The current greater economic cooperation among the Arab states, though directly and indirectly precipitated by the world energy crisis, has a relatively long history of ebbs and flows. Aside from political factors,[1] the drive for regional integration has rested, and still does, on the potential benefits accruing to the individual Arab states from a regional approach to economic development. This involves the mobilization and efficient utilization of regional resources—in particular, surplus petrofunds—the establishment of wider markets for industrial and to a less extent agricultural products, and the functioning as an economic bloc vis-a-vis the rest of the world. However, regional planning, if carried out at once, would entail significant—albeit transitory—costs for some Arab countries. Therefore, it is imperative to stress simultaneously the long-term community and convergence of interests among the Arab states, as well as the need for creating a viable regional institutional structure within which potential economic conflicts can be resolved and compromises reached.

Historically, aside from some general sentiments, immediate material incentives for cooperation, that is, visible gains of expanded economic and trade relations, were notably small among the Arab states which for the most part, economically as well as politically, were not oriented toward each other. Recently, and particularly under the impact of the newly discovered wealth, oil, this picture has been changing. In the absence of capital shortages, industrialization hinges directly on the efficient utilization and/or expansion of the supply of existing regional cooperant factors of production, special manpower resources, and the amalgamation of isolated and generally small national markets. This has contributed to the growing awareness of the potential benefits derivable from regional cooperation. Thus, at present economic cooperation is actively practiced in the hope that it will eventuate in economic integration, instead of waiting until an appropriate framework for economic integration can be created. In order to put current developments in perspective, it is essential to trace briefly the evolution of regional integration among the Arab states. Such an analysis will highlight the opportunities and impediments regional integration has encountered in the Arab world.

THE EVOLUTION OF REGIONAL INTEGRATION
IN THE ARAB MIDDLE EAST

The history of economic cooperation among the Arab states may be conveniently divided into four periods: the Ottoman and the mandate period, the World War II years, the postindependence years extending into the early 1970s, and the current period. During the Ottoman and early mandate period, a semblance of a regional market existed whereby goods could move freely between the Arab countries, and a uniform ad valorem tariff rate was levied on imports from outside the Ottoman Empire.[2] However, the absence of quantitative or qualitative restrictions on the movement of goods among the various contiguous Arab countries did not stimulate significant trade for at least three important reasons: lack of adequate transportation facilities, the predominantly nonmonetized nature of Arab economies, and the virtual absence of significant industrial production. In fact the de facto customs union area was essentially to facilitate trade of certain European powers—notably Britain and to a lesser extent France—with the Ottoman Empire, rather than to promote the movement of domestic products within the Empire.[3]

Until 1930, this picture remained essentially intact despite the dissolution of the Ottoman Empire and the emergence of new states under British and French mandatory authorities.[4] The mandatory powers, while recognizing the existence of economic ties between certain neighboring Arab countries, made no attempt to foster economic integration among these countries within a broader regional framework. During the 1930s, however, and under the combined impact of the Great Depression and the imposition of protective tariffs and other trade restrictions, the then existing regional market was considerably narrowed. Monetary developments reflected in the adoption of new national currencies tied to the pound sterling or the French franc resulted in further deterioration of inter-Arab trade. The emerging states needed revenues, and foreign trade presented an easily accessible as well as lucrative source. Therefore, it was only natural that tariffs and duties were raised or newly imposed on various imported and exported commodities. These measures were also conceived of as a necessary means to promote industrialization for they tended to shelter potential industrial establishments from fierce competition from abroad. Although the protective motive was seemingly important, the basic underlying reason for higher tariffs was undoubtedly the collection of revenues.

The impact of these developments was mirrored in significant reduction in inter-Arab trade; consequently, there was little semblance of a regional market in the Middle East by the close of this period, 1939. Nevertheless, some important Arab economic ties persisted within the framework of the free-trade relations between Syria and Lebanon under the French mandate, between Egypt and the Sudan under the Anglo-Egyptian condominium, and between Transjordan and Palestine under the British mandate for Palestine.[5]

The outbreak of World War II soon arrested further economic disintegration among the Arab countries as Egypt, Sudan, Greater Syria, Iraq, and the countries of the Arabian Peninsula came under the jurisdiction of a regional planning agency, the Middle East Supply Center—a joint Anglo-American agency entrusted with the task of ensuring, on the one hand, the availability of adequate transport and quay space for incoming war materials and, on the other hand, the provision of essential supplies to the civilian population of the Middle East. Within an international wartime framework, the Middle East Supply Center succeeded in effecting once again some functional integration among the Arab countries.[6] But because of the limited economic base of the Arab countries, in particular their industrial base, inter-Arab trade remained small in real value and limited in composition. Nevertheless, the existence of the Middle East Supply Center and the disruption of normal supply lines because of the war maintained a regional market to some extent. This loose regional framework could not withstand, however, the rebirth of economic nationalism soon after the war was ended and the supply center terminated.

As the war ended the apparent economic integration among the Arab countries was being gradually but steadily eroded, notwithstanding the emergence of many Arab countries as independent states and the creation of the Arab League in 1945.

In fact, independence appears to have fostered nationalism; state after state introduced new qualitative and quantitative trade restrictions and raised the levels of existing ones. Moreover, Arab multilateral trade relations suffered a severe setback due to the loss of Palestine which was the hub of a network of trade relations among many Arab countries. Palestine's trade with other Arab countries was both considerable and diversified, as it was probably one of the most industrialized countries in the region. The cessation of trade with Palestine subsequent to the creation of Israel and the mounting political and military tension in the Arab world which followed were factors responsible for the sharp decline in multilateral trade in the region. However, several Arab countries, including Egypt, Saudi Arabia, Syria, Jordan, Iraq, Lebanon, and others, concluded bilateral agreements with one or more Arab countries to facilitate and expand their trade and to conserve precious foreign exchange.[7] These agreements may be classified into three categories.[8] The first includes agreements expressing the desire of the contracting parties to intensify trade relations with each other on the basis of the most-favored-nation clause. The second category comprises agreements providing preferential trade treatment involving lower tariff rates for commodities originating with either party, as well as exemption of import and export licensing for selected commodities. In most cases a commodity was considered of local origin when Arab raw materials and domestic labor costs were not less than 50 percent of total production costs. The third type of trade agreement established free trade as a matter of general principle but retained qualitative and/or quantitative restrictions on specific commodities. These agreements suffered from two major weaknesses: almost all of them were of short duration, ranging from six months to one year subject to automatic extension, and the commodities receiving most preferential treatment were those classified as farm products and livestock and their products.[9] Consequently, their impact on the volume and composition of trade among the Arab countries was limited. In other words, the lack of permanency or at least a sufficiently long time horizon in these agreements frustrated their basic objective, the creation of a semi-integrated economic environment less restrictive to growth and industrialization. Moreover, the emphasis on agricultural products perpetuated the lopsided composition of trade between Arab countries, thus giving existing and potential industries little if any encouragement. Generally inter-Arab trade increased in absolute value but the impact of the several bilateral agreements was not sufficiently strong to bring about a rise in regional trade vis-a-vis the rest of the world. In fact, regional trade decreased in proportional terms because of a substantial increase in trade with countries outside the region.[10]

Inter-Arab trade was also closely influenced by political relations between contracting partners. When such relations were good, trade increased, and when political relations deteriorated trade declined precipitously and almost instantly. Such was the pattern of trade between Egypt and Syria, Egypt and Saudi Arabia, Egypt and Sudan, Iraq and Kuwait, among others.

Thus, by the early 1960s, the evolution of the economic and political relations among the Arab countries had placed these countries ". . . in a position of being for the most part neither politically nor economically oriented toward each other for a common market undertaking."[11]

Interest in multilateralism rekindled in the 1960s, perhaps as a response to the initiation on March 25, 1957 of the European Common Market. Egypt, Iraq, Syria, Jordan, and Kuwait finally ratified by June 1964 the Economic Unity Agreement initialed two years earlier by a larger group of Arab states. The agreement constituted basically a declaration of intent on the part of the signatories to undertake certain general steps at an unspecified future date to effect complete economic unity among themselves. The principal measure envisaged in the direction of economic unity was the creation in stages of a common market. The first phase, providing for the establishment of a free-trade area among the signatories of the agreement on January 1, 1965, was accepted only in principle. In practice, trade relations among the Arab countries continued to be dominated by bilateral agreements of short duration, mainly motivated by the desire to find outlets for surplus production or access to imports for which payment could be made in inconvertible domestic currencies. The failure to effectively implement the Economic Unity and related agreements may be attributed to a multiplicity of factors, including the hasty adoption of an overly ambitious form of economic integration, the absence of detailed studies regarding the benefits and costs of integration for individual states, the mounting political strain in Arab relations subsequent to the 1967 Middle East conflict, the lack of an adequate multilateral payments system, the increasing involvement of the government in the economy in Egypt, Iraq, and Syria (thus substituting planned trade for market-motivated foreign-sector flows), and the concern of some states about the latent dangers of economic polarization elsewhere and backwash effects at home. Thus, it is not surprising that regional economic integration in the Arab world did not make many inroads during the 1960s.

OBSTACLES AND RATIONALE
FOR REGIONAL DEVELOPMENT

Obstacles

The tracing of the evolution of regional integration in the Arab world indicated some of the difficulties encountered in its realization. This section briefly outlines some of the major obstacles and assesses their significance.

The following are the most important obstacles to economic integration: (1) different economic systems; (2) different stages of industrial development; (3) shortage of foreign exchange and absence of a multilateral payment mechanism; (4) the importance of tariff as a source of government revenue; (5) variations in trade and exchange controls and economic relations with Third World countries; and (6) absence of adequate regional infrastructure, scarcity of skilled labor, and the difficulty of acquiring foreign technology.

There are, in general, three groups of Arab countries. Lebanon and the Gulf countries, for instance, enjoy market-oriented, free, and open economies. Countries such as Algeria, Egypt, Syria, and Iraq are characterized by planned, state-dominated, and controlled economies. The third group comprises countries like Tunisia, Morocco, and the Sudan with various shades of market orientation and planning and a significant degree of government control. The removal of qualitative and quantitative restrictions and the opening up of the domestic markets of the planned economies to investment from the market-oriented free economies may present a basic conflict in economic organization. Moreover, the potential benefits from economic integration between states in different stages of industrial and general development tend to be polarized; the relatively advanced countries offer better investment environments and are better equipped to take advantage of the wider markets and opportunities provided by the region. Such polarization raises questions of equity and acts as a deterrent to integration. This is precisely the case with respect to the Arab states. Countries like Saudi Arabia, North Yemen, the Sudan, and to a lesser extent Iraq and Jordan feel that their industrial development may be jeopardized if industrial products from Egypt and Syria are granted free access to their domestic markets. Furthermore, Arab governments with the exception of a few oil exporters depend heavily on revenues from customs duties, which amount to about 20 to 40 percent of the total revenues of their ordinary budgets.[12] These governments are either unable or unwilling to replace any possible diminution in import duties as a result of integration by introducing new domestic taxes or raising the levels of old ones. Thus, they are loath to implement integrative measures without adequate assurances that their economic and fiscal interests will be safeguarded.

Greater economic ties between Arab states are also frustrated by the lack of an efficient and modern regional transportation network, the scarcity of skilled manpower, and the difficulty in mobilizing sufficient capital and in acquiring foreign technology.

These impediments to Arab economic integration are not insurmountable; however, given the current economic fabric of the various Arab states, it seems that these hurdles may be resolved only within a regional planning framework. Regional planning could ensure an equitable and optimum distribution of industries that is in consonance with regional factors endowment. But it must be pointed out that:

> The achievement of such an optimum would, however, meet with both technical and political problems. The evaluation of dynamic comparative advantages within the region involves complex technical issues. The question becomes more complicated if the distribution of activities among countries has to be modified, as dictated by the principles of dynamic comparative advantage, in order to assure a certain degree of politically balanced regional allocation of resources.[13]

The necessary modification of the industrial structure of certain countries must be accomplished in a gradual manner and with adequate compensation paid to those members suffering significant economic losses. This could be achieved if each member state agreed to liquidate its own inefficient industries in the long run by letting depreciation and obsolescence take their course.[14] Meanwhile, in addition to paying compensation, the regional grouping would assist its members in the expansion of their more efficient lines of production.

Furthermore, for a regional-planning approach to be successful, no fundamental or substantial changes in the economic system of any Arab state are required; each member state could accommodate the adopted regional distribution of economic activities within its existing framework of economic organization. This obviously obliterates a major obstacle in the way of economic integration. However, the feasibility of such an approach was until recently constrained by the inadequacy of capital resources at the disposal of the Arab countries, including the major oil exporters. Most Arab countries devoted the bulk of their resources to the creation of a modern physical and social infrastructure, an activity that, unlike industrialization, requires little formal regional cooperation. With the exception of Kuwait, the capital resources of the Arab countries, including the oil exporters, were hardly sufficient to sustain their own development on a modest scale. Consequently, the incentive for economic involvement in the region and in joint ventures on an impressive scale was lacking. Thus, until the early 1970s, capital transfers were comparatively small and most Arab joint enterprises were restricted in scope and very limited in terms of capitalization.[15]

The Rationale for Regional Development

The benefits accruing from economic integration relate essentially to three factors: greater efficiency of production, higher levels of growth and industrialization, and improvements in the terms of trade and economic relations with the rest of the world.[16]

Production efficiency in the Arab world is low due in part to the limited size of the market. The market for most industrial products is small, not only because of the small population, but more significantly because of the low per capita income and the disintegrated character of markets, caused primarily by poor transportation facilities. Such conditions tend to constrain the possibility of exploiting economies of large-scale production or lead to the underutilization of existing production capacities, thereby increasing per unit cost. As a result, producers earn lower profit margins and final and intermediate users must pay higher prices for the products. Economic integration by widening the market eliminates most or possibly all of these problems.

Economic integration in the form of a common market arrangement may also quicken the pace of growth and industrialization in the region for reasons quite different from those related to the broadening of the market. Such an economic grouping would increase and diversify the resource base, thus permitting the establishment of certain efficient and competitive industries. Take for example the development of a weapons industry in Egypt which must import large amounts of war materials and weapons every year. Labor, iron ore, technical skills, and to a lesser extent, energy are available in Egypt. However, capital is extremely scarce, rendering the development of this vital and highly capital-intensive industry by Egypt alone virtually impossible. The recent accord between Saudi Arabia, Qatar, and Egypt establishing such an industry in Egypt with a capital exceeding $1 billion is a vivid demonstration of the benefits of regional cooperation. This study will document other instances in which regional cooperation has been instrumental in the creation of new industries and facilities in the Arab world. Generally, however, it is evident that the resource base of most Arab countries is extremely skewed. Some countries, notably the small Gulf states, have almost nothing except oil and natural and associated gas. Others are very well endowed with agricultural land and water resources (the Sudan, Iraq, Syria). Still others have an abundant labor supply (Egypt, Morocco, Algeria). Economic cooperation among the Arab countries may not only alleviate the detrimental impact of this pronounced skew of the resource base, but also, provided such cooperation is sufficiently extensive, turn the skew to an advantage rather than an impediment to economic development. In fact, it is hardly possible to envisage the small Gulf states attaining the present stage of economic and social development without the substantial labor inputs of the labor-surplus countries of Egypt, Lebanon, and in particular of the Palestinian people.[17]

Regional cooperation can also be a potent element in promoting efficient industrialization; the capital-surplus countries may insist on a regional capital utilization plan that pays explicit attention to the factors endowment of the region.* In making the flow of capital contingent upon adherence to an optimal regional distribution of economic activities, the capital-surplus countries perform a necessary and crucial role in fostering regional integration, because the recipient countries are made fully aware of the benefits accruing to them from active regional economic cooperation.

The economic weight of an integrated Arab bloc in international economic and political relations would be much greater than the sum total of the economic and political weights of the individual Arab states. The foreign trade of any Arab country (oil export excluded) with any major industrialized country or bloc of countries is relatively small compared to the total foreign trade of the latter. Thus, the bargaining position of the individual Arab state is rather weak. If, however, the Arab world is viewed collectively, its economic weight would undoubtedly be much greater; thus the bargaining position of an integrated Arab economic bloc would be considerably enhanced. In fact, in one vital export commodity, oil, the combined weight of the Arab producers is of global consequence. This may explain the relatively early cooperation of the Arab states on oil matters.[18]

Recently, the acquisition of modern technology and the securing of markets in the developed countries have become at least as important as the

---

*The concept of factors endowment must be perceived in a dynamic context and should incorporate, among other things, the element of locational advantage of potential industries.

improvement in the terms of trade for most developing countries, including the Arab states. Many Arab states are in the process of establishing several new industries, a few of which require sophisticated technology and wider markets than the region can provide.* It is, therefore, essential that the developed Western nations acquiesce in the transfer of modern technology and the opening up of their markets for certain Arab industrial products. The creation of an economically integrated Arab bloc would obviously augment the incentives for Western nations to act cooperatively.

Moreover, a larger economic entity would more easily attract capital from various sources including international lending institutions, bilateral and multilateral official aid, and private investment. This factor must have been very important in the past but the recent dramatic increases in oil prices and producers' revenues have decreased its weight. The shift in the capital status of the Arab region, however, puts into sharp relief the growing need for technical skills and technical assistance. A regional grouping would be in a better situation to acquire such skills and assistance not only because of its superior bargaining position, but also because of its ability to establish more efficient and profitable industries.

Although the Arab states stand to profit appreciably from an appropriately fashioned regional integration scheme, such an arrangement has been hindered by a variety of factors, most of which were outlined above. The recent emergence of many Arab oil exporters as important capital-surplus countries has infused new life, urgency, and interest into regional cooperation. The Arab countries, however, do not seem to favor the immediate revival of old integration blueprints or the hasty construction of new ones.† Their relatively long span of development as sovereign states with a few, albeit growing, economic contacts with each other appears to caution against any egregious overhaul in economic relations. Moreover, they have come to realize that greater economic cooperation must not await the establishment of an appropriate framework; instead, it should proceed as far as possible within the existing framework in the

---

*A case in point is the petrochemical industries. Another example may be the weapons industry referred to above.

†A high and distinguished Kuwaiti official emphasized that Arab economic integration "and what it could ultimately represent in terms of practical achievements, are too important to be left in the limbo of good intentions, or, even worse, used to justify hasty decisions that pave the way for still more frustrations." He goes on to stress the need for an "Arab Economic Integration Research Institute" that could specifically "investigate the real possibilities of Arab regional or subregional integration; study the various problems raised by economic integration; identify and prepare specific integration projects; elaborate a doctrine of Arab economic integration capable of taking the subject out of the rhetoric and the impotence of previous experiments into the area of sober analysis, realistic proposals and well-founded hopes."[19]

hope that such cooperation may in due time lead to an appropriate form of economic integration. Thus, economic cooperation has proceeded on several fronts: joint ventures, provision of bilateral and multilateral aid for general and development purposes, the creation of a number of developmental aid-extending institutions to channel capital funds on concessional terms more efficiently and on an ongoing basis, and the establishment of several private financial and investment institutions with a regional and international vista. There has also been growing interest in the coordination and harmonization of monetary and financial structures and policies of the various Arab states, and in the effective management of their balance-of-payments problems as mirrored in the recent establishment of an Arab Monetary Fund along lines similar to those of the IMF. All indications considered, regional economic cooperation among the Arab states does not appear to be an ephemeral phenomenon but rather one that is here to stay and probably intensify.

Regional cooperation, however, has not been confined to increased economic relations among the Arab countries, but has embraced greater economic cooperation between a few Arab countries and some non-Arab countries in the region, notably Iran and to a lesser extent Turkey. Iran appears to be drawing nearer to the region as witnessed by the recent Iranian joint ventures with, and aid extended to, Egypt and Syria. The relaxation of tension between Iran and Iraq subsequent to the settlement of their long lasting border dispute may prove serendipitous to greater and broader regional cooperation. The Arab policy, in particular Egyptian policy, appears to be emphasizing, for various reasons, that Iran is an integral part of the region. If the present political situation improves and stability prevails in the Middle East, the next decade will probably show a perceptible increase in regional cooperation on both the economic and political fronts.

MIDDLE EASTERN REGIONAL DEVELOPMENT
AND THE UNITED STATES

The extent to which the Middle East countries are willing to invest in the United States, to export petroleum products to the United States, and to import goods and services from the United States is a function of their level of financial surpluses and reserves. An analysis of these surpluses has been conducted in terms of the domestic absorptive capacity of these economies. However, existing studies of absorptive capacity have not adequately taken into account the opportunities for investment by the oil-producing countries in joint ventures, investments, and capital transfer for regional development in the Middle East. The available evidence suggests that the flow of surplus funds into regional development and into Third World countries is an important and growing proportion of these funds. The oil-producing countries appear to place a higher priority on investment and aid designed to stimulate development in the Middle East than on investment and aid outside the Middle East. There is also evidence of a commitment on the part of these countries to provide investments and aid for development of Third World countries. In this sense absorptive capacity reflects not only the commitments of the oil-producing country to domestic development but also to development within the region and in Third World countries. According to one source, the creation of an Arab financial system will have to be accompanied by the parallel blossoming of investment opportunities throughout the Arab world.[20] Sheikh Yamani of Saudi Arabia has long since drawn attention to this objective:

> The real solution to surplus funds lies in properly channelling them out into world investment opportunities on a long-term basis, spread over as many areas as possible. Unfortunately, most financial institutions concerned with the problem came with recommendations of investment opportunities which may become available in major industrialized countries alone. We certainly welcome these recommendations, *but they do not rank highest in the list of our priorities.* If an even distribution is sought, our countries should be recipients of the largest share. Since our financial markets are limited and can absorb only a part of our surplus funds, massive industrialization of our countries (in the region) can be the answer.[21]

It is this concept of absorptive capacity that is lacking in the existing literature which concentrates on absorptive capacity within the domestic economies of the oil-producing countries. To ignore the flow of investment, aid, and grants from the oil producers to other countries in the region and in the Third World is to ignore an important and growing outlet for surplus funds. This narrow approach to absorptive capacity is not a realistic appraisal, in the sense that it is likely to underestimate levels of oil production, exports, and imports in the oil-producing countries, and to overestimate the surplus funds available for investment in the United States and other OECD countries. From the standpoint of the United States this narrow approach to absorptive capacity is likely to severely bias projections of the level of oil imports from the producer countries in the Middle East, levels of exports to the region, flows of capital between the United States and the Middle East, and deficits in the U.S. balance of payments.

Absorptive capacity in this broader sense includes the following:

(a) Domestic absorptive capacity—the capacity of the oil-producing country to absorb revenues from the production and sale of petroleum products in outlets within the domestic economy, for example, in gross domestic investment, in consumption (including defense and welfare expenditures), and in imports.

(b) Joint ventures—with other oil-rich and/or oil-poor countries in the region.

(c) Regional investment and aid—in non-oil-producing countries in the region.

(d) Direct Third World investment and aid—direct investment and aid to developing countries outside the region.

(e) Indirect Third World investment and aid—investment and aid channelled through international agencies such as OPEC, the World Bank, and Arab Bank for Africa, among others.

(f) Direct investment in the developed world—purchase of equity interests in companies in OECD countries.

(g) Portfolio investment in the developed world—purchase of nonequity financial assets in OECD countries.

This study proposes to examine the above components of absorptive capacity concentrating on (a), (b) and (c). From the standpoint of the United States it is parts (f) and (g) that have the most important economic impact. However, these components of absorptive capacity are obviously interdependent, making the flow of surplus funds to the United States functionally related to the share of those funds that are allocated by the oil producers to regional development in the Middle East. Thus, the analysis is extended to explore the relationships between the flow of funds into regional development and the flow of funds into Third World countries and into the developed countries including the United States. Finally, the study provides a preliminary analysis of the implications of regional developments and cooperation in the Middle East for U.S. trade, capital flows, and balance of payments. The volume and pattern of U.S. trade with the countries investigated will be studied to ascertain how it will be affected by the projected regional developments and cooperation among capital-surplus and capital-deficit countries of the Middle East.

NOTES

1. Arab political unity has been a cherished goal of the Arab people since World War I. See Ahmed Tarbeen, *Arab Unity between 1916-1945* (Cairo: Al Kamalia Publishing House, 1959). (In Arabic.)

2. Alfred G. Musrey, *An Arab Common Market: A Study in Inter-Arab Trade Relations, 1920-67* (New York: Praeger, 1969), p. 7.

3. For an early economic history of the Middle East, see Charles Issawi, *The Economic History of the Middle East, 1800-1941* (Chicago: University of Chicago Press, 1966).

4. Mohammed A. Diab, *Inter-Arab Economic Co-operation, 1951-1960* (Beirut: Economic Research Institute, American University of Beirut, n.d.).

5. Musrey, op. cit., pp. 28-29.

6. Ibid., pp. 30-34. The agency was first British; it became a joint agency in 1942.

7. See ibid., p. 150, for a list of these agreements.

8. Diab, op. cit., pp. 22-23.

9. Ibid., p. 23.

10. Musrey, op. cit., p. 70.

11. Ibid., p. 106.

12. Ibid., p. 126.

13. United Nations, *Studies on Development Problems in Countries of Western Asia, 1974* (New York: United Nations, 1975), p. 47.

14. Ibid.

15. Diab, op. cit., pp. 20-23.

16. For these and other non-economic benefits, see Fadhil Zaky Mohamad, "Prospects for Arab Federation" (Ph.D. diss., University of Colorado, 1956).

17. See Ragaei El Mallakh, *Economic Development and Regional Cooperation: Kuwait* (Chicago: University of Chicago Press, 1968), for a discussion of the contribution of expatriate labor to the economic development of Kuwait; also Ragaei El Mallakh, "Energy and Economic Upsurge: The Arab States of the Gulf," (forthcoming), with respect to Qatar, the United Arab Emirates and Bahrain.

18. The Arab League sponsored a Committee of Oil Experts, which first convened on June 14, 1952. Further cooperation continued through the annual Arab Petroleum Congresses and OAPEC (Organization of Arab Petroleum Exporting Countries). See Abdul Amir Q. Kubbah, *OPEC: Past and Present* (Vienna: Petro-Economic Research Center, 1974), Ch. I.

19. See Abdlatif Y. Al-Hamad, *Building Up Development-Oriented Institutions in the Arab Countries* (Kuwait: Kuwait Fund for Arab Economic Development, October 1972), p. 8. The author is the director general of the Kuwait Fund for Arab Economic Development.

20. *International Currency Review*, November-December, 1974.

21. Ibid.

2

DOMESTIC ABSORPTIVE CAPACITY OF THE OIL PRODUCERS

THE CONCEPT OF ABSORPTIVE CAPACITY

The central analytical tool in this study is the concept of absorptive capacity. The concept of absorptive capacity can be elusive in the light of the existing economic literature; no less than nine different definitions of the concept were offered at a conference on capital movements, organized in 1965 by the International Economic Association. To make the concept operational in the present study, John H. Adler's definition of absorptive capacity is useful.

> Absorptive capacity may then be defined as that amount of invest-ment or that rate of gross domestic investment expressed as a proportion of GNP, that can be made at an acceptable rate of return, with the supply of co-operant factors considered as given.[1]

In order to examine the impact of regional cooperation on absorptive capacity, it is necessary to elaborate the concept in greater detail. In addition to those limiting factors that have traditionally been identified in the literature on absorptive capacity, there is a wider range of factors to be explored, whose constraints on absorptive capacity are especially important from the standpoint of regional cooperation. Traditionally, the constraints on absorptive capacity fall into four broad categories: (1) those related to the size of the demand and the markets; (2) impediments due to inadequate infrastructure and shortage of complementary inputs; (3) planning and implementation inadequacies; and (4) political, institutional and sociocultural restrictions. As R. F. Mikesell has pointed out, apart from the lack of financial resources itself, the alleged limita-tions of absorptive capacity virtually coincide with the gamut of growth-inhibiting factors.[2] The one limitation that is not included is the supply of financial resources. Here a distinction is made between absorptive capacity and capital formation. The latter term as normally used refers both to the supply of financial resources and to their transformation into real capital goods. Absorptive capacity in the usual sense covers the transformation act and the subsequent use of the capital goods formed. The generation or the transfer of the financial resources is not usually incorporated in the analysis of limitations of absorptive capacity.

While the above distinction may be relevant from the standpoint of an individual country, such is not the case when a regional accounting framework is adopted. When asking what are the constraints on absorptive capacity in the context of a regional grouping of sovereign states, the constraint on the supply of financial resources cannot be ignored. Without further anticipating the discussion in later chapters, it suffices here to note that in a regional context it is necessary not only that capital be accumulated, but also that it be mobilized for productive use.

The following section outlines and appraises some important studies of domestic absorptive capacity of the oil-based economies in the Middle East. These studies generally assume either explicitly or implicitly a rather high degree of regional labor mobility. The analysis, moreover, is usually not restricted to "pure" investment but encompasses practically all types of government expenditures including subsidies and transfer payments.* This deviation from the investment approach referred to above is deemed necessary for the following reasons.

First, the investment approach focuses on the expected productivity of capital on the margin and the prevailing market price of loanable funds. The equilibrium condition, and thus maximum absorptive capacity, is attained when the rate of return on incremental investment is just equal to the price of capital, the interest rate. But this assumes that the expected rate of return on capital is easily ascertainable—an assumption difficult to maintain in a developing context, where investment generates substantial external economies, thus creating a sizable wedge between the social and the private rate of return.

Second, the investment approach is more appropriate to an advanced and predominantly private enterprise economy with limited direct government involvement in economic activities. However, oil-based economies are basically developing economies in which oil revenues accrue directly to the government. As a result, the government plays a pervasive and extremely large role in the economy. Moreover, the objectives and preferences of a government are generally different from those of private entrepreneurs. Thus, government perception of the needs of the economy, and not a profit calculus, is the major determinant of absorptive capacity.

---

*Models emphasizing investment will be further discussed later in this chapter.

Third, the preoccupation with investment has tended to stress expenditures on physical plants and facilities and not outlays on social services and human resources development. Generally, the former are equated with investment proper and the latter with consumption. This narrow view of what constitutes investment and consumption may be relevant to developed economies that already enjoy a high standard of living. In those economies, moderate variations in consumption levels or expenditures on social services are unlikely to impact appreciably on labor productivity. In the developing economies, however, the situation is drastically different. The standard of living for the bulk of the population is low; thus additional expenditures on food, other consumptive items, and social welfare services including health and education could materially enhance labor productivity, and a fortiori the economy's growth potential. To construe absorptive capacity solely in terms of the ability of the developing countries to undertake tangible and technologically advanced investment is tantamount not only to being occupied—to use a familiar metaphor—with the body to the exclusion of the soul, but also to misunderstanding the complex and intricate relationship between the two.

Mindful of these criticisms and motivated by practical considerations, the studies reviewed below have retreated from the investment or demand-for-capital method to what may be termed the expenditure approach to absorptive capacity. Thus, investment and consumption are treated on an equal footing, the central concern being the magnitude of oil revenues necessary to sustain a feasible level of public expenditures consistent with government's preferences and objectives.

EXISTING ESTIMATES OF ABSORPTIVE CAPACITY OF FOREIGN EXCHANGE

Estimates exist of foreign exchange absorptive capacity for Iran, Iraq, Kuwait, Libya, Saudi Arabia, and the United Arab Emirates. The methodology employed in arriving at these estimates varies from very simple extrapolation of recent imports figures to relatively sophisticated general equilibrium econometric modeling. The following is a brief survey of these estimates on a country-by-country basis, starting with the most involved estimates and ending with the comparatively simple ones.

Iran

Iranian total imports in 1974 approached the $8 billion mark. Iran is experiencing a period of unprecedented growth under extremely favorable conditions including $20 billion of oil revenues in 1974 alone and relatively stable and development-oriented government. Most observers think that Iran's present current-account surpluses are an ephemeral phenomenon that will soon disappear, possibly as early as 1977 or at the latest 1980. These predictions are essentially based on the following factors: the exceedingly high growth of imports in recent years, the ambitious development plans of the government, and the expected leveling off of oil revenues in the next five years. In many cases, ambitious development plans fail to be implemented for they often underestimate the bottlenecks and obstacles to successful development. However, Iran has many plus marks on its side: a pool of unskilled labor, a well-diversified resource base, abundant capital, adequate and rapidly expanding infrastructure, and above all a disciplined government machinery fully committed to development.

Two studies offer estimates of foreign exchange needed to sustain the projected development of the economy in the next decade or so. The first study is a general equilibrium model consisting of 45 equations, of which 22 are behavioral and 23 definitional.[3] The foreign sector is represented by the following equations:

Oil exports

$$Eo = 3.127 + 1.113 \ TOR \tag{2.1}$$

Non-oil exports

$$Eno = 0.163 + 0.295 \ Ip(m) + 0.118 \ VAM \tag{2.2}$$

Total exports

$$E = Eo + Eno \tag{2.3}$$

Imports of consumer goods

$$Mc = 4.043 + 0.30 \ GNP - 1.122 \ Time \tag{2.4}$$

Imports of capital and intermediate goods

$$M_{k+I} = 12.081 + 0.313 \ E + 1.499 \ Ip(m)(-1) \tag{2.5}$$

Net imports of goods and services

$$NMS = VAM/10 \tag{2.6}$$

Total imports

$$M = Mc + M_{k+I} + NMS \tag{2.7}$$

Net factor income from abroad

$$Tf \quad = 5.690 + 0.459 \, TOR \tag{2.8}$$

Import-export gap

$$GEX = E - M - Tf \tag{2.9}$$

where

$Ip(m)$ = private investment-machinery
Eo = oil and gas exports
Eno = non-oil and gas exports
E = total exports
Mc = imports of consumer goods
M_{k+I} = imports of capital and intermediate goods
NMS = net imports of goods and services
TOR = post-price-market price differential
GEX = export-import gap
VAM = value-added in manufacturing
M = total imports
GNP = gross national product

A simultaneous solution of the general model based on a given set of assumptions regarding the exogenous variables in the model gave estimates in constant 1972 prices of total imports, shown in Table 2.1. The assumptions

TABLE 2.1

Import Absorptive Capacity of Iran: Variant I, 1972-92

	1972	1977	1982	1987	1992
M (billions of dollars)	3.6	13.25	23.73	31.42	37.92
M (billions of riyals)	240.1	883.1	1,581.9	2,094.6	2,528.4
M/GNP (percent)	20.2	23.6	23.7	21.1	15.8

Sources: Firouz Vakil, *A Macro-Economic Projection for Iran, 1973-1992* (Tehran, Iran: Plan and Budget Organization, April 1974); data calculations made by staff of the International Research Center for Energy and Economic Development, Boulder, Colorado (hereafter cited as ICEED staff). Data calculations by ICEED staff available upon request for this and subsequent tables.

TABLE 2.2

Import Absorptive Capacity of Iran: Variant II, 1972-92

	1972	1977	1982	1987	1992
M (billions of dollars)	3.6	12.7	24.21	32.64	39.22
M(billions of riyals)	240.0	846.7	1,614.4	2,176.0	2,614.5
M/GNP (percent)	20.2	22.2	23.7	21.6	16.1

Sources: Firouz Vakil, *A Macro-Economic Projection for Iran, 1973-1992* (Tehran, Iran: 1974); calculations by the ICEED staff.

include: low government revenues (oil, gas, refined oil and petrochemicals), high population, a depreciation rate of 7 percent value-added in agriculture, growth at about 8 percent in current prices, various rates of growth in manufacturing, a price floor, net imports of services equal to VAM/10 for each year of projection, and no policy targets other than those implied by the above assumptions.[4]

Another simulation of the model based on the same assumptions as above, except for government revenues which are assumed high, gave the results shown in Table 2.2.[5]

The model demonstrates that Iran's import absorptive capacity is primarily a function of time. The need for foreign exchange to sustain a rapid pace of import growth rises rapidly as the time horizon lengthens. However, the rate of growth of imports between the various subperiods is constantly declining, indicating in part the setting in of external diseconomies as the economy advances to higher stages of economic growth. The second run of the model premised on higher government revenues does not appear to have increased imports appreciably. Total imports in the whole period are only 2.2 percent higher for the second run, while total government revenues were 4.2 percent higher than in the first run. Thus, the growth of imports seems to be basically determined by the growth of the economy, in particular the level of investment, rather than by the availability of greater amounts of foreign exchange. The projected level of imports in 1977 appears to be in line with the level of imports achieved in 1974. This indicates that the model does give reasonable predictions at least for the immediate future.

The share of imports in GNP rises in the first decade and then starts declining. The initial increase is mainly explained by the sizable need for capital goods imports. As the country develops its own capital goods industries and progresses in implementing import substitution policies with respect to the consumer goods sector, the need for imports will decline.

The model contains eight exogenous variables, some of which are crucial. Among them are value-added in agriculture, gross revenue from oil and gas, rate of growth of the labor supply, and the rate of growth of manufacturing labor supply.[6] Evidently, the accurateness of the projections of the model hinges on whether or not these exogenous variables will assume the values predicted for them.

The model is based on the recent experience of Iran beginning in 1960 and ending in 1973. Thus the projections assume implicitly that there will be no significant changes in the structural equations estimated until 1992. Although this assumption is rather restrictive, it is nevertheless inherent in any projection and does not necessarily detract from the usefulness of the model.

Another study of the Iranian economy defines the domestic absorptive capacity for foreign exchange as the sum total of the various components of imports (capital, intermediate, and consumption goods, and imports of services). The levels of these imports, however, are not projected by fitting statistical equations to historical data; instead, their values are ascertained using the input-output technique.[7] The analysis singles out the lack of adequate skilled labor and infrastructure as the key bottlenecks in economic growth. The next step consists essentially of using the 1972 input-output table as a starting point to prepare similar tables for the forecast years desired. Foreign exchange requirement, that is, domestic absorptive capacity, is deduced from the input-output table by subtracting non-oil exports from the sum of consumption, investment, and intermediate imports.

> The general approach to making these forecasts is to first develop a preliminary estimate of the level of total output for the economy, use the input-output model to calculate industry output, compute the resultant labor demand and compare with exogenous forecasts of labor supply. The procedure then iteratively revises total output forecasts until a match is obtained between total final demand and a fully employed labor force allocated among the sectors so as to produce what is demanded. In short, the method insists upon full employment, so the size of the labor force and its improvement in productivity are primary constraints on economic growth.[8]

According to this method, domestic foreign exchange requirements that must be satisfied from oil revenues are estimated to be $5.3 and $8.5 billion in 1975 and 1980, respectively.[9]

The main problems with this approach are two. First, the input-output table assumes linear relationships with fixed coefficients of production; thus, neither are future changes in the structure of the economy adequately accounted for, nor is the possibility of factor substitution permitted. In an economy undergoing a rapid process of development under conditions of surplus capital, these assumptions are generally unrealistic. Second, the forecast need for oil revenues in 1975 is considerably less than the volume of foreign exchange Iran spent on imports in 1974. Thus, these estimates seem to contain a large margin of error.

Iraq

Iraqi total imports soared from about $630 million in 1970 to some $4 billion in 1974. Such a dramatic growth of imports represents a discontinuity attributable to the huge oil revenues received in 1974 ($6-7 billion) and the initial low level of imports. While oil revenues are expected to continue at this high level and probably increase in future years, the real growth rate of imports is likely to be in line with the growth of national product.

Domestic absorptive capacity for Iraq is defined as the maximum level of government spending consistent with government objectives and the constraints in the economy, less government revenues from sources other than oil exports.[10] This definition was adopted because oil revenues accrue to the government which, moreover, closely controls the economy and monopolizes the foreign trade sector. Time series data for Iraq beginning with 1958 and extending into the 1970s are used to fit statistical equations pertaining to private investment, private consumption, non-oil government revenues, and net income (non-oil GDP at factor cost minus capital depreciation and direct taxes). The basic approach is to estimate government investment and government consumption that are consistent with a maximum growth rate of non-oil GDP. This rate is derived from a detailed analysis of projected population growth, the labor force and labor participation rate, labor productivity trends, government policy on expatriate labor, and the prospects for utilizing currently unemployed and underemployed labor.

Total investment required by the maximum rate of growth of output is then calculated by estimating the gross value-added (GVA) for the agricultural, industrial and services sectors from total non-oil GDP and the 1970-74 National Development Plan objectives, and then multiplying by the appropriate sectoral capital/output ratios. Government investment is obtained by subtracting private investment (derived from the model's respective statistical equation) from total investment as determined above. Government consumption expenditures are computed as a fraction of estimated private consumption, a relationship that showed significant stability and consistency during the 1960s. Private consumption is derived from the statistical equation relating private consumption to net income.

Total government revenue requirements are then the sum of government consumption and investment, plus investment in the nationalized oil industry; the latter is estimated separately, taking into account announced targets of

FIGURE 2.1

Model for Estimating Domestic Absorptive Capacity, Iraq

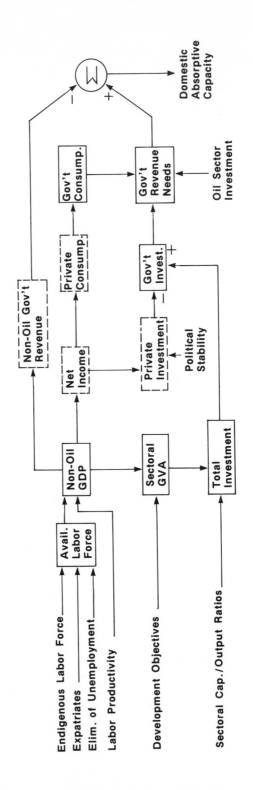

Source: C. A. Gebelein, "Forecasting Absorptive Capacity for Oil Revenues: Practical Techniques for Policy Analysis," paper presented to the Annual Meeting of the Western Economic Association, San Diego, California, June 25-28, 1975.

TABLE 2.3

Domestic Absorptive Capacity of Iraq, 1975-92
(millions of 1974 dollars)

1975	1980	1985	1990
3,233	6,437	9,437	17,244
(3,692)*	(7,372)	(10,945)	(20,302)

*Figures in parentheses assume a moderately liberal government policy with respect to public consumption, along with a moderately higher capital/output ratio.

Source: C. A. Gebelein, "Forecasting Absorptive Capacity for Oil Revenues: Practical Techniques for Policy Analysis," paper presented to the Annual Meeting of the Western Economic Association, San Diego, California, June 25-28, 1975.

oil production capacity and average per barrel development expenses in the Middle East.

Finally, the domestic absorptive capacity for oil revenues is calculated as the difference of government revenue needs and government non-oil sector revenue, which is also estimated from non-oil GDP.[11]

The model outlined above is depicted in Figure 2.1. Using this model, estimates of domestic absorptive capacity for Iraq are obtained, as shown in Table 2.3.[12]

It appears from these estimates that the rate of expansion in domestic absorptive capacity will accelerate during 1975-80, proceed at a slower pace in 1980-85, and then revert to its earlier rate of growth in 1985-90. This course reflects the projected development of the Iraqi economy. The first period will be dominated by huge infrastructural investments; the second will be characterized by continued investment in infrastructure and in industrial and agricultural pursuits, but at a lower pace; and finally, the third will witness industrialization on a large scale and substantial investment in social infrastructure and the upgrading of manpower resources. In 1985-90, most growth-inhibiting bottlenecks will probably have been alleviated and this will basically account for the resumption of the rate of expansion in absorptive capacity.

The basic limitation of this approach is that the statistical relationships may show structural discontinuity as a result of the radical change in foreign exchange availability. In particular, the given estimates of absorptive capacity are based on established government development objectives and policies. Thus, public policy pertaining to imports of consumption goods is not expected to change drastically. Indeed, if present tariffs are significantly lowered and import quotas and foreign exchange restrictions eliminated, a surge in consumption imports seems inevitable. Moreover, if the government decides to disseminate a larger portion of its oil revenues to the private sector, imports will rise even further, for there is a substantial pent-up demand for a great variety of foreign products. In fact, the Iraqi per capita import level is very low compared either to that in neighboring countries or to per capita imports of the leading industrialized nations of the world.[13]

The model of absorptive capacity, although it incorporates a macroframe-work, is nevertheless not a true general-equilibrium approach; the oil sector together with the revenues it generates and the investment it requires are either dealt with separately or accounted for only indirectly. But such an approach is perfectly appropriate, because the oil sector during most of the period under study is not expected to become a fully integral part of the domestic economy.

Saudi Arabia

Saudi Arabia, the world's largest oil reservoir, received close to $27 billion in oil revenues in 1974 alone, out of which the country managed to spend on imports of goods and net services only some $4 billion. Although present development plans in Saudi Arabia call for truly huge expenditures over the next five years ($144 billion), it is very unlikely that actual expenditures will even approach this magnitude. The country is still in the incipient stages of development with pronounced cultural unpreparedness and infrastructural bottlenecks permeating the social and economic fabric. One of the foremost and basic hindrances to rapid development in Saudi Arabia is the scarcity of manpower. This scarcity, however, is in large part due to traditional social attitudes that virtually exclude the female population from the labor force. In a country with acute labor short-age, rapid development can be attained only by pursuing a liberal immigration policy; however, changing the population mix may create undesirable social friction and tension, which the government wants to minimize. In other words, if rapid development is to be accomplished, many traditional social attitudes and barriers must give way; otherwise social unrest and political instability may ensue.

The obstacles to accelerated development are not only social in character, but include such factors as an undiversified resource base, inhospitable physical environment, primitive infrastructure, and rudimentary government machinery and institutions incapable of dealing effectively with the multidimensional prob-lems associated with speedy economic growth and social transformation.[14] Given these conditions and in the light of the expected continuation and probable rise of oil revenues accruing to Saudi Arabia, the country will find itself with con-siderable surplus capital that must be invested abroad.

Due to its huge oil reserves and production capacity Saudi Arabia plays a critical role in fashioning the pricing policy of OPEC. However, Saudi Arabia's oil production policy is shaped at least in part by the foreign exchange requirements of her domestic economy. Thus, an accurate assessment of domestic capital absorptive capacity is an extremely important issue, the impact of which far transcends the Saudi scene.

Unfortunately, historical data on Saudi national acounts and other relevant statistics are unavailable. In fact, even the precise size of the population is unknown, with estimates ranging from 4.3 to 8.2 million. One study views domestic absorptive capacity for oil revenues in Saudi Arabia as:

> ... the maximum annual level of government current and capital spending possible, subject to constraints on the availability of skilled labor, knowledge of natural resources, and technology, management and entrepreneurial experience, institutional capabilities, and social and cultural factors, less any non-oil revenue.[15]

The analysis of absorptive capacity then focuses on the labor constraint because of its facility for quantification, and tries to incorporate the other constraints indirectly.[16] The method employed consists of the following steps.

1. The available labor supply in each year is estimated from the rate of growth of the indigenous population, labor participation rates, and government policy on expatriate labor.

2. Three categories of government spending opportunities are identified: oil participation costs, defense, and domestic expenditures which include spending on infrastructure and administration.

3. Generally, maximum expenditure is determined by the availability of labor and the labor intensiveness of the particular spending category; the labor-intensiveness of the given categories is, however, assumed fixed. Moreover, the total labor requirements associated with the independently determined defense spending as well as with the private non-oil-sector spending are estimated separately. And spending for acquiring participation in oil production is not related to labor availability. Thus, the labor supply available to sustain spending on infrastructure and administration is arrived at by subtracting the labor requirements associated with defense and private non-oil-sector spending from the total labor supply as determined in step one.

4. Since labor requirement per dollar spending in administration and infrastructure is assumed fixed, maximization of total spending implies that all labor must be utilized in just one category, that is, either administration or infrastructure depending on which category possesses the lowest labor requirement per dollar of expenditure. Such an unrealistic solution is avoided by introducing two new constraints, which "prevent public administration employment from

FIGURE 2.2

Model for Estimating Domestic Absorptive Capacity, Saudi Arabia

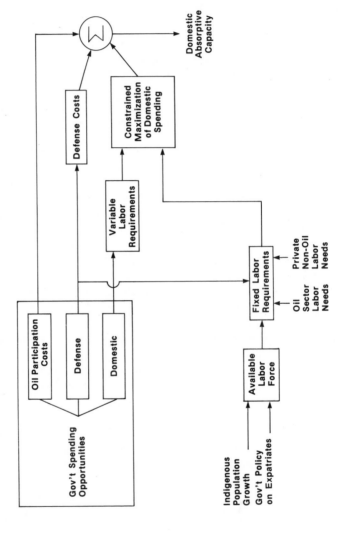

Source: C. A. Gebelein, "Forecasting Absorptive Capacity for Oil Revenues: Practical Techniques for Policy Analysis," paper presented to the Annual Meeting of the Western Economic Association, San Diego, California, June 25-28, 1975.

falling below present levels and from exceeding a selected maximum fraction of the labor force."[17] The model is schematically presented in Figure 2.2.

The model gives the following projections of the need for oil revenues to satisfy domestic Saudi requirements: $5.5 and $9.4 billion in 1975 and 1980, respectively.[18] (Figures are in 1974 dollars.)

This study uses a great deal of sound intuition and enlightened judgment to project the absorptive capacity of Saudi Arabia; in fact, with the paucity of data and their degree of reliability, the approach followed is perhaps a most productive one. Theoretically, however, the assumptions made with respect to fixed labor coefficients and fixed total labor requirements of certain categories of expenditures are generally indefensible, especially in the context of growth and development.

Libya

Libya became a major oil exporter in the 1960s. Since then foreign exchange derived from oil exports has dominated the pace of economic and social development in the country. When oil revenues suddenly rose to an unprecedented level of about $6.5 billion in 1974, the contrast between such a high level of revenues and the narrow resource base, inadequate infrastructure, limited population size (2.25 million in 1973), and inefficient administrative machinery became exceedingly visible. Thus, the question of how much current and prospective oil revenues Libya could effectively utilize to transform, diversify, and develop its oil-based economy assumed critical importance for such issues as oil-production programming, investment alternatives and planning policy.

Dr. Taher El Jehaimi has constructed a macro-econometric model that provides new and interesting estimates of the absorptive capacity of the Libyan economy.[19] Before presenting Dr. El Jehaimi's results a brief outline of his approach and the model is appropriate. He observes that the demand-for-capital approach to the problem of absorptive capacity in a developing economy is inadequate and impractical for a variety of reasons, including absence of detailed information and statistics needed for conducting benefit-cost analysis of prospective projects, the difficulty of drawing a clear demarcation line between investment and consumption, and the appropriateness of using micro-economic tools in analyzing the profitability of projects whose effects may be either very difficult to quantify or are generally pervasive and widely diffused. He advances instead an expenditure approach which involves measuring absorptive capacity in terms of the total claims the society places on the supplies of its domestic resources over a specified span of time. The magnitude of domestic absorption (domestic investment and consumption) is associated with a given level of external absorption (imports, transfers, and changes in foreign reserves).

TABLE 2.4

Absorptive Capacity of Libya, 1975-85
(millions of constant 1964 Libyan dinars)

	1975	1980	1985
Total consumption	1,066.88	1,702.90	2,427.46
Private	638.65	1,156.36	1,729.92
Public	428.23	546.54	697.54
Total investment	700.00	881.70	993.43
Private	100.00	115.93	147.96
Public	600.00	765.77	845.47
Domestic absorption	1,766.88	2,584.60	3,420.89
Total imports	779.35	1,162.53	1,514.08
Consumer	262.79	508.24	780.17
Capital	516.56	654.29	733.91
Exports	1,246.26	2,874.30	4,674.68
Gross domestic product	2,233.79	4,296.37	6,581.49

Note: The Libyan dinar-dollar exchange rate is: 1 LD = approximately $3.40.

Source: Taher El Jehaimi, "Absorptive Capacity and Alternative Investment Policies: The Case of Libya" (Ph.D. diss., University of Colorado, 1975).

Domestic as well as external absorption are determined within a simultaneous equation econometric model that includes 14 structural equations and 8 identities. The model is based on the simple Keynesian theory of effective demand and income determination and employs national account statistics pertaining to the 1962-71 period. In the relevant version of the model (variant II), investment is assumed exogenous and is disaggregated into private investment and public investment. The former is assumed to grow in real terms at 3 percent annually in 1971-80 and at 5 percent annually thereafter up to 1985. Public investment, however, is assumed to grow in real terms at 5 percent annually up to 1980 and at 2 percent thereafter. Dr. El Jehaimi admits that the selection of these rates is arbitrary but he maintains that they are "reasonable in terms of current policy as well as in terms of physical capacities displayed over the last several years."

Given the above assumptions, future levels of investment are projected and used as exogenous variables to determine the values of the remaining variables in the model. The results are given in Table 2.4.

Dr. El Jehaimi proposes that absorptive capacity thus determined be checked against the level of inflation the community is willing to tolerate. This test serves in effect as a proxy for the appropriateness of the marginal efficiency of investment. He specifies a statistical relationship between levels of aggregate expenditure and the price level and uses historical data to test this relationship, obtaining a statistically significant equation of the following form:

$$P(t) = 56.548 + 0.142 \, Ex(t) \qquad\qquad\qquad (2.10)$$
$$(8.843) \qquad\qquad R^2_{adj.} = .90$$

where $P(t)$ and $Ex(t)$ stand for price and expenditure in time t respectively.

Dr. El Jehaimi then makes the assumption that the maximum tolerable rate of inflation in the planning period is 10 percent annually and demonstrates with the aid of Equation (2.10) that the projected levels of domestic and external absorption do not produce an excessive rate of inflation.

According to the model, the gap between total exports and imports widens from LD 466.91 million in 1975 to LD 3,160.6 million in 1985, exhibiting a tendency toward higher transfers abroad as the economy develops. Dr. El Jehaimi points out that "independence from oil, as a national objective, may be achieved only at the expense of increasing dependence on foreign skills."

The projected absorptive capacity seems to be too high in light of the resource and population base of Libya, thus casting some doubt on the absence of future structural shifts in the parameters and/or on the assumptions of the model.

Kuwait

The overriding constraints on domestic absorptive capacity in Kuwait are basically related to three factors: small physical size (total area including Kuwait's share in the neutral zone is about 9,000 square miles), limited population (under one million), and a very skewed natural resource base (oil and natural gas and practically nothing else). Other important restraining factors include a mature social and physical infrastructure, the expansion and modernization of which is becoming increasingly difficult because of very high levels of past investment that were made possible by more than two decades of high oil revenues; high levels of annual import per capita (about $1,600 in 1974); and government restrictions on immigration. These factors, taken together, indicate that while the level of imports will continue to be very high, future expansion in imports will not be dramatic; in fact, the expansion of imports in real terms may very probably be akin to the rate of growth of imports experienced in the 1960s.

Aside from some recent estimates by the U.S. Treasury and Mitchell, Hutchins, Inc., there are practically no projections of Kuwait's import requirement in the next decade.* Therefore, a simple model has been constructed to

---

*These will be analyzed later in a separate section.

forecast Kuwait's absorptive capacity of foreign exchange. The model utilizes Kuwaiti time series data for the period 1962-72 and defines absorptive capacity as

$$AC = IMc + IMi + R \tag{2.11}$$

where

      AC = domestic absorptive capacity of foreign exchange
      IMc = imports of consumption goods and services other than the services of resident foreign labor
      IMi = investment goods imports (capital goods plus intermediate products)
      R   = remittances of expatriate labor abroad

A linear stochastic relationship is assumed to exist between IMc, IMi and NNP, $GNP_{non\text{-}oil}$, respectively. The relationship between IMc and NNP is straightforward and needs little explanation. Given the limited industrial and agricultural base of the country, higher NNP when filtered to the population results in increased demand for imports. Capital goods imports are naturally a rising function of domestic investment which itself is organically linked to the growth of domestic output in the non-oil sectors. For the purpose of forecasting the level of investment associated with a given increment in output, the oil sector must be treated as an enclave sector with minor direct linkages to the rest of the economy.

Kuwait, like other small Gulf countries, suffers from acute labor shortages and has had and still has to import substantial numbers of foreign workers in order to sustain her rapid developmental pace. Expatriate laborers, mostly from other Arab countries, usually view their residency in Kuwait as transitory and ephemeral and as a means of supporting families left behind. Thus, they save a substantial portion of their income and almost all these savings are remitted to their mother countries. Domestic absorptive capacity of foreign exchange must therefore include these remittances of expatriate labor as well as the usual annual import bill.

The equations below are fitted to estimate consumption goods and investment goods imports:

$$IMc = 28.18 + .074 \, NNP \tag{2.12}$$
$$ (4.64) \qquad\qquad R^2 = .71$$

$$IMi = 15.48 + .16 \, GNP_{non\text{-}oil} \tag{2.13}$$
$$ (3.393) \qquad\qquad R^2 = .56$$

The following assumptions are made in estimating remittances of expatriate labor. First, the present labor participation rate of 67 percent of the non-Kuwaiti population is assumed to continue until 1985. Strictly speaking, the labor participation rate stands for the number of persons employed over the number of potentially employable population, that is, those in the productive age groups. However, total non-Kuwaiti population is here substituted for potentially active population.[20] Second, the average annual wage ($6,000 in 1974) of the dominant sector in the economy, the government, is taken as the representative average wage for the economy and is assumed to remain constant in real terms until 1985. Third, the population projection adopted in variant II is 5 percent, and 5.5 percent rates of growth for Kuwaitis and non-Kuwaitis, respectively.[21] Fourth, about one-third of earned income is assumed to be saved and transferred abroad. The latter savings rate is assumed to be lower than the national average of between 40 and 45 percent in order to compensate for the income differential between Kuwaitis and non-Kuwaitis. Given these assumptions, the earned income of expatriate labor and the magnitude of remittances abroad become fully determinate. (See Table 2.5.)

To forecast future imports of consumption and capital goods, it is assumed that Kuwait's oil revenues of about $8.25 billion in 1974 will not increase in real terms during the period under investigation. This assumption is based on several factors. The global demand for OPEC oil is expected to exhibit a modest increase of about 2 to 3 percent starting late in the 1970s, as the world economy pulls out of the current recession. Production capacity, in contrast, is

TABLE 2.5

Non-Kuwaiti Population, Labor Force, Income, and Remittances Abroad in Selected Years

Year	Population	Labor Force	Income*	Remittances*
	(thousands)		(millions of dollars)	
1975	552.2	370.0	2,220	732.6
1980	683.2	457.7	2,746	906.3
1985	851.5	570.5	3,432	1,129.6

*Figures in constant 1974 prices.

Sources: Government of Kuwait, The Planning Board, *Statistical Yearbook of Kuwait* (Kuwait: The Planning Board, 1974); calculations made by the ICEED staff.

anticipated to grow at a much higher rate, thus accentuating the problem of excess production capacity. This necessitates devising a formula for allocating shut-in capacity among OPEC members if present oil prices are to be preserved. Countries with relatively low domestic absorptive capacity will probably be the natural candidates for absorbing any slack in the world demand for oil. These countries are likely to maintain their current production levels and let the high absorbers increase their production rates in accordance with the anticipated modest growth in world demand for several reasons, including the scarcity of attractive and secure investment opportunities abroad and the growing advocacy of conservation, especially in virtually single-resource economies. One may, of course, argue that the low absorbers, having the highest reserves among OPEC members, may resist losing market shares and may not even be interested in keeping prices high for fear that high prices may accelerate the development of alternate sources of energy. But such a scenario is probably unlikely given the substantial lead time required in developing other sources of energy, the growing worldwide concern about depletion of natural resources, and the many nonenergy uses of petroleum.

Non-oil GNP is expected to grow at a rate of 8 percent per year in real terms, a rate that is in line both with the expectations of the Kuwaiti planning authorities and the growth experience of the Kuwaiti economy in the 1960s.[22] Given the historical annual depreciation rate of about 6 percent, $NNP_{non-oil}$ can be calculated. (See Tables 2.6 and 2.7.)

Pulling the various elements together and using our two fundamental statistical equations, (2.12) and (2.13), domestic absorptive capacity can be estimated as follows. Given the high level of oil revenues projected to accrue to the

TABLE 2.6

Kuwaiti Non-Oil GNP, Non-Oil NNP, and NNP for Selected Years (millions of 1974 dollars)

Year	$GNP_{non-oil}$	$NNP_{non-oil}$	NNP
1975	3,903	3,669	11,919
1980	5,739	5,395	13,645
1985	8,436	7,930	16,180

Source: Riad El Sheikh, *Kuwait: Economic Growth of the Oil State, Problems and Policies* (Kuwait: Kuwait University, 1973); Government of Kuwait, The Planning Board, *Statistical Yearbook of Kuwait* (Kuwait: The Planning Board, 1974); calculations made by the ICEED staff.

TABLE 2.7

Domestic Foreign Exchange Requirements of Kuwait, 1975-85
(millions of 1974 dollars)

Year	Consumption Goods Imports	Capital Goods Imports	Remittances Abroad	Total*
1975	910.17	639.95	732.6	2,283
1980	1,038.0	933.72	906.3	2,878
1985	1,226.0	1,365.24	1,129.6	3,721

*These estimates may be biased downward by some 10 percent because military imports in the 1960s were negligible. Imports for defense purposes are estimated at $500 million in 1975.

Source: Calculations made by the ICEED staff.

government until 1985 ($8.25 billion annually), Kuwait will generate an annual sizable surplus ranging from about $5.5 billion in 1975 to about $4.0 billion in 1985. Thus, the cumulative surplus in the next decade is likely to approach the $50 billion mark.

United Arab Emirates

The United Arab Emirates is a federation, established in December 1971, of the seven sheikdoms previously known as the Trucial States: Abu Dhabi, Dubai, Sharjah, Ajman, Ras Al-Khaimah, Umm Al-Qawain and Fujairah. Presently, only the first three emirates produce crude petroleum.

The country is small in area and population. Total area is 30,000 square miles and total population was estimated at 350,000 inhabitants in 1974. The majority of the population consists, moreover, of expatriates largely from the Arab world, Iran, Pakistan, and India. The natural resource base is extremely skewed; aside from petroleum and natural gas the country possesses hardly anything of major significance. Oil revenues, which reached an all-time high of about $5 billion in 1974, are the basic impetus in the economic development of the country. Abu Dhabi started oil export in 1962 followed by Dubai in 1969. Most of the accruing oil revenues in the 1960s were devoted to infrastructural development in the oil-producing emirates themselves; consequently Abu Dhabi and Dubai became by far the most socially and economically developed emirates. Since the establishment of the federation, however, there is a conscious and vigorous attempt on the part of the federal government, the budget of which is largely supported by Abu Dhabi, to accelerate the development of the non-oil producing emirates.

The structure of government is still autocratic; however, through the establishment of the National Federal Council the base of inputs to the governmental processes has been broadened and popular participation introduced, albeit on a limited scale. The bureaucracy is still not very well developed and is beset with the familiar problems usually encountered in all developing countries.

Statistical information, including national income accounting data, is very scarce and leaves many gaps. Thus no detailed analysis of the economic profile and its evolution is possible on the basis of past experience. Moreover, the recent egregious changes, both with respect to oil revenues and the form of government and institutions, signify pronounced discontinuities, thereby limiting the usefulness of an analysis based principally on historical experience. Therefore, in assessing future requirements for foreign exchange the analysis will draw liberally on Kuwait's experience and postulate several reasonable assumptions when necessary.

Basically, absorptive capacity for foreign exchange is defined as the sum of total imports of goods and services other than the services of resident expatriate labor plus remittances abroad. Per capita imports in 1975 are assumed to have been double those of Kuwait and this level of imports per capita ($3,200) is projected to be the average for the next five years. During 1980-85, per capita imports are expected to decline; they are assumed to average $2,550, that is, 50 percent higher than the Kuwaiti level of $1,700. The rationale for these assumptions is that the United Arab Emirates will still have to invest heavily in building and expanding its physical infrastructure and that these expenditures will be much higher than those in Kuwait, particularly in the next five years, for

TABLE 2.8

United Arab Emirates: Projected Population, Income, and Remittances Abroad, 1975-85

	Year		
	1975	1980	1985
Total population (thousands)	385	620	998
Expatriates (thousands)	231.0	372.0	598.8
Expatriate labor (thousands)	161.70	260.40	419.16
Expatriate income (millions of 1974 dollars)	1,455.3	2,343.6	3,772.4
Remittances (millions of 1974 dollars)	485.1	781.2	1,257.5

Source: Calculations made by the ICEED staff.

TABLE 2.9

United Arab Emirates: Absorptive Capacity
of Foreign Exchange, 1975-85
(millions of constant 1974 dollars)

Year	Total Imports of Goods and Services	Remittances Abroad	Total
1975	1,232.0	485.1	1,717.1
1980	1,984.0	781.2	2,765.2
1985	2,544.9	1,257.5	3,802.4

Source: Calculations made by the ICEED staff.

at least three important reasons: the larger size of the United Arab Emirates, the federal structure of government, and the relatively underdeveloped infrastructure. In the light of the acute scarcity of educated people and the limited span of the contemporary era of prosperity, investment per capita in human resources and outlays for social welfare are also expected to be much higher than in Kuwait. In point of fact, the Kuwaiti economy is in a sense a "mature" economy with a long history of capital surplus dating back to the mid-1950s. As the United Arab Emirates continue to develop under virtually no capital constraint, the growth of capital expenditures and other outlays must eventually level off as the fundamental barriers to higher absorption, reflected in area, population, and the resource base, forcefully assert themselves. This is the reason it is assumed that the level of per capita imports in 1980-85 will be lower than in 1975-80.

In projecting total population of the United Arab Emirates, the ratio of expatriates, the percentage of the labor force in the expatriate population, and the average rate of saving, Kuwait has been taken more or less as a model.* However, the average annual wage in constant 1974 prices is assumed to be 50 percent higher during 1975-85 than its Kuwaiti counterpart because of

---

*The rate of population growth in 1974-1985 is assumed to be 10 percent, similar to Kuwait's rate during the 1960s. The ratio of expatriates in total population is assumed to be 60 percent, slightly higher than Kuwait's 55 percent. The labor participation rate of the expatriate population is assumed to be 70 percent, slightly higher than Kuwait's 67 percent. As in the Kuwaiti case, one-third of earned income of the expatriate workers is assumed to be saved and transferred abroad.

two factors: the substantially higher per capita income of the United Arab Emirates, and the relative unfamiliarity of foreign labor with the country, which acts as a hindrance to extensive labor migration. Higher wages may then play the role of an offsetting factor. Given these assumptions, the results shown in Tables 2.8 and 2.9 are obtained.

OTHER MODELS OF ABSORPTIVE CAPACITY

Models Emphasizing Investment

Economists emphasize the role of capital formation in expanding the productive capacity of the economy. Thus, many models tend to view absorptive capacity exclusively in terms of the need for savings to finance additional investment. The demand for capital, moreover, is traditionally assumed to be constrained by capital availability at a reasonable price. Such a perception of investment implies a Say's Law relationship between the demand and supply of capital, thereby denying the very existence of the absorptive capacity problem. In normal circumstances, that is, when capital is generated endogenously, the economy should encounter little difficulty in absorbing the capital provided. However, in the case of the oil-producing countries, capital is for all practical purposes accumulated outside the national economy proper; it originates in the oil sector enclave with its few and ineffective direct linkages to the national economy. Thus, capital is thrust on a domestic economy with a resource base and structure that may be either underdeveloped or even primitive. Such a setting evidently precludes the operation of the normal relationship between supply and demand in the capital market, thereby raising the question of absorptive capacity.

Viewed differently, the investment process involves an important element of learning.[23] The current low capital absorption of some oil-producing nations must be attributed at least in part to the relatively low rate of past investment. The relation between the past rate of investment and prospective rates is intricate and complex because a higher historical rate not only implies greater familiarity and practice in the investment field, but also a larger economic system that can digest a considerably greater amount of capital, even in the limiting case of a constant future rate of investment. While some of the aforementioned difficulties confronting oil-producing countries in their attempt to absorb greater volumes of capital may be alleviated by pursuing judicious outward-looking policies, especially with respect to labor importation or the attraction of foreign management and entrepreneurship, the fundamental problem is likely to resist such quick solutions, even if the social costs of those solutions can be accepted.

FIGURE 2.3

Capital-Labor Ratios and Relative Factor Prices

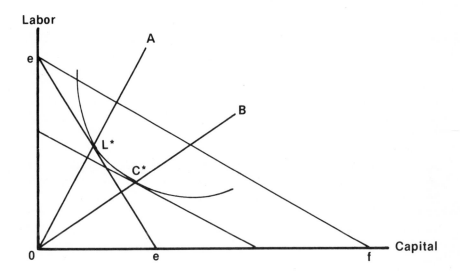

Source: Compiled by the authors.

The problem of absorptive capacity may also be perceived as a branch of capital adjustment theory. To elucidate this view, it is instructive to envisage the problem in a microsetting. Assume that a producer faces the labor situation portrayed in Figure 2.3 with the initial equilibrium at point L*. Allow for a decline in the price of capital, that is, a movement from ee to ef. Assume for simplicity that the producer is not allowed to expand his output; under these circumstances, the point of equilibrium shifts from L* on ray OA (the labor-intensive technique) to point C* on ray OB (the capital-intensive technique). The transition from ray OA to OB or alternatively from point L* to C* is not instantaneous as the graph may lead us to believe. It takes time to adjust prevailing techniques of production to the new factor price ratio even in highly industrialized economies with well-functioning capital markets. In a developing economy with rudimentary financial institutions and/or inexperience with capital-intensive techniques coupled with the difficulty of obtaining Western technology, the process of adjustment must take a much longer time span to be completed. This analysis is equally relevant for the economy as a whole; the economy needs time to attain its optimum capital-labor ratio as factor prices change.

The bulk of investment in the oil-based economies is undertaken by the government, which is also the sole recipient of oil revenues. Furthermore, higher oil revenues not only permit greater public investment outlays, but in addition exert considerable political pressures on the respective ministries to increase investment expenditures. Thus, the magnitude of oil revenues appears to be of critical importance in determining the volume of public investment outlays. To show the historical relation of oil revenues to public domestic investment and the implications of this relation for absorptive capacity, the following econometric analysis is conducted.

Government investment spending is assumed to be a linear stochastic function of the country's oil revenues. However, since oil revenues for the oil-producing countries have attained their present-day magnitudes only recently, and since this occurred in a fairly discontinuous manner, one might expect a significant structural change in the investment spending patterns of these countries in the last few years. Thus the following government investment function is fitted using Ordinary Least Squares Regression Analysis.*

$$G_i = a + \beta_1 R_i + \beta_2 D_i R_i + u_i \qquad\qquad (2.14)$$

where:

G = government investment
R = annual oil revenues
D = 0, 1 depending on the year
i = year, normally starting with 1962 and ending with 1974[†]
u = disturbance term

Hence β_2 would indicate whether the government investment spending coefficient with respect to oil revenues, β_1, had undergone any significant change.

To obtain a more complete estimate of domestic investment, a private investment function was also fitted where possible. Private investment is assumed to be linearly related to government investment as in the following equation:

$$P_i = a + \beta G_i + u_i \qquad\qquad (2.15)$$

---

*Raw data for the regression analyses are derived principally from various national sources, and are in billions of Iranian riyals, millions of Kuwaiti dinars, and millions of Saudi riyals.
†In the case of Saudi Arabia, the starting year is 1963.

where P_i, G_i are annual domestic private and government investments during the period under investigation and u_i is a stochastic term.

Total domestic investment spending is then the sum of government domestic investment spending and private domestic investment expenditures.

The regression results for three major oil-based countries in the Middle East, namely, Iran, Kuwait, and Saudi Arabia, are reported in Table 2.10. The ensuing remarks discuss the findings and highlight their implications.

First, the coefficients, β_1, β_2, as well as R^2 are everywhere significant at the 5 percent level, confirming the hypothesis that oil revenues are a statistically significant argument explaining variations in public investment spending. The generally high magnitude of R^2, moreover, indicates that a large proportion of the variation in public investment expenditures may be attributed to fluctuations in oil revenues.

Second, the relation between government investment and oil revenues has undergone a visible structural change in all three countries beginning in 1974. Equation (2.14a) in each case covers the whole period 1962-74, including 1974. Equation (2.14b), however, recognizes two subperiods, namely 1962-73, and thereafter. The coefficient of the dummy variable, β_2, is relevant to the second subperiod only. It says that government investment as a proportion of oil revenues decreased considerably in 1974; the change in government investment spending associated with a change in oil revenues in 1974 was 0.29 in Iran, 0.037 in Kuwait, and 0.159 in Saudi Arabia as opposed to 0.438, 0.101, and 0.641, respectively, before that. Thus, looking at equation (2.14a) alone masks this pronounced structural change and obfuscates the true evolution of the relation between government investment and oil revenues. It is also important to observe that the inclusion of the dummy variable has generally improved the statistical fit.

Third, the structural change in the three countries is not of equal magnitude. This can be ascertained by calculating from equation (2.14b) what may be termed the absorption ratio, $\beta_1/(\beta_1 - \beta_2)$. The higher this ratio, the greater is the deterioration in the responsiveness of public investment to increases in oil revenues. This ratio was 1.51 in Iran, 2.73 in Kuwait, and 4.03 in Saudi Arabia. The analysis confirms intuition in that Iran, a large and relatively developed country with a diversified resources base, has the smallest ratio.

Fourth, the coefficient of oil revenues, β_1, even for the initial period alone, 1962-73, is rather low, suggesting that these countries may have been either unwilling to commit a higher percentage of their oil revenues to public investment or that a larger volume of oil revenues could not be invested for reasons that we have noted above. Given the central role of the public sector in these economies, the second explanation appears more plausible especially in Kuwait, which enjoyed a sizable capital surplus throughout the whole period. The precipitous drop of this coefficient in 1974 from β_1 to $(\beta_1 - \beta_2)$ is indicative of the acute bottlenecks experienced by these countries, preventing additional

TABLE 2.10

Government Investment Function in Selected Oil-Based Economies in the Middle East

Country	Equation Number	a	β_1	β_2	R^2	D-W[a]
Iran	2.14a[c]	63.9794	0.262 (23.1234)[b]		0.98	1.1445
	2.14b[c]	34.554	0.4378 (5.8549)	-0.1443 (2.1848)	0.98	1.3586
Kuwait	2.14a	36.2055	0.0312 (5.4306)		0.73	1.4660
	2.14b	16.3415	0.1005 (4.5154)	-0.0631 (3.1710)	0.87	1.9696
Saudi Arabia	2.14a	2,059.97	0.1389 (6.0997)		0.78	1.1734
	2.14b	-621.71	0.6411 (23.9916)	-0.4822 (18.9783)	0.99	2.1177

Note: A single Rho transformation is applied to adjust for serial autocorrelation.
[a]Durbin-Watson.
[b]Figures in parentheses are Student t ratios.
[c]Equation 2.14a covers the whole period 1962-74; equation 2.14b recognizes two subperiods, 1962-73 and thereafter.
Source: Calculations made by the ICEED staff.

investment spending at the current levels of oil revenues. In the case of Kuwait, this has unequivocally accentuated an already existing situation.

Fifth, although the analysis indicates that government domestic investment is not able to keep pace with the increase in oil revenues, it does not say that other investment spending is not occurring in accordance with the higher levels of revenues. Specifically, investment in the private sector may have increased over the past two years as a result of greater volume of government investment since the latter plays an important role in determining the volume and direction of private investment in Iran. Thus, a regression equation fitting private investment to government investment was run. Another equation with a dummy variable relating private investment to government investment is also fitted to ascertain whether there has been any significant change in this relationship over the past two years. The results are indicated below:

$$P_i = 25.3 + .469 \, G_i \tag{2.16}$$
$$(12.99) \qquad\qquad R^2 = .92$$

$$P_i = 26.9 + .43 \, G_i + .05 \, D_i G_i \tag{2.17}$$
$$(7.40) \quad (.926) \qquad\qquad R^2 = .92$$

The dummy variable is not really significant except at the 20 percent level but its sign is suggestive, indicating a tendency for private investment to increase as the level of government investment rises.

Although domestic investments in the oil producing countries seem to be largely unresponsive to the sudden and enormous rise in oil revenues, regional and international investments are steadily expanding. These countries are investing in other countries in the region and elsewhere or in joint ventures such as financial and productive facilities. But these types of investment projects are not counted in the government investment variable which seems to have exhibited a decrease with respect to oil revenues. The magnitude and types of investment of the oil producers directed toward other economies will be addressed later in this study.

Estimates of Import Capacities from Cross-Sectional Regression Data

The approach followed in this section is highly aggregative and thus contains a number of pitfalls. However, its simplicity and facility for projection compensates for its inherent deficiencies. One of the basic limitations of this approach is that it does not distinguish between consumption and investment. Investment is, of course, much harder to push to new heights than consumption because it is an activity requiring intensive familiarity with and understanding of markets, managerial capabilities, and technological know-how. These factors are scarce in developing countries and may pose insurmountable difficulties for small-sized developing nations. The evidence from economic history suggests that the ratio of investment to GNP has never exceeded 30 to 35 percent in any country, even in the most rapid phase of its development. Branko Horvat[24] mentions the Soviet Union (1920-40) and the Yugoslav economy (1952) as probably approaching these limits. Horvat, however, shows that these countries were in fact overinvesting because the contribution of investment at the margin to total output was in both cases distinctly negative. As a limiting case, and considering the unusual circumstances prevailing in the oil-producing countries we have assumed that the maximum share of domestic investment in income is 40 percent. Implicit in this assumption is a zero marginal return to capital. If this assumption is not accepted then the above share of domestic investment in income would be considered excessive.

The value of consumption imports on the other hand is constrained by logistic bottlenecks—harbors, airports, roads, and railway facilities—as well as domestic income distribution and the tastes of the population. Oil revenues accrue directly to the governments. Thus, the extent that the respective governments are able and willing to disseminate these revenues to the population at large or to certain specific groups affects the volume and pattern of demand for imports. Wealth and income concentration leads to higher demand for luxury products, the value of which is considerably higher for any given volume of imports, thus tending to increase absorptive capacity. Similarly, if tastes can be shifted toward high value, small-volume products, whether through a particular income distribution policy or otherwise, the capacity of ports and other facilities will be less strained for any given volume of imports. Consumption goods imports are therefore highly susceptible to changes in government policies even in the absence of a revenue constraint.

Fully aware of these reservations and admonitions an equation has been fitted that expresses per capita imports in value terms as a function of per capita GNP, utilizing cross-sectional data of the Arab oil-producing countries and Iran in 1974.*

$$\frac{M}{P} = 122.457 + .149 \frac{GNP}{P} \tag{2.18}$$

$$(8.255) \qquad\qquad R^2 = .92$$

---

*The Arab oil producers include Algeria, Iraq, Kuwait, Libya, Qatar, Saudi Arabia, and the United Arab Emirates. When all OPEC countries were included the estimated parameters of the equation did not change significantly.

Given the equation, total imports of goods and services other than the services of resident expatriate labor would equal

$$M = P(122.457) + .149 \text{ GNP} \qquad\qquad (2.19)$$

The latter formulation makes explicit the impact of population size on the level of imports.

In order to use the above equation for import projection for the next decade, certain assumptions must be made with respect to the growth in oil revenues and the growth of non-oil GNP as well as the rate of population growth. Although probably the oil revenues of the Arab states in real terms will be increasing moderately at the rate of 2 to 3 percent annually, beginning toward the end of the 1970s, a rather pessimistic view is taken here: oil revenues are assumed to remain constant at their 1974 level. It is estimated that in the light of the declared planning objectives, the resource base, the historical record, policies on immigration, and the experience of other countries, the maximum attainable real rate of growth of non-oil GNP and the rate of population growth during the next decade for the Arab oil producers and Iran will be as shown in Table 2.11.

Given these rates and the assumption of constant oil revenues in real terms, the future size of population and the level of real GNP can be predicted. Table 2.12 thus provides estimates of the size of population and GNP of the respective countries in 1974, 1975, 1980 and 1985.

Using our fundamental equation (2.13), together with the relevant estimates of population and GNP in future years, import absorptive capacity can be estimated. The results, in billions of dollars, are given in Table 2.13.

TABLE 2.11

Projected Rates of Growth of Non-Oil GNP and Population for Selected Countries
(in percent)

Country	Rate of Growth of Non-oil GNP	Rate of Population Growth
Saudi Arabia	15.0	10.0
Iraq	15.0	5.0
Iran	15.0	4.0
Libya	12.0	10.0
Qatar	8.0	6.3

Source: Calculations made by the ICEED staff.

TABLE 2.12

Population, Oil Revenues, and GNP for Selected Countries

Country and Year	Population (thousands)	Oil Revenues (billions of dollars)	Non-Oil GNP (billions of dollars)	Total GNP (billions of dollars)
Saudi Arabia				
1974	5,500	27.0	2.500	29.500
1975	6,050	27.0	2.875	29.875
1980	9,744	27.0	5.783	32.783
1985	15,692	27.0	11.631	38.631
Iraq				
1974	10,406	7.0	5.500	12.500
1975	10,926	7.0	6.325	13.325
1980	13,945	7.0	12.722	19.722
1985	17,798	7.0	25.588	32.588
Iran				
1974	31,467	20.0	12.600	32.600
1975	32,726	20.0	14.490	34.490
1980	39,816	20.0	29.145	49.145
1985	48,442	20.0	58.620	78.620
Libya				
1974	2,386	6.5	4.167	10.667
1975	2,625	6.5	4.667	11.167
1980	4,227	6.5	8.225	14.725
1985	6,808	6.5	14.495	20.995
Qatar				
1974	130	1.7	0.500	2.200
1975	138	1.7	0.540	2.240
1980	188	1.7	0.793	2.493
1985	255	1.7	1.166	2.866

Sources: Calculations made by the ICEED staff using base-year statistics from International Monetary Fund, *IMF Surveys* (Washington, D.C.: International Monetary Fund, selected issues); United Nations, *National Account Statistics* (New York: United Nations, selected years); International Monetary Fund, *International Financial Statistics, 1974* (Washington, D.C.: International Monetary Fund, 1975); Mitchell, Hutchins, Inc., *OPEC Expenditures: Size, Timing, Nature and Beneficiaries* (New York: Mitchell, Hutchins, Inc., August 20, 1975).

A few observations must be kept in mind in comparing the estimates in Tables 2.11-2.13 with other estimates, especially those of the U.S. Treasury Department for OPEC imports, f.o.b.* given in Table 2.14.

---

*Free on board.

TABLE 2.13

Import Absorptive Capacity for Selected
Oil Producing Countries, 1975-85
(billions of 1974 dollars)

Country	1975	1980	1985
Saudi Arabia	5.200	6.080	7.680
Iraq	3.320	4.650	7.040
Iran	9.150	12.200	17.650
Kuwait	1.550	1.970	2.590
Libya	1.990	2.710	3.960
Qatar	0.350	0.400	0.460
UAE	1.230	1.980	2.545

Source: Calculations made by the ICEED staff.

First, with the exception of Iran and Libya, all the other estimates are derived from partial analysis—not from a simultaneous equation model. To that extent, problems of consistency are outflanked. However, estimates that try to relate imports to GNP, albeit crudely, are evidently better than those that merely stipulate a given rate of growth in imports, as the Treasury study apparently does.

Second, the estimates are not strictly comparable because of varying degrees of coverage and comprehensiveness. Some do include remittances of

TABLE 2.14

OPEC Imports f.o.b.
(billions of 1974 dollars)

Country	1974	1980	1985
Iran	8.0	24.4	32.0
Iraq	3.5	9.5	14.0
Kuwait	1.5	3.4	6.4
Libya	3.0	5.2	6.5
Qatar	0.3	0.6	0.9
Saudi Arabia	3.5	7.5	17.4
UAE	1.6	3.9	6.9

Source: U.S. Department of the Treasury, *The Absorptive Capacity of the OPEC Countries*, mimeographed (Washington, D.C.: Department of the Treasury, Sept. 5, 1975).

TABLE 2.15

Absorptive Capacity of Oil Revenues for Selected Countries, 1975-85
(billions of 1974 dollars)

Country and Source	1975	1980	1985
Iran			
Vakil	13.25	23.73	31.42
Gebelein[a]	5.30	8.50	–
U.S. Treasury[b]	8.00	24.40	32.00
El Mallakh et al.[b]	9.20	12.20	17.70
Iraq			
Gebelein	3.70	7.40	10.90
U.S. Treasury	3.50	9.50	14.00
El Mallakh et al.	3.32	4.70	7.00
Saudi Arabia			
Gebelein	5.50	9.40	–
U.S. Treasury	3.50	7.50	17.40
El Mallakh et al.	5.20	6.10	7.70
Libya			
El Jehaimi[c]	7.56	17.64	28.62
U.S. Treasury	3.00	5.20	6.50
El Mallakh et al.	2.00	2.70	4.00
Kuwait			
U.S. Treasury	1.50	3.40	6.40
El Mallakh et al.	1.60	2.00	2.60
United Arab Emirates			
U.S. Treasury	1.60	3.90	6.90
El Mallakh et al.	1.23	2.00	2.60
Qatar			
U.S. Treasury	0.30	0.60	0.90
El Mallakh et al.	0.35	0.40	0.46

[a]Estimates are for 1977, 1982, and 1987 and are in constant 1972 prices. Figures represent total imports that are partially financed by non-oil exports.

[b]Total imports may be in part financed by non-oil exports. In most cases, however, non-oil exports are negligible.

[c]Total exports are estimated to satisfy a given level of investment in the model.

Sources: U.S. Department of the Treasury, The Absorptive Capacity of the OPEC Countries, mimeographed (Washington, D.C.: Department of the Treasury, September 5, 1975); Firouz Vakil, *A Macro-Economic Projection for Iran, 1973-1992* (Tehran, Iran: Plan and Budget Organization, April 1974); C. A. Gebelein, "Forecasting Absorptive Capacity for Oil Revenues: Practical Techniques for Policy Analysis," paper presented to the Annual Meeting of the Western Economic Association, San Diego, California, June 25-28, 1975; Taher El Jehaimi, "Absorptive Capacity and Alternative Investment Policies: The Case of Libya" (Ph.D. diss., University of Colorado, 1975); El Mallakh et al. refers to calculations by the ICEED staff.

expatriate labor and other transfers, military imports, and foreign aid, and some do not. The cross-sectional analysis in this section does not, for example, embrace these elements. Thus, in comparing these estimates, one must keep in mind these differences along with the various assumptions employed in each case with regard to the strategic factors or the exogenous variables in the respective models.

Third, the structural relation between import and GNP may shift over time, in which case obvious biases in the estimates are introduced. Moreover, the cross-sectional analysis tests this relationship, employing data from various countries that have one overriding characteristic in common—dependence on oil—but nevertheless vary greatly as to the resource base and the structure of the economy. Using intercountry relationships in a national setting may again produce inaccurate estimates. Thus, levels of imports derived from the cross-sectional analysis must be viewed with caution and perhaps only as useful first approximations.

SUMMARY OF THE RESULTS

Table 2.15 presents the various estimates of absorptive capacity of the Arab oil-producing countries under investigation, and of Iran.

NOTES

1. John H. Adler, *Absorptive Capacity: The Concept and Its Determinants* (Washington, D.C.: The Brookings Institution, 1965), p. 5.

2. R. F. Mikesell, *Foreign Investment in Latin America* (Washington, D.C.: Pan American Union, 1965), Ch. 13.

3. Firouz Vakil, *A Macro-Econometric Projection for Iran, 1973-1992* (Tehran, Iran: Plan and Budget Organization, April, 1974).

4. Ibid., p. 19. See also p. 22 for the estimates. Estimates of M are reported on p. 22 in current prices; they are converted to constant 1972 prices using the GNP deflator as may be calculated from Table 6, p. 21.

5. Ibid., pp. 34-36. Figures were converted to constant prices.

6. Ibid., p. 7.

7. Christopher A. Gebelein, "Forecasting Absorptive Capacity for Oil Revenues: Practical Techniques for Policy Analysis," paper presented to the Annual Meeting of the Western Economic Association, San Diego, California, June 25-28, 1975, pp. 23-29.

8. Ibid., p. 26.

9. Christopher A. Gebelein, "Effects of Conservation on Oil Prices: Analysis of Misconceptions," *Journal of Energy and Development* 1 Autumn 1975, Table 2, p. 62. Figures are in constant 1974 prices.

10. Gebelein, "Forecasting Absorptive Capacity," op. cit., pp. 19-23.

11. Ibid., p. 23.

12. Notice that Gebelein, "Effects of Conservation," op. cit., p. 16, gives the lower bound estimates of domestic absorptive capacity.

13. In 1972, Iraqi imports per capita were $71 as compared to $929 for Kuwait. Central Bank of Kuwait, *Annual Report* (Kuwait: Al-Assriya Printing Press, 1973), p. 145.

14. For a discussion of the political and other noneconomic factors affecting Saudi Arabia's development, see Rosalie Avery, "Saudi Arabia: A Capabilities Analysis" (M.A. thesis, University of Colorado, 1973).

15. Gebelein, "Forecasting Absorptive Capacity," op. cit., p. 13. Non-oil revenues are relatively small and are therefore ignored in the analysis.

16. Ibid.

17. Ibid., p. 17.

18. Gebelein, "Effect of Conservation," op. cit., p. 19.

19. Taher El Jehaimi, "Absorptive Capacity and Alternative Investment Policies: The Case of Libya" (Ph.D. diss., University of Colorado, 1975).

20. See Planning Board, *Statistical Yearbook of Kuwait* (Kuwait: The Planning Board, 1974), pp. 30, 44.

21. Ibid., p. 62.

22. Riad El Sheikh, *Kuwait: Economic Growth of the Oil State, Problems and Policies* (Kuwait: Kuwait University, 1973), pp. 122-24.

23. This is probably what motivated Chenery to advocate his "past rate of investment" as the basic determinant of domestic absorptive capacity. See Willy J. Stevens, *Capital Absorptive Capacity in Developing Countries* (Leiden: A. W. Sijthaff, 1971), pp. 110-14. Hirschman also recognized that "the ability to invest is acquired and increased primarily by practice. . . ." See Albert Hirschman, *The Strategy of Economic Development* (New Haven: Yale University Press, 1958), p. 36.

24. Branko Horvat, "The Optimum Rate of Investment," *Economic Journal* 68 (December 1958): 747-67.

3

REGIONAL COOPERATION
AND ABSORPTIVE CAPACITY
IN THE MIDDLE EAST:
SOME ECONOMETRIC TESTS

REGIONAL COOPERATION AND TRADE
IN THE MIDDLE EAST

Theory

The purpose of this chapter is to test the impact of regional cooperation on Arab countries in the Middle East. The major discontinuity in regional cooperation for these countries was the formation of OAPEC and OPEC, and the increase in the price of oil associated with the increased bargaining power of the Arab oil producers in the context of these organizations. While in the long run the effects of regional cooperation are by no means limited to the increased prices and revenues for oil producers, the near-term effects are more easily identifiable in terms of this discontinuity. For this reason our tests hypothesize a discontinuity associated with regional cooperation in 1973 when the price of oil increased. The first series of tests examines the effects of regional cooperation on trade in the Middle East. The second series of tests examines the effects of regional cooperation on capital markets in the Middle East.

While the focus of attention seems to be on the effects of regional cooperation in the production and pricing of oil, this has tended to obscure more basic economic impacts of regional cooperation. Traditionally, one of the most important effects of regional cooperation has been liberalization of trade.[1] Trade liberalization in turn provides access to an enlarged market for producers. For some producers liberalization of trade may result in increased competition from lower priced imports; at the extreme, these producers may not be able to compete successfully with imported goods and services and may be forced out of business. However, for the group as a whole the expectation is that the increased

specialization and trade based upon comparative advantage will increase the total
volume of trade among the cooperating nations.

Methodology

The methodology involves testing two basic propositions regarding the
impact of regional cooperation on trade in the Middle East: that regional integration in the area as measured by intraregional trade flows is increasing; and
that regional integration in the area is having an impact on U.S. exports to the
region.

The form of our tests is straightforward. We assume that changes in trade
patterns are a function of time and structural changes, with the latter represented
when appropriate by a dummy variable. The dependent variable is always represented as a ratio. This in turn transforms the raw data expressed in nominal
terms into a dimensionless ratio. Our sample consists of yearly observations
starting in 1966 and ending in 1974.

The first tests were to determine the increase in AOPEC imports in relation to total world imports and AOPEC exports in relation to total world
exports. A dummy variable was added to the AOPEC exports/world exports
regression and was set equal to 1 in 1974 only. No dummy was added to the
import regression.

Data

Data for intraregional trade and extraregional trade were collected for each
year from 1966 through 1974 from various issues of the *Direction of Trade.*
(Supplemental trade statistics were obtained from *International Financial Statistics.*) Every attempt was made to check the data for consistency. The countries included were Libya, Iran, United Arab Emirates, Iraq, Saudi Arabia,
Kuwait, Lebanon, Jordan, Egypt, Sudan, Algeria, Bahrain, Qatar, Tunisia, and
Syria. For each country, the imports from and exports to all the other above-
mentioned countries were computed on a yearly basis. The compiled tables also
include yearly trade data with the United States and total trade with the rest of
the world.

The data have to be judged somewhat unreliable. In many cases country
A's reported exports to country B will differ substantially from country B's
reported imports from country A. This source of error might not be so trouble-
some if separate data were available for every year for countries A and B, which
was not the case. If, for instance, no data from country A were available with
respect to trade with country B, but data were available from country B sources,
then country B's data were used for country A's data also.

While the data collected could be used to investigate trade patterns on a country-by-country basis, the decision was made to work with broader aggregates. The following conventions are used when referring to groups of countries:

1. AOPEC refers to the study countries of Iran, Iraq, Kuwait, United Arab Emirates, Libya, and Saudi Arabia. Iran, a non-Arab country, is included here because of its growing regional role and trade relations.

2. All-Arab refers to all the countries included in the trade-flow study.

3. Non-AOPEC-Arab refers to the countries included in the trade-flow study that are not AOPEC countries.

When the data were aggregated on a broader scale a great deal of inconsistency appears to have washed out. By definition all-Arab intratrade imports equal all-Arab intratrade exports plus transport costs. Table 3.1 presents the aggregated intratrade data for the study years, and shows the dramatic and consistent growth in intraregional trade, which rose from slightly more than $1 billion in 1966 to well above the $4-billion mark in 1974—a ratio of more

TABLE 3.1

Data on Arab Trade Flows
(millions of U.S. dollars)

Year	Intratrade Exports (All-Arab)	Intratrade Imports (All-Arab)	Intraregional Trade	Absolute Difference[a]	Percent Discrepancy[b]
1966	464	548	1,012	+84	17
1967	495	532	1,027	+37	7
1968	562	624	1,186	+62	10
1969	548	647	1,195	+99	17
1970	575	686	1,261	+111	18
1971	730	727	1,457	+3	0.4
1972	908.78	1,087.72	1,996.50	+178.94	17.9
1973	1,047.51	1,259.02	2,306.02	+211.51	18.3
1974	1,820.09	2,411.94	4,232.03	+591.85	28

[a]Column 2 – Column 1: Imports minus exports.
[b]Column 4/Column 3/2: Imports minus exports divided by average intraregional trade.

Sources: United Nations, *Yearbook of International Trade Statistics* (New York: United Nations, various issues, 1966-74); International Monetary Fund, *International Financial Statistics* (Washington, D.C.: International Monetary Funds, various issues, 1966-74); idem, *Direction of International Trade* (Washington, D.C.: International Monetary Fund, various issues, 1966-74).

than 1 to 4. Given moderate inflationary trends in most of this period, the major part of the increment in intraregional trade must represent a growth in real terms. The table also indicates that the aggregated differences obtain a high of 28 percent in 1974 and a low of 0.4 percent in 1971. The average discrepancy is 14.8 percent. If transport and insurance costs are assumed to equal 10 to 15 percent of the import bill, it appears that much of the discrepancy between import and export values can be explained by reference to transport outlays. While this explanation is not fully satisfactory, it is believed that the aggregated data are reliable enough to perform the simple tests that follow.

Econometric Tests

The results of the econometric tests are reported in Table 3.2.

It comes as no surprise that AOPEC exports have risen in relation to world exports. At the 5 percent level, AOPEC imports/world imports show significance as a function of time.

The initial hypothesis is that there is increasing intraregional trade in the Arab world. This hypothesis was tested in several ways with the regressions reported in Table 3.3.

Regression 3 indicates that the ratio of total intratrade exports to total world exports has declined as a function of time. Regression 4 indicates that if only Arab-world exports are considered, the decline has been even more pronounced. Regression 5 presents similar findings with respect to imports. All three regressions tend to dispute the hypothesis of increasing intraregional trade and in fact show a tendency toward increasing regional trade disintegration. Several qualifications are, however, in order.

TABLE 3.2

Econometric Tests: AOPEC/World Exports and Imports
($Y = a_0 + bt + cD$ where t is time and D represents a dummy variable)

Dependent Variable	a_0	b	c	R^2
1. Exports AOPEC/world exports	.033	.0018 (4.29)	.0437 (12.80)	.983
2. Imports AOPEC/world imports	.0137	.00088 (2.42)		.455

Note: Figures in parentheses are t scores.
Source: Calculations made by the ICEED staff.

TABLE 3.3

Econometric Tests: All-Arab Exports
$(Y = a_0 + bt)$

Dependent Variable	a	b	R^2
3. $\dfrac{\text{Total intratrade exports—all-Arab}}{\text{Total world exports}}$	0.0033	−0.00015 (3.29)	.61
4. $\dfrac{\text{Total intratrade exports—all-Arab}}{\text{Total all-Arab world exports}}$	0.067	−0.0044 (5.93)	.83
5. $\dfrac{\text{Total intratrade imports—all-Arab}}{\text{Total all-Arab world imports}}$	0.094	−0.002 (4.27)	.72

Note: Figures in parentheses are t scores.
Source: Calculations made by the ICEED staff.

1. The regressions do not include any data for 1975 or 1976. It is possible that system changes have occurred in these years.

2. A finer breakdown of the data might show increasing trade integration among groups of countries. For example, dividing the countries into Arab-African and Arab-non-African categories might be a fruitful exercise. Analysis of individual countries' behavior might also reveal changing trade patterns. Future studies may well want to investigate these conjectures.

3. The increasing importance of oil exports in all-Arab world exports may be the main factor behind these results. Given the present narrow industrial base of the Arab world, higher oil proceeds are largely directed by necessity to Western markets. Imports of machinery and high technology inputs required for rapid development cannot be procured elsewhere. As significant industries are established in the Arab world, however, intraregional trade is likely to grow at a faster rate than extraregional trade. This conclusion is in accord with the historical trend, which shows that apart from oil and a few other commodities, most Arab exports, especially processed goods, were intraregional.

This study is also concerned with the impact of regional integration on the U.S. trade account. Two experiments were conducted to discern any changes between Arab imports and U.S. exports. Table 3.4 presents the results of these experiments.

The regression coefficient of equation 7 in Table 3.4 is significant at the 10 percent level. Regression 8 is, however, not significant, nor does it have the "correct" sign. But regression 7 appears to confirm our second proposition,

TABLE 3.4

Econometric Tests: All-Arab/AOPEC Imports from the United States
$(Y = a_0 + bt)$

Dependent Variable	a	b	R^2
7. $\dfrac{\text{Total all-Arab imports from the United States}}{\text{Total U.S. exports}}$	.021	.0019 (1.92)	.35
8. $\dfrac{\text{AOPEC imports from the United States}}{\text{Total AOPEC imports}}$	.17	−.00093 (0.475)	.03

Source: Calculations made by the ICEED staff.

namely, that regional cooperation in the Middle East is having an impact on U.S. exports to the region.

Conclusions

In summary, the results of this section show:

1. That annual intraregional trade flows have been consistently increasing in absolute terms during the period 1966-74. However, in relative terms, that is, compared to the growth of extraregional trade, they seem to have suffered a visible decline. This decline is probably more apparent than real because the distorting impact of precipitously rising oil exports is not accounted for. Furthermore, disaggregation by subregion (such as the Gulf area, Egypt and the Gulf, the North African states) and/or by type of commodity (agricultural versus nonagricultural commodities, commodities versus services including tourism) may reveal results consistent with the hypothesis of increasing intraregional trade volumes. Evidently this is an area in which further research could yield fruitful results.

2. That regional cooperation in the Middle East does have a positive impact on U.S. exports to the region. In fact, the Middle East is likely to become one of the major customers of the United States during the coming decade, as will be discussed in the final chapter of this study.

3. That it should be kept in mind, however, that the above experiments represent only a look at what has occurred and may be very unreliable guides as to what may occur in the future precisely because of the new realities in the area, reflected in the emergence of the Arab oil producers as capital-surplus countries, and in the current greater economic and political coordination of policies among the Arab states. These developments will be analyzed later in this volume.

REGIONAL COOPERATION AND CAPITAL MARKETS IN THE MIDDLE EAST

Theory

The impact of regional integration on the volume of investment was first examined by C. P. Kindleberger, who points out that economic integration may render resources more mobile:

> There is something to be said for the view that customs union makes its contribution to European recovery by rendering resources more mobile among occupations. If customs union were accompanied by some elements of political and monetary union, as some think inevitable, necessary or desirable, it might be that migration across national boundaries would be rendered easier. Increased competition derived from the broadening of the market in space makes demand curves more elastic for the single producer. This increased competition at the same time may encourage easier entry and hence contribute to factor mobility locally, as well as internationally.[2]

Kindleberger also emphasizes that there is nothing inevitable about the relationship between economic integration and factor mobility. Factor mobility is a function of many factors other than size of market. The widening of the cultural unit and the broadening of the market may contribute to mobility at a given standard of living, but they contribute little to the immobilizing qualities of tradition and continuity in older countries and poverty in relatively underdeveloped areas.

Perhaps the most comprehensive view of the impact of economic integration on absorptive capacity is provided by Bela Balassa.[3] He argues that in addition to its effects on commodity trade, the lessening of uncertainty associated with national frontiers will influence investment activity through its impact on investments in export industries and on foreign investments. Furthermore, economic integration will affect investment through the reallocation of production and changes in production methods that follow the removal of tariff barriers within an integrated area. Finally, in a common market, the flow of funds between member countries is facilitated by the establishment of an integrated capital market. As a result, both the volume of investment and the allocation of investment funds among industries and countries can be affected.

In the case of the Middle East the mobilization problem is extremely complex. Not only does capital have to move from the oil-producing industry to other industries, but mobilization frequently involves geographic movement as well. In general, most of the savings accrue in the oil-producing regions, but the demand for capital is often in the non-oil producing regions. Accumulations from the oil industry must be transferred into other industries and regions. A fund of qualitative information suggests that these countries have encountered substantial problems in their attempts to mobilize capital across regional and industrial boundaries. Indeed the interregional flow of private capital may even have been perverse. External economies and general benefits derived from agglomeration of capital projects in the relatively rich regions may cause capital to migrate from the poorer to the richer regions, tending to accentuate interregional inequality. High apparent risk premiums, lack of entrepreneurial ability, and immature capital markets may further depress investment activity and capital accumulation in the poorer regions. The latter, immature development of financial institutions, may prove to be not only important, but also the most easily measurable of these factors in explaining perverse capital flows.

Along with economic growth in the region have come more efficient capital markets. If perverse interregional private capital flows have been typical of early growth, the development of more sophisticated capital markets should help to deter the net outflow of capital from poorer regions. External economies and benefits accruing from agglomeration of capital projects may eventually become exhausted at the margin in the richer regions, while they begin to assert themselves in the poorer regions as development proceeds there (albeit, perhaps at a slower pace). Finally, if growth becomes relatively rapid in the poorer regions due to any other factors, the capital flow will most likely undergo a natural reversal.

Methodology

The purpose of this section is to test for regional capital market integration among the Arab countries of the Middle East. The test involves several different hypotheses. The first hypothesis states that capital markets within these Arab countries have become more closely integrated and that, ceteris paribus, interest rates on similar assets in these countries should converge. In particular, tests need to be made for convergence of interest rates between the oil-producing Arab countries, and between these countries and the non-oil producing Arab countries, on the assumption that regional cooperation should provide a much greater mobility of capital funds between these countries than would have existed without regional cooperation.

A second hypothesis is that capital markets of the Arab countries will diverge from capital markets in the non-Arab countries of the region that are not integrated into regional cooperation with the Arab countries. Tests are made for divergence of interest rates between the Arab countries and other underdeveloped countries in the region on the assumption that there are greater barriers to the mobility of capital between these countries than among the Arab countries. Those barriers reflect the cultural differences and lack of institutions comparable to those emerging through regional cooperation among the Arab countries.

A third hypothesis is that capital markets of the Arab countries have also diverged from the capital markets in the United States and Western Europe. Tests are done for divergence of interest rates between the group of Arab countries and a representative group of developed countries in Western Europe and the United States. The assumption is that regional cooperation is resulting not only in greater mobility of capital among the Arab countries, but also in similar and coordinated policies regarding capital flows with the developed economies. As the latter group of countries has experienced increasing instability, as reflected in currency devaluation and restriction on capital flows, the Arab countries have responded by developing financial institutions to coordinate policies regarding capital flows within the region and with developed economies.

This latter hypothesis is also tested using a more rigorous test based on portfolio analysis. The previous tests make no assumptions about investment behavior on the part of Arab investors, other than the assumption that investors are maximizing expected returns in capital markets where regional cooperation is reducing the barriers to capital flows between Arab countries relative to capital flows outside the Arab countries. The more rigorous test from portfolio analysis is based on the hypothesis that traditionally Arab investors and capital market institutions have been biased in favor of assets in the developed countries of the West. However, with regional cooperation and the development of capital market institutions capable of mobilizing capital within the region, the bias should shift from those assets to assets inside the region. The latter test requires a more explicit statement of the underlying assumptions.[4]

Economic theory has long postulated the existence of a relationship between asset risk and return. The risk attaching to a particular asset may be viewed as the probability distributions of possible rewards accruing to the asset's owner at future points in time. Uncertainty refers to the degree of confidence the investor places in his perception of these distributions. The usual hypothesis is that in the absence of barriers to competition in the capital market (including an unequal distribution of knowledge) differences between the returns from various assets depend on the relative degrees of risk and uncertainty associated with each asset. Recently, a fully articulated theory of the relationship between relative degree of risk and return has appeared, an outgrowth of the mean-standard deviation models of portfolio choice first evolved by Markowitz and Tobin.[5] The new model of capital asset pricing makes possible a test of the proposition that regional cooperation is having an impact on the financial resources of Arab countries in the Middle East.

The first method of testing these hypotheses is a relatively simple procedure. If the dispersion between interest rates is decreasing over time it is assumed that this is a result of capital market integration. Hence, if $|Xr_1 t - Yr_2 t|$

is decreasing over time, it is assumed that this is a valid test for capital market integration, where Xr_1t, Yr_2t represent similar assets in countries X and Y with interest rates r_1 and r_2 in time t, and the vertical bars represent absolute value.

Several problems arise with this kind of analysis. No distinction is made between nominal and real interest rates. If the various countries are experiencing different rates of inflation this would tend to bias the results. Secondly, the use of absolute as opposed to a weighted difference implies that convergence in our context is an absolute narrowing of differences. The assumption here is that a risk premium is an absolute as opposed to a relative difference. With these qualifications in mind, the results of the various tests are presented.

Data

The first question that can be asked is whether the data are adequate to support these tests of capital market integration. It is well known that capital markets in some of these countries are dominated by the public sector and that political factors loom large for the region as a whole. For example, the 1967 war disrupted capital markets throughout the region. However, it is also true that a number of these countries maintain open capital markets that reflect market forces in both the domestic and international economy. In several of these capital markets financial institutions from the developed countries play an active role in integrating the markets into the international capital market. For example, the Central Bank of Kuwait characterized the Kuwaiti capital market as follows:

> Kuwait financial market is highly sensitive in view of its limited size and its exposure to international economic developments whose repercussions are of great impact on the local market. A drop in interest rates abroad or a disruption in international financial markets would push up both prices and volume of shares transacted in the local market. Such international events would bring about substantial inflow of funds invested abroad in chase of higher interest rates or more security against losses that might result from the fluctuations in the exchange rates of some currencies. However, the local market is too limited to absorb such large inflows. Therefore the local stock market, which is the only left investment alternative, would be subjected to great pressures thus pushing up both prices and volume of shares transacted in the local market.[6]

In addition to Kuwait, other countries having open capital markets are Abu Dhabi, Dubai, Sharjah, Qatar, Bahrain, Saudi Arabia, and Lebanon. Note that Lebanon is a non-oil-producing Arab country that has an extensive history as a financial center in the Middle East, whereas the other countries are oil-producing countries with a more recent development of capital markets. Data on prime short-term bank rate, commercial paper rate, long-term (three- to five-year) rate, and rediscount rate have been obtained for each of these countries.[7]

Econometric Tests

The first test is for convergence of interest rates among the Middle East oil-producing nations, for which a regression in the form

$$\Sigma(Xrt - \bar{X}rt)^2 = a + bt + cZ \tag{3.1}$$

is used. This test differs slightly from the test mentioned earlier in that the use of squared deviations is regressed on time and a dummy variable Z has been inserted on the right hand side. The equation is defined as follows:

1. Xrt represents an observation on an asset in country r in period t.
2. $\bar{X}t$ represents the average of all i in period t.
3. t represents time.
4. Z is a dummy variable set equal to zero from May 1971 until May 1973. From August 1973 to and including May 1975, the dummy was set at 1.

The time period for this regression is May 1971 to May 1975. Quarterly data were used based on observations in February, May, August and November of each full year. The countries chosen were Abu Dhabi, Bahrain, Qatar, and Saudi Arabia. The interest rate used for this study was the short-term prime rate in each country. The results are given below, with t scores in parentheses.

Dependent Variable	b	c	R^2/DW	Observations
$\Sigma(Xrt - \bar{X}rt)^2$	.04 (.33)	2.9 (2.35)	.62/1.78	17

These results contradict the hypothesis that interest rates are converging in the Middle East. The b term, while insignificant, has the wrong sign. The c term yields a significant score but obtains the wrong sign. Several qualifications, however, are in order. First, the sample of countries is limited, and may not represent the true picture of Middle Eastern capital markets. Second, a closer look at the data reveals a tendency toward convergence in late 1974 and early 1975. It should be emphasized that the dummy variable was inserted during the 1973 Arab-Israeli war. We speculate that the period immediately following the war tended, at least initially, to disrupt whatever, if any, capital market integration was taking place. This would not be inconsistent with a longer-run tendency toward capital market integration.

The first hypothesis also states that via regional cooperation and regional integration one would expect a convergence between interest rates among the

Arab oil- and Arab non-oil-producing nations in the Middle East. In this test the form

$$|MErt - LEBrt| = a + bt + cx \tag{3.2}$$

is used, where t, x are defined as before. MErt represents the average short-term prime interest rate in period t for a group of oil-producing nations. These nations are Abu Dhabi, Bahrain, Dubai, Qatar, Saudi Arabia and Sharjah, from August 1971 to May 1974. From August 1974 to February 1975, the ME is redefined to include only Abu Dhabi, Bahrain, Qatar, and Saudi Arabia. This redefinition was utilized to take into account the currency union formed between Abu Dhabi, Dubai, and Sharjah in June 1974. LEBrt represents the prime short-term Lebanese interest rate in period t. Lebanon is used to represent an Arab (or predominantly Arab) non-oil-producing nation in the region. X is a dummy variable set at 0 until November 1973. In February 1974 the value was set at 1.

Dependent Variable	b	c	R^2/DW	R^2	Observations
|MErt - LEBrt|	-.001	-1.92	.946/2.78		16
	(.54)	(8.39)			
Rho transformation	-.001	-1.97		.977	
	(.69)	(11.7)			

The results indicate a tendency for convergence. While the b term is insignificant at .25 level in both cases, it has a negative sign which is consistent with convergence. The dummy variable is not only significant at the .01 level, but it also obtains a negative coefficient. The explanatory value of the regression is high. The regression results are consistent with a convergence of the Middle East-Lebanese interest rates. It is worth noting that this convergence need not be due to capital market integration, but may be caused by other factors as well.

The second hypothesis states that the Middle East capital market will tend to diverge from less developed non-oil-producing, non-Arab nations. Because of the availability of comparable data we chose to test the relationship between a Middle East interest rate and a Pakistani interest rate. The form of the test was

$$|MErt - PAKrt| = a + bt \tag{3.3}$$

All interest rates are prime short-term rates. The Middle East is defined as in Equation (3.2). The time period is the same as in the above test, except that the initial observation is from May 1971. The results are given below.

Dependent Variable	b	R^2/DW	R^2	Observations
|MErt – PAKrt|	.37	.81/1.18		17
	(6.82)			
Rho transformation	.329		.75	
	(8.52)			

The results obtained are consistent with a divergence between Middle East and Pakistani capital markets. While no further testing was done utilizing less developed non-Arab states, it is believed that a further testing of this nature may be warranted.

The third hypothesis states that regional integration in the Middle East will lead to a divergence between interest rates in the Middle East and the developed nations.

The first test defined the Middle East as Abu Dhabi, Saudi Arabia, Bahrain, Qatar and Kuwait. For all countries except Kuwait the prime short-term interest rate was used. For Kuwait a local bank credit rate was utilized. Due to limitations on Kuwaiti data only nine sample observations were obtained. The sample period covers March, June, September, December of 1972 and 1973, and March of 1974.

The developed nations consist of the United States, United Kingdom, Canada, Japan, Germany, Italy, Belgium, Switzerland, Sweden, and the Eurodollar rate is used. (All country rates are prime short-term rates.) The equation tested is in the form

$$|MErt - Drt| = a_0 + bt \qquad (3.4)$$

where MErt, Drt represent average short-term rates in the Middle East and the developed nations, respectively, in time t. The results are presented below.

Dependent Variable	b	R^2/DW	Observations
|MErt – Drt|	.016	.02/1.79	9
	(.388)		

The results are insignificant at the .25 level. The test shows no statistically significant evidence of divergence over time. It should be emphasized that the sample is of small size. Further, the b coefficient, while insignificant, was positive, indicating the possibility of divergence.

A further test was conducted by utilizing an average Middle East short-term prime rate and the United States short-term business loan rate. The Middle East was defined as on page 60, and the sample period is from May 1971 to February 1975. The results are shown below.

Dependent Variable	b	R^2/DW	R^2	Observations
|MErt – USrt|	.046	.05/.88		16
	(.887)			
Rho transformation	.058		.027	
	(.607)			

The results are again statistically insignificant. The b term is positive, indicating a tendency for divergence; however, the t score is not significant at the .25 level.

The final test of the third hypothesis is based on the proposition of regional bias in capital markets in the Middle East. We assume that (1) the Middle East capital market consists of risk averters who maximized their expected utility from end-of-period wealth; (2) portfolio decisions are made solely on the basis of expected returns and standard deviations of returns; (3) that all investors have similar time horizons and similar expectations; and (4) that all capital markets are perfect in the sense that there are many buyers and sellers and equal interest rates for borrowing and lending. Then it can be shown that in equilibrium the relationship between the expected return on an asset and a riskless asset Rf is given by

$$E(Rj) = Rf + \lambda \, Cov \, (Rj, Rm)$$

or

$$\frac{E(Rj) - Rf}{Cov \, (Rj, Rm)} = \lambda \tag{3.5}$$

where $E(Rj - Rf)$ is the risk premium on the jth asset above the riskless asset Rf, and Cov (Rj, Rm) is defined as the covariance of the jth asset to the portfolio of all m assets, where m also includes the jth asset.

The equation states that the relationship between an asset's expected return and risk is proportional. Furthermore this proportion is constant across all assets. However, if assets of differing regions are considered to be imperfect substitutes, the λ would not be constant. Therefore, a test is made to see if the λ differs between Middle East and developed countries' securities.

The form of the test is as follows:

$$\frac{Rj - Rc}{Cov \, (Rj, rim)} = a_0 + a_2 x \tag{3.6}$$

where

1. Rj is the compound rate of growth of asset j for the years 1971-74. The Rj's used in this study were calculated from the discount trade-paper rates of Abu Dhabi, Bahrian, Qatar, Saudi Arabia; the prime short-term rates of Abu Dhabi, Bahrain, Qatar, and Saudi Arabia; both the United States short-term bank rate and the commercial prime-paper rates; the prime short-term rates of the United Kingdom, France, and Germany; and the Eurodollar rate.

2. Rc is a compound rate computed by using the long-term rate for Abu Dhabi, Bahrain, Qatar, and Saudi Arabia.

3. Rj, rim is the covariance between the jth asset and the average rate on all assets.

4. X is a dummy variable set at 0 if the investment is foreign, 1 if it is domestic (Middle East). Therefore, if investment is biased toward regional assets, the sign on a_2 would be negative. The results are given below.

Dependent Variable	a_2	adj R^2/DW	Observations
$\dfrac{\text{Rj} - \text{Rc}}{\text{Cov (Rj, rim)}}$	6.16 (1.47)	.097/1.88	13

Note that the explanatory power of the equation is slight. The a_2 coefficient indicates a bias toward foreign assets; however, it is insignificant at the .10 level. While this test rests on rather stringent assumptions it is believed that further testing along these lines might be useful, especially if additional data could be obtained.[8] Furthermore, the above equation might be tested over different time periods.

Conclusions

In summary, an attempt has been made to demonstrate the incipient development of a capital market among Arab countries in the Middle East and a divergence of this regional market from capital markets in both less developed non-Arab nations and the developed world. The tests were not conclusive but several points stand out.

1. There appears to be a narrowing of interest rate differentials between the Arab oil and non-oil producers in the region.

2. There appears to be a divergence between the Middle East and less developed countries.

3. The results are inconclusive as regards a convergence of a Middle East oil producer's capital market, a divergence of a Middle East oil producer's capital markets from capital markets in developed countries, and the bias of investment either toward or away from Middle East capital markets.

It is again emphasized that these tests represent only a preliminary first attempt to test the hypotheses stated at the outset.

NOTES

1. Charles P. Kindleberger, "European Economic Integration" in *Money, Trade, and Economic Growth*, ed. John Henry Williams (New York: Macmillan, 1951).

2. Ibid., p. 66.

3. Bela Balassa, *Economic Development and Integration*, Centro de Estudios Monetarios Latinoamericanos, Mexico, 1965; and idem, *The Theory of Economic Integration* (Homewood, Ill.: Irwin, 1961).

4. For an application of this test to the British capital market, see Michael Edelstein, "Rigidity and Bias in the British Capital Market, 1870-1913" in *Essays on a Mature Economy Nation after 1840*, ed. Donald N. McCloskey (Princeton, N.J.: Princeton University Press, 1971), pp. 83-106.

5. Harry Markowitz, *Portfolio Selection: Efficient Diversification of Investments* (New York: John Wiley, 1959); James Tobin, "Liquidity Preference as Behavior Toward Risk," *Review of Economic Studies*, 1959, pp. 65-86.

6. Central Bank of Kuwait, *Fourth Annual Report* (Kuwait: Magahiwi Press, 1973).

7. Prime short-term bank rate: Abu Dhabi, Bahrain, Dubai, Lebanon, Pakistan, Qatar, Saudi Arabia, Sharjah—First National City Bank, Foreign Information Service, "Middle Eastern Money Market Conditions," *Monthly Economic Report*, various issues, 1971-75; Kuwait—Central Bank of Kuwait, *Annual Report*, 1971-74; United States, United Kingdom, Canada, Japan, France, Germany, Italy, Belgium, Switzerland, Sweden, Eurodollar market—Morgan Guaranty Trust Company of New York, *World Financial Markets*, various issues, 1971-74.

Commercial paper rate: Abu Dhabi, Bahrain, Dubai, Lebanon, Pakistan, Qatar, Saudi Arabia, Sharjah—First National City Bank, Foreign Information Service, "Middle Eastern Money Market Conditions," *Monthly Economic Report*, various issues, 1971-75; U.S. Department of Commerce, *Survey of Current Business*, various issues, 1971-75.

Long-term (three- to five-year) rate: Abu Dhabi, Bahrain, Dubai, Lebanon, Pakistan, Qatar, Saudi Arabia, Sharjah—First National City Bank, Foreign Information Service, "Middle Eastern Money Market Conditions," *Monthly Economic Report*, various issues, 1971-75; U.S. Department of Commerce, *Survey of Current Business*, various issues, 1971-75.

Rediscount rate: Abu Dhabi, Bahrain, Dubai, Lebanon, Pakistan, Qatar, Saudi Arabia, Sharjah—First National City Bank, Foreign Information Service, "Middle Eastern Money Market Conditions," *Monthly Economic Report*, various issues, 1971-75; Kuwait—Central Bank of Kuwait, *Annual Report*, 1971-74; United States, United Kingdom, Canada, Japan, France, Germany, Italy, Belgium, Switzerland, Sweden—International Monetary Fund, *International Financial Statistics*, various issues, 1971-75.

8. A further series of tests was attempted using analysis of variance analogous to the tests used by Lance E. Davis, "The Investment Market, 1870-1914: The Evolution of a National Market," *Journal of Economic History* 15 (September, 1965), pp. 355-93. Due to problems of data availability and small sample size properties in the tests these results are not reported.

4

FINANCING THE
CAPITAL REQUIREMENTS
OF THE NON-OIL PRODUCERS

ASSESSING THE SIZE OF THE CAPITAL SURPLUS

The size of surplus oil revenues depends basically on two variables: the magnitude of oil revenues received by the government and the domestic absorptive capacity of the economy. Given the level of oil revenues, the greater the capacity of the major oil producers to use these revenues domestically, the smaller the surplus capital. Such a perception of the allocation of oil revenues accords with the order of priorities declared by all oil-exporting countries in the Middle East: investment is first to be directed toward satisfying the needs of the national economy with the balance flowing to the region, the developing world, and the industrialized nations in that order. A fairly precise idea has already been obtained of where the limits of domestic absorptive capacity of the oil producers may lie. It has also become apparent that domestic absorptive capacity is basically and foremost a function of time; the economy of each and every state is normally capable of absorbing a greater volume of capital in later periods than at the present time or in the immediate future. However, as the time horizon lengthens, estimates of absorptive capacity become less dependable because of the difficulty associated with forecasting possible shifts in the structural parameters of statistical equations. Not only is absorptive capacity subject to a wide margin of error in the long run, but also the oil demand-supply equation cannot be predicted with certitude, thus rendering any projection of long-run oil revenues a hazardous and unreliable exercise at best. Due to these considerations, the analysis in this chapter is confined to the period of 1975-80.

In the light of the following discussion, two assumptions appear plausible, albeit somewhat conservative: oil prices will be maintained at their current levels and the present global demand for oil will stay unchanged during 1975-80. It follows that the Middle East countries can easily continue oil production at current levels with no diminution in revenues, provided the supply of oil from other sources remains constant. The prospects for substantial surge in oil supplies from non-Middle-East sources appear at least until 1980 very remote. Middle East oil is obviously accessible and competititve compared to oil from such alternative sources as the North Sea and Alaska. Such alternative sources are not only expensive but also face significant logistic problems and involve considerable lead time that may exceed ten years.

> Exploration of the major oil reserves found in the industrialized world has involved very substantial lead times despite the crucial need for captive and more secure supplies. For example, about ten to fifteen years have been required to bring up major new oil in the North Slope of Alaska. The history of development of [Alaska's North Slope and the North Sea petroleum reserves] should be particularly enlightening for those who look toward unforeseen developments to diminish the world oil problem.[1]

Thus, given a stable world demand for oil and a relatively constant supply of non-Middle-East oil, present production levels in the Middle East can be maintained at stable prices. This would ensure that current oil revenues remain constant, ceteris paribus.

Many factors may be cited that could effectively reduce the global demand for oil. These include prolonged economic stagnation in the West, successful and extensive conservation efforts, and rapid substitution of other energy sources for oil or any combination of the above. If any of these conditions materializes, then the future of oil prices, production, and revenues will hinge again on the behavior of oil supply from non-Middle-East sources. In the event the latter supply remains constant, the oil-producing states in the Middle East must curtail their production levels if present oil prices are to be preserved. The manner in which production cutbacks are apportioned among the various oil exporters bears important implications for the size of the capital surplus. If the low absorbers—Kuwait, Qatar, the United Arab Emirates, and Saudi Arabia—shoulder the bulk of the necessary reduction in demand, while the high absorbers—Iran, Iraq, and Algeria—maintain their production levels intact, the size of capital surplus may diminish appreciably and may even be wiped out altogether. If, on the other hand, shut-in capacity is allocated on the basis of current market shares, the size of the capital surplus will evidently be reduced by less.* It should

----

*The interest here is in the size of the capital surplus available to finance development in the Arab non-oil producing states. Specifically, the possibility is ruled out that diminished oil revenues accruing to the high absorbers due to production cutbacks would be compensated for by capital inflows from the low absorbing oil countries.

be emphasized, however, that if the oil producers are viewed as one group, then the size of the surplus would not be susceptible to variations in the distribution of production cutbacks.

Some would argue that if demand for OPEC oil could be sufficiently reduced, the solidarity of OPEC would be eroded and oil prices would start a downward spiral, as each country would strive to hold its market share by offering oil at slightly lower prices. However, at least until 1980, such a scenario of price war must be regarded as tenuous and highly improbable for the following reasons.

First, the possibility of a drastic leftward shift in the demand curve for oil during the next five years is exceedingly remote. The lead time required to develop and more importantly to convert the contemporary economic life to a new source of energy certainly is much longer. Those who naively believe in such miracles must be reminded that coal is still a major source of energy, notwithstanding the discovery and development of crude petroleum about a century ago.

Second, moderate leftward shifts in the demand for oil would in all probability be offset by output restrictions on the part of the producers as recent experience clearly illustrates. In fact, as long as the demand curve shifts symmetrically, that is, without significantly changing its slope, the best course of action OPEC members can pursue is to maintain prices and further cut back production. This is indeed a corollary of a distinctly inelastic demand in the relevant range. Possible long-run asymmetrical shifts must be counteracted with extensive industrialization in the field of petrochemicals.

It must be emphasized, moreover, that the interests of the high absorbers and the low absorbers as to the appropriate levels of prices and production are not diametrically opposed as is commonly but erroneously contended. True, the high absorbers require greater revenues to sustain a rapid pace of economic and social development; however, this desire must be balanced against their limited and dwindling petroleum reserves. The low absorbers, in turn, would not be greatly averse to production cutbacks for the sake of holding prices at present levels, despite their large reserves, because of the following factors: constrained domestic avenues for productive investment, high risks involved in international investment, and the almost single resource nature of their economy. These motives individually and in combination make a policy of conservation both feasible and attractive, especially if one keeps in mind the multifarious products that can be manufactured from crude petroleum and natural gas.

Finally, the West has very little to gain from significantly lower oil prices because such prices tend—as they forcefully did in the recent past—to decelerate not only exploration and development of oil reserves outside the Middle East, but also the development of alternate sources of energy. Consequently, lower oil prices would increase and prolong the dependence of Europe, Japan, and the United States on the Middle East. The U.S. government is cognizant of this

TABLE 4.1

Estimates of the Capital Surplus
of Major Arab Oil Exporters, 1975-85
(billions of 1974 dollars)

	1975	1980	1985
Oil revenues	55.79	55.79	55.79
Less payment for nationalized			
foreign oil interest	1.00	1.00	–
Less absorptive capacity			
Minimum	12.22	19.60	26.66
Maximum	16.55	32.00	52.10
Equals surplus capital			
Minimum	38.24	22.79	3.69
Maximum	42.57	35.19	29.13

Note: Estimates are for Iraq, Kuwait, Libya, Qatar, Saudi Arabia, and the United Arab Emirates.
Source: Calculations made by the ICEED staff.

fact—witness its advocacy of a floor price for oil that does not frustrate the basic objective of greater self-sufficiency in energy.

In the light of this discussion it appears plausible to assume that oil revenues of the major oil producers in the Middle East will continue at their current level of approximately $56 billion until 1980 and possibly even 1985. Given the level of oil revenues and the projections of domestic absorptive capacity developed above, the size of the capital surplus may be estimated.*

Taking a rather conservative viewpoint, it is assumed that the size of the surplus would be close to its minimum levels, that is, about $38 billion, $23 billion, and $4 billion in 1975, 1980, and 1985, respectively. The validity of the subsequent argument would, of course, be enhanced if the magnitudes of the surplus were larger.

---

*Iran is excluded here in order to focus on the Arab world. By now, most Middle East governments have nationalized slightly more than 50 percent of the foreign oil interests and agreed to pay compensation totaling some $3.3 billion. There are indications, however, that these governments will soon assume full ownership of foreign oil interests operating within their borders. Thus, payments to Western oil companies for sequestered property are expected to average about $1 billion annually during 1975-80.

REGIONAL INVESTMENT AND/OR DEVELOPMENT AID: AN ANALYSIS OF OBJECTIVES AND MOTIVATION

To ascertain the broad objectives of regional investment and aid programs is a complex task because these objectives are almost always intertwined, thus precluding a neat separation, let alone ranking of individual motives. Moreover, different investors and donors may have very special reasons for or assign different weights to individual motives in their investment and aid-giving activities. Generally, the following four factors, listed in order of importance, appear to be the basic and most significant underlying motives behind all Arab investment and development aid: the political, the cultural, the economic, and the humanitarian motives.

The political and cultural/religious motives behind Arab oil producers' investment and/or aid to Arab non-oil-producing countries are obvious: the people of the two groups share close affinities in language, religion, background, and history. In fact, all Arab countries view themselves as part and parcel of the Arab world. Any Arab oil-producing country, especially if small, finds itself under enormous pressures both from within and from the rest of the Arab world to contribute to the economic development of the Arab people—a sentiment echoed in the national slogan, "Arab oil for Arab people." This explains why such nations as Saudi Arabia, Kuwait, and Abu Dhabi consider the orderly economic development of fellow Arab states as an effective deterrent to social and political instability in the region.

The economic rationale for channeling surplus capital to the region has been spelled out earlier in some detail. Thus, it suffices here to reiterate briefly some of the major arguments. With the possible exception of Algeria, the leading Arab oil producers are labor-deficit countries. To accelerate their own economic and social development they have been relying increasingly on expatriate labor, notably, Palestinians, Egyptians, and Lebanese.* Investment in and aid to labor-surplus Arab countries may be cited as a potent means of competition for labor, especially skilled manpower. Furthermore, economic cooperation between the Arab oil producers and non-oil states, particularly at the commodity and sectoral levels, could be of great potential benefit to all parties concerned. There is greater realization that cooperation enlarges the size of the market and reduces market uncertainty, thereby permitting the exploitation of economies of large-scale production. It also allows specialization along the principle of comparative advantage, contributing to more efficient allocation of resources.

----

*Expatriate labor in many Gulf states often constitutes much higher than 50 percent of the total labor force.

The recent surge in oil prices created egregious disparities in human wealth and human welfare conditions between the oil haves and have-nots. The cleavage between these two groups is most dramatic in the Arab world. Countries with relatively small populations like Abu Dhabi, Qatar, Kuwait, Libya, Saudi Arabia, and to a lesser extent Iraq, suddenly have found themselves with enormous financial resources far exceeding their domestic capital absorptive capacities (at least in the immediate future), while the people of Egypt, Sudan, Yemen, Morocco, Jordan, Syria, and Tunisia are still living close to subsistence or even starvation levels. Thus, humanitarian considerations reflected in the moral principle of relative egalitarianism normally accepted within a single country and community must be recognized as an important factor in Arab investment and aid-giving activities.

The motives for channeling investment and/or aid to non-Arab developing countries are not different from those listed above, though the accent is heavily on the religious and political aspects. The bond of Islam is still a powerful force, especially in such traditional states as Saudi Arabia. Thus, the sizable assistance provided by the Arab oil exporters to the Moslem countries and communities must be viewed in this light. The political rationale for investment and aid extension to developing countries outside the Arab and Islamic worlds lies in the desire to marshal Third World support for the Arab position in the Middle East crisis and on such issues as commodity pricing for raw materials in the field of international economic relations. Another factor is said to be that the Arab countries share with the Third World a long history of colonialism, poverty, deprivation, and backwardness—a past and present kinship.

It is important to observe that the economic motive behind Arab investment and/or aid to the region and to the developing countries is gradually but steadily gaining in significance, due both to the growing monetary and financial vicissitudes in West European and U.S. markets and to the recent efforts by many developing countries to attract additional foreign investment. Arab investment and/or development aid, by strengthening the economic and political relations with recipient countries, would enhance the security and prospects of channeling Arab surplus capital to profitable investment in Third World countries, thereby permitting a greater diversification of Arab portfolio holdings.

CAPITAL REQUIREMENTS
OF THE ARAB NON-OIL-EXPORTING STATES

It is apparent that at least until 1980 the major Arab oil producers will sustain substantial capital accumulation over and above their domestic requirements. But the projected size of the surplus gets progressively smaller as the bottlenecks hindering greater capital utilization in these countries are effectively overcome. Meanwhile, these countries will be looking for remunerative investment avenues outside their borders.* High on their scale of priorities stands regional investment for reasons already outlined above. If regional cooperation, as all indications seem to point out, is not an evanescent phenomenon but one which is here to stay and grow, then it becomes imperative to assess the potential demand for and supply of capital in the Arab non-oil countries.

A 10 percent annual real compound rate of growth of GNP in the Arab non-oil economies for the period 1975-80 is assumed. This rate is admittedly high and must be considered as the maximum rate these countries could achieve, given their resource base, economic structure, and institutional capabilities, provided the supply of capital is highly elastic. In fact, with the current average rate of population growth in the Arab world, a 10 percent rate of growth in GNP would ensure the doubling of per capita income in the non-oil-producing countries in about ten years. Moreover the assumed rate of growth is in line with planners' preferences and aspirations in many states in the area, thus serving well as a point of departure for an analysis of the magnitude of the capital gap in these economies.

Analysis of capital requirements of the Arab non-oil economies proceeds within the general framework of the Harrod-Domar model. The basic relationship is spelled out in the following familiar equation:

Rate of growth in GNP = Rate of investment/Incremental capital-output ratio

The estimation procedure is outlined below:

The necessary data on current GNP, recent incremental capital-output ratios, marginal saving rates, and current rates of investment are collected and evaluated for consistency and reliability.

The rate of required future investment is simply the product of multiplying the projected rate of growth of GNP by the respective incremental capital-output ratio.

The capital requirement of each state is easily arrived at by multiplying the future rate of investment by the projected level of GNP during the period 1975-80.

The capital available to each non-oil economy is calculated in the following manner: the historical capital formation rate is multiplied by GNP in 1974 and the resulting magnitude is added to the annual incremental savings. The latter is procured by multiplying the marginal saving rate by the appropriate increment in GNP in each year.

------

*Regional investment must be evaluated not only in terms of pecuniary benefits but also in terms of its contribution to the multifarious objectives of the investing country. The rationale for this perception is the fact that oil revenues accrue to governments that, unlike their private citizens, are not narrowly motivated.

The capital gap for every state is then obtained by subtracting available capital resources from the capital requirement necessary to sustain the projected rate of growth in GNP as previously determined.

Finally, the regional capital gap is defined as the sum of the capital gaps of the individual countries under investigation (Egypt, Sudan, Morocco, Tunisia, Syria, Yemen Arab Republic, Lebanon, and Jordan).

It must be emphasized that the results obtained here reflect the net additional or incremental volume of capital transfer to the regional non-oil economies which must take place if these economies are to realize the stipulated rate of growth in GNP indicated above. In other words, the net additional capital requirements represent a volume of capital transfer over and above current levels received by the non-oil economies from the major oil producers and from other sources. Thus, should nonregional capital transfers for development purposes dry up or decrease, albeit an unlikely possibility, then regional capital transfers must compensate for the emerging capital deficiency. The current level of capital transfer from the major oil producers to the region and elsewhere will be analyzed separately in the ensuing sections.

The limitations of the analysis are recognized. Specifically, the organic link assumed between output growth and capital formation may be questioned. Certainly, capital is a critical factor in the growth process but it is not the only factor. Thus an oversimplification may be involved in relegating other factors, namely, skilled labor, administrative and managerial capacities, and entrepreneurial talent, to the background despite their crucial role in the process of development. One may further object to the assumption of constant incremental capital-output ratios in basically agrarian economies. In such economies, changes in weather conditions usually produce significant variations in the overall capital-output ratio. Moreover, and apart from its highly aggregative nature, the capital-output ratio technique does not adequately account for gestation periods of diverse investment projects.

There is no wish to deny the partial validity of these criticisms. However, there are significant balancing factors. First, if capital could be removed as a binding constraint on the growth process, the investigator would be able to appraise the effectiveness of government policies pertaining to the necessary institutional reforms and the mobilization of other existing and dormant resources. Thus, the social costs of inefficient government bureaucracy and of growth-inhibiting public policies would be directly reflected in the output foregone. Evidently, one can no longer contend that capital shortage is at the heart of the inadequate performance of most of these economies.

Second, some of the shortcomings of the capital-output ratio technique, namely, its aggregative nature and its simplicity, are precisely the attributes responsible for its current extensive use. For the purpose of procuring approximate answers to development problems of considerable complexity, it is often useful to employ simple and aggregative tools.

Third, a given technique or theory should not be evaluated in terms of the correspondence of its premises to exact factual conditions. Rather, a theory must be appraised in terms of its capacity to predict future phenomena with a reasonable margin of error. As a tool of analysis, the capital-output ratio technique has proved productive in formulating the aggregative framework of many plans in numerous developing countries. Thus, at the present level of generality and for the purpose of contrasting the capital gap of the non-oil economies in the region with the capital surplus of the Arab oil producers, the capital-output ratio technique is adequate and legitimate.

The relevant statistics and the results of the analysis are indicated in Tables 4.2, 4.3, and 4.4.

Several observations may be made on the basis of these results. Absorptive capacity in the Arab non-oil countries must be defined in terms of capital accumulation as well as capital formation. The dearth of available capital resources

TABLE 4.2

GNP, Rates of Investment and Saving, and the Capital-Output Ratio in Selected Arab Countries

	GNP (billions of 1974 dollars)	Rate of Investment[a] (percent)	Marginal Saving Rate[b] (percent)	Incremental Capital-Output Ratio[c]
Egypt	10.00	11.10	10.08	3.04
Sudan	2.40	11.00	13.87	3.90
Morocco	5.70	13.30	10.54	2.50
Tunisia	3.00	21.40	18.18	2.60
Syria	2.66	19.90	6.00	2.25
Lebanon	2.60	19.10	2.00	3.20
Jordan	0.90	19.40	0.00	3.75
Yemen Arab Republic	0.55	13.10	0.00	2.85

[a]Investment rates are reported for the early 1970s.

[b]Marginal saving rates are taken from Abdul-Rasool with the exception of those for Jordan and the Yemen Arab Republic which were assumed zero because of the prevalence of negative rates in the past.

[c]Abdul-Rasool's ratios are moderately revised in the light of new developments.

Sources: Kuwait Fund for Arab Economic Development, The Arab World: Key Indicators (Kuwait: Kuwait Fund, 1975); F. Abdul-Rasool, "The Role of Arab Monetary Reserves in Arab Economic Integration" (Baghdad: Central Bank of Iraq, 1974) (Memo in Arabic, 1974); U.S. Department of State, Bureau of Public Affairs, Office of Media Services, Special Report No. 22, November 1975; calculations made by the ICEED staff.

TABLE 4.3

Capital Requirements of Selected Arab Countries, 1975-80
(billions of 1974 dollars)

Country	Capital Requirement	Available Capital	Capital Gap	Percent Available
Egypt	23.470	9.280	14.190	39.5
Sudan	7.210	2.411	4.799	33.4
Morocco	11.020	6.044	4.976	54.8
Tunisia	6.030	5.210	0.820	86.4
Syria	4.600	3.571	1.029	77.6
Lebanon	6.432	3.111	3.321	48.4
Jordan	2.600	1.152	1.448	44.3
Yemen Arab Republic	1.200	0.480	0.720	40.0
Total	62.562	31.259	31.303	50.0

Source: Calculations made by the ICEED staff.

TABLE 4.4

Total Capital Requirements of Selected Arab Countries, 1975-80
(billions of 1974 dollars)

Year	Capital Requirement	Available Capital	Capital Gap	Percent Available
1975	8.142	4.341	3.801	53
1976	8.920	4.658	4.262	52
1977	9.750	4.991	4.759	51
1978	10.840	5.346	5.494	49
1979	11.890	5.745	6.145	48
1980	13.020	6.178	6.842	47
Total	62.562	31.259	31.303	50

Source: Calculations made by the ICEED staff.

is the basic constraint on absorptive capacity. The oil exporters, on the other hand, face a strikingly dissimilar structural disequilibrium: absorptive capacity is restrained by acute labor shortage and not by the scarcity of capital resources. Estimates of capital absorptive capacity of the major oil producers were predicated on sizable labor importation from the region, thus making regional cooperation an indispensable means of investment expansion. Similarly, the projected rate of growth in GNP for the Arab non-oil economies cannot be attained in the absence of the stipulated net capital transfer, principally from the leading oil producers.[2] The reciprocity of interests between the two groups of countries— the Arab oil producers and the non-oil-based economies—is becoming increasingly clear. These countries can hardly realistically hope to achieve their full economic potential without extensive regional cooperation. A rough measure of the contribution of regional cooperation to the expansion of the absorptive capacity of the major oil producers may be gleaned from the composition of the labor force with respect to its national origin. The percentage of expatriate labor in the small littoral states is presently in excess of 60 percent and it is more than 25 percent in Saudi Arabia and Libya. In Iraq, the proportion is expected to range between 5 and 10 percent in the next decade.

The actual and potential contribution of regional cooperation to increasing the absorptive capacity of the Arab non-oil economies may be measured in terms of the current level of capital transfer and the size of the projected capital gap. An additional $31.3 billion net capital transfer from the leading oil producers to the region would more than double the rate of growth of GNP in recipient countries.

The estimates of the required capital transfers are net. Thus, it is assumed that repatriation of debt and interest thereon is accomplished by one or a combination of such policies as postponement of repatriation beyond 1980, raising the marginal saving rate to neutralize reverse capital flows, and encouraging foreign equity investment in the domestic economy but with restricted profit transfer at least in the initial period.

The average net additional capital transfer necessary to accelerate the rate of growth in the non-oil economies to a level of 10 percent is about $5.2 billion annually during 1975-80. The minimum estimate of surplus capital in the leading oil-producing states ranges between $38 billion in 1975 and $23 billion in 1980, thus averaging about $30.5 billion annually. The annual volume of capital transfer is therefore only 16.5 percent of the annual capital surplus. Given that current investment in and aid to the region is relatively small, such an additional level of capital transfer obviously is not an unwise investment strategy for the major oil producers. This is so because the dividends from regional investment are likely to exceed the rate of return on additional investment in the West. Regional investment permits portfolio diversification, thus decreasing risk for any given rate of return, and it provides considerable nonpecuniary benefits as well.

The countries most in need of additional capital transfer are the Sudan and Egypt. In fact, about 45 percent of the total additional capital transfer must be channeled to Egypt, the country suffering from the most serious shortage of capital, given its abundant labor supply. Tunisia and Syria are better situated, displaying greater capacity in marshaling capital resources for development. This may be partially explained by their higher per capita income, relatively efficient government institutions, and favorable growth prospects.

The capital gap during 1975-80 steadily increases from about $3.8 billion in 1975 to $6.8 billion in 1980. On the other hand, the minimum size of the capital surplus progressively declines from $38 billion in 1975 to $23 billion in 1980. This conflicting time profile of the two variables is likely to decrease the future willingness of the oil producers to finance development in the capital-deficit countries. The Arab non-oil countries must, therefore, strive to enhance the profitability prospects of investment within their own economies, if they seriously wish to receive adequate support from their fellow oil-exporting countries.

As a first approximation, the recipient countries would be better off borrowing and paying a real rate of interest on borrowed funds that does not exceed eight percent. Such a rate of interest implies cumulative interest payments during the period under consideration of about $9 billion which is roughly equivalent to the increment in the GNP of the non-oil producers accruing as a result of additional capital transfer.* Obviously, the lower the rate of interest charged, the greater would be the benefits derived by the non-oil economies. Similarly, the burden of the debt would also depend on the evolution of the terms of trade of the recipient countries, as well as the success of their import substitution and export expansion policies.

From the point of view of the oil producers, investment in the region seems to yield not only considerable nonpecuniary benefits but also significant return, especially if one recalls that the rate of interest in the Eurodollar market where a substantial amount of surplus capital is invested is around 10 percent. In the light of the contemporary two-digit inflation prevailing in most Western economies, the real rate of interest on investment there must be zero or distinctly negative.

It may also be argued that proper allowance for risk would enhance the attractiveness of regional investment because of possible clash of political

---

*The incremental GNP is calculated on the assumption that, without additional capital transfer, GNP would be growing at 5 percent. The availability of capital increases the rate of growth of GNP to 10 percent, thus contributing an additional $9.4 billion. This argument must be viewed, however, as tentative and preliminary because it neither takes into account the benefits of investment beyond 1980 nor the rate of amortization of debt.

interests between the West and the oil-exporting countries. Proponents of this view also advocate the creation of multinational specialized institutions entrusted with channeling capital to the region because such an approach would, among other things, reduce significantly the hazards of noneconomic risks that regional investment might encounter.[3]

The prospects for continuity in the level of capital transfer from the oil producers to the region in the 1980s are limited. The estimated minimum capital surplus in 1985 is about $4 billion. As we have emphasized, however, this estimate is subject to a wide margin of error. Nevertheless, current rates of growth in the domestic absorptive capacity of the oil producers and in their oil revenues make an optimistic projection of regional investment in the 1980s unwarranted. The non-oil economies should therefore expect a significant drop in the level of regional investment in the 1980s along with stringent credit terms.*

THE DEBT PROBLEM
OF THE ARAB NON-OIL COUNTRIES

This section does not address the central questions that arise in the context of debt analysis, namely, why and how countries get involved in debt situations, the extent to which foreign capital is indispensable for their economic development, where the boundaries lie for financing domestic development through external capital inflows, and what the respective roles of resource providers and recipients are in promoting economic development and sound debt management practices. Important as they are, these issues are not the main concern here, but rather, the magnitude of indebtedness of the Arab non-oil countries to countries, groups of countries, and organizations and institutions outside the region. Obviously, the capital status of the region cannot be appropriately evaluated without explicit reference to the external debt accumulated in the past.

The magnitude of the external public debt of the Arab oil producers with the exception of Algeria is negligible in relation to their present financial resources and may, therefore, be ignored. The external public debt of the Arab non-oil countries is, however, substantial. Unfortunately, information as to its size and composition is available only as of December 31, 1972.†

---

*Of course, such a conclusion could be invalidated if the world demand for OPEC oil resumed its previous growth pattern at prevailing prices, or if the oil producers failed to maintain their own growth momentum in the 1980s.

† All of these Arab countries are planned economies in which the public sector plays a leading and dominant role. The movement of capital across national boundaries is strictly controlled. Consequently, private external indebtedness is insignificant and may, therefore, be ignored.

TABLE 4.5

Outstanding External Public Debt of Selected Arab Countries as of December 31, 1972
(millions of dollars)

Country	Disbursed Only	Including Undisbursed						Service payments on external public debt as percent of exports of goods and nonfactor services	
		Total	Bilateral Official	Multilateral	Suppliers	Banks	Other	1965	1972
Algeria	1,625.0	2,827.0	1,227.8	16.9	1,152.2	368.0	62.1	–	14.2
Egypt	1,571.1	2,040.9	1,622.4	67.2	105.9	44.9	200.4	15.3	31.5
Jordan	161.1	221.6	193.9	22.3	–	5.4	–	1.2	7.0
Morocco	852.1	1,112.2	678.7	282.7	49.3	63.9	37.9	4.8	8.5
Sudan	297.6	382.1	190.7	137.6	9.1	44.7	0.2	5.5	12.3
Syria	243.2	510.4	455.7	22.9	31.8	–	–	5.5	10.5
Tunisia	697.7	1,091.1	700.8	199.6	70.4	112.5	7.8	7.7	16.2
Total	5,447.8	8,185.3	5,070.0	749.2	1,418.7	639.4	308.4	–	–

Sources: The World Bank, *Annual Report 1974* (Washington, D.C.: World Bank, 1975); Kuwait Fund for Arab Economic Development, *The Arab World: Key Indicators* (Kuwait: Kuwait Fund, April 1975), p. 52.

Table 4.5 reveals the following important points:

1. The most heavily indebted countries in the group with respect to the absolute size of the debt (whether total or disbursed only) are Algeria and Egypt. If, however, the debt-service ratio is considered, Egypt will come first with Tunisia as a distant second.

2. The debt-service ratio in all the countries under investigation has risen precipitously, in the majority of cases more than doubling during 1965-72. This indicates the rising demand for capital in the region and the inability of the respective countries to marshal sufficient domestic resources. Generally, the higher the debt-service ratio, the lower is the capacity of the respective country to attract additional foreign capital. These countries must, therefore, initiate policies capable of restraining the rapid growth in their debt-service ratios.

3. The composition of the debt reveals a preponderance of bilateral aid and commercial credits, amounting to over 90 percent of the total. Bilateral aid is generally less desirable from the political standpoint, whereas commercial credits severely tax the repayment capacity of the country.

At least with respect to one major country, Egypt, the outstanding external public debt in convertible currencies must have grown dramatically in the previous three years. The Egyptian government recently announced in Parliament that the size of such debt, excluding military debts, is 2,218.6 million Egyptian pounds or about $5,674 million.[4] The size of the military debts of Egypt and Syria to the Soviet Union is not officially revealed, but it is believed to be on the order of $3 to $5 billion. On the basis of this and other fragmentary evidence and incomplete data, it is estimated that the total external public debt of the countries under investigation to nonregional countries is in the neighborhood of $16 billion as of January 1975. Evidently, the extent to which the region as a whole may be considered capital-surplus is diminished by the magnitude of this debt.

Another point is worth emphasizing here. One or more of the Arab major oil producers may wish to see significant reduction in the political leverage of foreign powers in the area, especially that of the Soviet Union. The fact that Egypt and Syria are deeply in debt to the Soviet Union obviously runs counter to this objective. Thus, the oil producers either collectively or individually may find it politically expedient to finance all or at least part of the outstanding bilateral debt of the Arab non-oil countries to the Soviet Union and other East bloc states. Such a policy would claim up to $6 billion or an average of $1 billion annually of the capital surplus of the oil producers during 1975-80. However, realistically speaking, the oil producers would probably not engage in such massive financing of existing debt. Nevertheless, some effort in this direction (perhaps as much as $3 billion during 1975-80) may be expected, especially in the light of the current Soviet pressure on Egypt using Egyptian military debts as a prime tool.

ANALYSIS OF ACTUAL REGIONAL CAPITAL FLOWS

This section endeavors to provide a quantitative analysis of actual or already initiated capital flows from the oil producers. Except for Arab institutionalized development aid, all the figures presented cover only the recent period of January 1973 to July 1975. Although special attention was made to consult all available published sources,[5] it cannot be claimed with certitude that the figures represent the exact and complete total capital flows because some capital transfer, particularly that related to military assistance to Egypt, Syria, and Jordan, is either inaccurately reported or simply not revealed. Nevertheless, the following taxonomy and detailed quantitative analysis should indicate clearly the order of magnitude of these capital flows and display their rapid expansion and growing significance.

Arab Development Aid Institutions

Tables 4.6 and 4.7 provide an exposition of the various Arab national and regional development aid institutions, indicating their resources and operations.* From these tables the following trends can be discerned among the national (KFAED, ADFAED, IFED, and SDF) and regional aid institutions.

1. Most loans are advanced to Arab countries, with Egypt, Sudan, Syria, Tunisia, and Bahrain being the major aid recipients. These countries occupy the center of political gravity in the Arab world and/or are relatively more developed, making them better equipped to absorb additional capital (Egypt, Syria, Tunisia); possess great agricultural potential (Sudan, Syria); or have close proximity and ethnic ties to the major Gulf oil producers (Bahrain). Nonetheless, the scope of operations of the newly established regional funds, and as of 1974 the KFAED and ADFAED as well, covers other developing countries in Africa and Asia.

2. The present paid-in capital of many of these institutions is one-half or even one-third of the authorized capital; however, these institutions are permitted to borrow additional resources when needed by issuing bonds.

3. The sum of outright grants provided is negligible, based on the reasoning that if these institutions are to function on an ongoing basis, their capital must be revolving. In their lending activities, the funds not only require appropriate guarantees of repayment from the borrowing countries, but also insist that feasibility and economic studies be carried out before any loans may be extended.

---

*The information contained in the tables does not go beyond July 1975.

TABLE 4.6

Arab National Development Aid Institutions: Resources and Operations

	Institution[a]			
	KFAED[b]	ADFAED	SDF	IFED
Headquarters and date established	Kuwait, December 1961	Abu Dhabi, July 1971	Riyadh, September 1974	Baghdad, June 1974
Capitalization (millions of dollars)	3,380	500	2,900	169
Types of operation	Project loans, provision of guarantees, technical assistance	Project loans, equity holdings, other forms of aid	Project loans	Project aid, technical assistance
Number and value of loans since inception (millions of dollars)	24 517[c]	27 279[d]	6 330[e]	1 10
Terms of loans and grant element (G.E)	3-4 percent interest, 0.5 percent service charge, generally 10-25 and 4-5 year repayment and grace periods respectively. G.E.: 29-48 percent	3-4.5 percent interest, 0.5 percent service charge, generally 11-19 and 2-4 year repayment and grace periods respectively. G.E.: Similar to the KFAED's	n.a.[f]	n.a.
Sectoral emphasis	Infrastructure, Agriculture, Industry	Infrastructure, Industry, Tourism, Agriculture	Infrastructure, Agriculture, Industry	n.a.
Special conditions	The Kuwaiti dinar is the unit of account; loans not to exceed 50 percent of total cost or 10 percent of the Fund's capital; generally, financing is restricted to foreign exchange requirements of projects; projects must not be in conflict with Kuwaiti or Arab economic interest.	Loans not to exceed 50 percent of total cost or 10 percent of the Fund's capital; generally, financing is restricted to foreign exchange requirements of projects.	The Saudi riyal is the unit of account; loans not to exceed 50 percent of total cost of project or 5 percent of the Fund's capital; at any time loans advanced to a single country must not exceed 10 percent of the Fund's capital.	n.a.

[a]KFAED, ADFAED, SDF, IFED stand for Kuwait Fund for Arab Economic Development, Abu Dhabi Fund for Arab Economic Development, Saudi Development Fund, and Iraq Fund for External Development, respectively.

[b]KFAED also extended grants for technical and feasibility studies totaling $4 million.

[c]Non-Arab recipients are Tanzania, Uganda, Rwanda, Sri Lanka, Malaysia, and Bangladesh, which jointly obtained a sum of about $35 million.

[d]Except for a recent $10 million loan to Bangladesh, the balance was extended to various Arab countries.

[e]Some $163 million represent two loans still under consideration.

[f]Data not available.

Sources: Middle East Economic Survey; Organization for Economic Cooperation and Development, *Flow of Resources from OPEC Members to Developing Countries*, December 6, 1974, and the *Addendum* dated April 23, 1975; Kuwait Fund for Arab Economic Development, *Basic Information*, November 1974; Hassan Selim, "Surplus Funds and Regional Development," in *Energy and Development*, ed. Ragaei El Mallakh and Carl McGuire (Boulder, Colo.: International Research Center for Energy and Economic Development, 1974).

TABLE 4.7

Arab Regional Development Aid Institutions:
Resources and Operations

Institu-tion[a]	Headquarters and date established	Capitalization (millions of dollars)	Types of operation	Number and Value of Loans Since Inception (millions of dollars)
AFESD	Kuwait, May, 1968[b]	347	Project loans Technical assistance	10 162
IDB	Jeddah (Saudi Arabia) August, 1974	910, may be increased to 2,500	Participation in equity capital; Loans and technical assistance for productive projects in the public and private sectors; Undertaking of research and promotion of foreign trade among member countries	Not operational yet
ABEDA	Khartoum, November 1973[c]	231	Provision of soft loans for medium- and small-size projects in cooperation with other regional and international lending agencies	n.a.[f]
AFTAF	Arab League (Cairo) January, 1974	25	Loans Technical know-how	n.a.[g]
AFOAF	ABEDA[d] March, 1974	200	Loans for oil imports	35 126
SFANOC	AFESD[e] June, 1974	80	Loans for oil imports	6 80

[a]AFESD (Arab Fund for Economic and Social Development), IDB (Islamic Development Bank), ABEDA (Arab Bank for Economic Development in Africa; also called Arab Bank for Industrial and Agricultural Development in Africa), AFTAF (Arab-African Technical Assistance Fund), AFOAF (Arab-African Oil Assistance Fund), SFANOC (Special Fund for Arab Non-Oil Exporting Countries).

[b]Commenced operation in 1972.

[c]Statutes approved in February, 1974.

[d]The administration of the allocated funds is entrusted to ABEDA.

[e]The administration of the allocated funds is entrusted to AFESD.

Terms of Loans and grant element (G. E.)	Sectoral emphasis	Special conditions
4–6% Interest; 18–20 and 4–5 year repayment and grace periods respectively. G. E.: 25–45%	Industry, Infrastructure	Recipient must be public or private organizations in Arab countries, equity participation by the Fund prohibited.
Loans extended must be interest free; Equity participation is emphasized	General directly productive activities	Recipient must be a Muslim country, or a Muslim community in non-Muslim countries.
n.a.	n.a.	Recipient must be a non-Arab nation.
1% Interest; 3-year grace period before repayment	Balance of payment support	Recipient must be a non-Arab nation.
1% Interest; 15 and 10 year repayment and grace periods respectively; G.E.: 71%	Balance of payment support	Previous oil import levels as basis for apportioning of financial assistance among individual states.
Zero Interest; Repayment over 10 years after initial 10-year grace period; G. E.: about 80%	Balance of payment support	Previous oil import levels as basis for apportioning of financial assistance among individual states.

fData not available.

gAs of November, 1974, five countries were in line to receive assistance: Liberia, Mali, Rwanda, Uganda, and Tanzania.

Sources: Middle East Economic Survey, Organization for Economic Cooperation and Development, *Flow of Resources from OPEC Members to Developing Countires*, December 6, 1974, and the *Addendum* dated April 23, 1975; United Nations Economic and Social Council, *Multilateral Institutions for Providing Financial and Technical Assistance to Developing Countries*, E/AC. 54/L. 75, March 28, 1975.

4. The condition that loans are paid out and must be repaid in the respective national currency seems to be intended to guard against possible adverse fluctuations in the foreign exchange rates of major currencies.

5. The stipulation that not more than 50 percent of the total costs of any project may be financed is designed to ensure the recipient's participation and interest in the project, elements generally essential to the success of the supported venture.

6. The provisions that any single loan must not exceed a given proportion of the capital of the respective fund and that at any one time loans extended to a single country may not exceed 10 percent of the fund's capital (in the SDF case) are intended to disseminate the services of the funds to the developing countries as well as to reduce the risk involved in lending.

7. Some of these funds perform other important services besides their main lending activities. For example, the ADFAED serves as a consultant and data source to the Abu Dhabi government on both international economic and financial matters and decisions concerning financial aid from the state reserves. Another example is the projected Investment Promotion Unit of the AFESD which will serve as a link between Arab entrepreneurs and investors in Arab capital-deficit countries.

8. There is a considerable degree of cofinancing between some of these funds and between them and other regional and international development lending agencies. For example, during the first full year of operations of the ADFAED, March 1973-March 1974, the fund approved 11 project loans, 9 of which were for financing schemes in cooperation with the KFAED, the AFESD, and the IBRD and its affiliates. Unfortunately, however, there exists at present no established framework for cooperation and coordination of the aid programs of these various institutions.

9. The supported projects must not be in conflict with the general economic interests of the Arab world. This condition, which currently poses little difficulty because most loans are concentrated in infrastructure and agriculture, is apparently designed to reduce the possibility of wasteful industrial duplication and to promote a semblance of regional integration by inducing the borrower to operate, to a certain extent, within the economic framework of the area. The impetus for regionalism would, however, be far greater were the regional aid institutions to receive the needed support and resources. These institutions are presently less significant than the national lending agencies in terms of capitalization as well as the number and value of loans extended.

10. The special oil assistance funds may not be permanent institutions, as they were created to alleviate the financial difficulties of certain countries resulting from the sharp increases in oil prices. Many factors, including future oil prices, levels of oil revenues, domestic capital absorptive capacities of the Arab oil exporters, and the regional political picture bear directly or indirectly on the possibility of these funds being operated on a continuous basis.

This rather lengthy list of aid agencies may increase even further in the near future as plans for the establishment of already proposed agencies are finalized.[6] None of these institutions should be confused with another long array of newly established investment companies, banks, and other financial institutions that have been marching across the Middle East stage: the Kuwait Investment Company, the Arab Petroleum Investment Company, the Arab Investment Company, the Arab Finance Corporation, among others. These are basically commercial institutions seeking profitable outlets for Arab surplus funds, particularly private funds, in the region and elsewhere. Their primary concern is not the initiation of development in recipient countries but return on investment. Nevertheless, the positive contribution of these largely commercial institutions to the socioeconomic development of Third World countries should not be minimized, for they tend to augment the worldwide availability and mobility of capital, thereby effecting a more efficient global allocation of a vital and scarce factor of production.

Aid and Soft Loans

Table 4.8 presents aid and soft loans provided by selected oil producers to the non-oil countries in the region, to the developing world, and to international organizations.

The total of about $11.6 billion in aid and soft loans extended by the oil producers is almost equally divided between the region and other developing countries. The share of the international organizations, principally the World Bank and the United Nations, is minor, amounting only to about $341 million. The time frame of this capital flow cannot be foreseen with precision. Nevertheless, most of the capital transfer will probably take place during 1975-80 because the majority of the recipient countries operate on the basis of quinquennium plans, the foreign exchange requirements of which are partially financed by borrowing abroad.

The composition of the capital flows is not known with accuracy. A tentative breakdown indicates that all of the aid and soft loans, save $1,248 million, are channeled to the region and other developing countries for the explicit purpose of fostering the economic and social development of recipient countries. The $1,248 million represent military assistance to Egypt, Syria, and to a very minor extent Oman.

In respect to the region, the major donor is Saudi Arabia, with Kuwait occupying the second place and Iran a close third. Iran, however, is by far the chief donor to the developing world, with Abu Dhabi and Saudi Arabia as distant second and third, respectively. If total aid and soft loans are considered, Iran conspicuously leads the group with Saudi Arabia as a distant second and Kuwait and Abu Dhabi as close third and fourth, respectively.

TABLE 4.8

Aid and Soft Loans of Selected Oil-Producing Countries
(millions of dollars)

Donor	Region	Recipient Developing World	Recipient International Organizations	Total
Iran	1,332.0	2,835	296.0	4,463.0
Saudi Arabia	2,022.0	615	31.3	2,668.3
Kuwait	1,406.0	460	–	1,866.0
United Arab Emirates (Abu Dhabi)	694.0	968	13.0	1,675.0
Libya	133.0	379	0.6	512.6
Iraq	202.4	203	–	405.4
Total	5,789.4	5,460	340.9	11,590.3

Sources: Organization for Economic Cooperation and Development, *Flow of Resources from OPEC Members to Developing Countries* (Paris: Organization for Economic Cooperation and Development, December 6, 1974) and *Addendum* (Paris: Organization for Economic Cooperation and Development, April 23, 1975); United Nations Economic and Social Council, *Multilateral Institutions for Providing Financial and Technical Assistance to Developing Countries*, E/AC.54/L.75 (New York: United Nations, March 28, 1975); Organization for Economic Cooperation and Development, *Development Cooperation, 1974 Review* (Paris: Organization for Economic Cooperation and Development, 1974).

Loans and Equity Investment

Table 4.9 displays loans and equity investment extended by the individual oil producers to the region and elsewhere. Table 4.10 shows the volume and the recipients of multicountry loans and investment classified by area.

A few comments on Tables 4.9 and 4.10 are in order.

Of a total of about $11.8 billion in loans and equity investment, the region received only some $1.22 billion, that is, about 10.4 percent. The major recipients were the OECD countries, the World Bank, and the IMF with a total sum of about $9.7 billion, that is, about 82 percent. The share of the developing world was only $866 million, amounting to 7.4 percent.

Although the share of the developing world is rather small, some of the funds made available to the World Bank and the IMF find their way to various developing countries. Thus, the positive contribution of petrodollars to the socioeconomic development of Third World countries involves in part the indirect benefits derived from greater worldwide availability and mobility of capital.

The region and the developing world are the major recipients of loans and investments extended by Arab institutions particularly in collaboration with Kuwaiti investment and financial institutions.

The time frame of these loans and equity investments cannot be discerned with certainty. However, with the exception of loans already consummated to the World Bank and the IMF, the bulk of capital transfer would probably be completed within a five-year period.

Moreover, some Arab financial institutions especially those of Kuwaiti origin have undertaken the underwriting of securities of Western and Japanese companies with total underwriting amounting to $355 million for the period under review.

TABLE 4.9

Loans and Equity Investment
(millions of dollars)

Donor	Recipients				
	Region	OECD	Developing World	Others[a]	Total[b]
Saudi Arabia	650.0	1,512.3	43.6	2,144.5	4,350.4
Iran	—	2,276.0	100.0	1,550.0	3,926.0
					(3,166.3)
Kuwait	—	1,127.7	68.8	765.5	1,962.0
Libya	47.8	—	653.7	199.0	900.5
					(512.0)
Abu Dhabi	523.0	16.3	—	76.0	615.3
					(854.0)
Total	1,220.8	4,932.3	866.1	4,735.0	11,754.2

[a]Includes contributions to international organizations, primarily the World Bank and the IMF.

[b]Figures in parentheses represent capital inflow into the respective oil-producing countries, which consists mostly of capital committed to oil exploration.

Sources: Organization for Economic Cooperation and Development, *Flow of Resources from OPEC Members to Developing Countries* (Paris: Organization for Economic Cooperation and Development, December 6, 1974) and *Addendum* (Paris: Organization for Economic Cooperation and Development, April 23, 1975); United Nations Economic and Social Council, *Multilateral Institutions for Providing Financial and Technical Assistance to Developing Countries*, E/AC.54/L.75 (New York: United Nations, March 28, 1975); Organization for Economic Cooperation and Development, *Development Cooperation, 1974 Review* (Paris: Organization for Economic Cooperation and Development, 1974).

TABLE 4.10

Recipients of Multicountry Loans and Investments
(millions of dollars)

Region[a]	Developing World	OECD	Other[b]	Total
813	669.7	161.71	126.7	1,771.0

[a]Includes $200 million extended by Libya and a Japanese firm to Iran.
[b]The World Bank.

Sources: Organization for Economic Cooperation and Development, *Flow of Resources from OPEC Members to Developing Countries* (Paris: Organization for Economic Cooperation and Development, December 6, 1974) and *Addendum* (Paris: Organization for Economic Cooperation and Development, April 23, 1975); United Nations Economic and Social Council, *Multilateral Institutions for Providing Financial and Technical Assistance to Developing Countries*, E/AC.54/L.75 (New York: United Nations, March 28, 1975); Organization for Economic Cooperation and Development, *Development Cooperation, 1974 Review* (Paris: Organization for Economic Cooperation and Development, 1974).

Joint Ventures

Joint ventures are one of the most important modes of regional and international cooperation. They involve collaboration between one or more oil producers on the one hand, and one or more developing countries, OECD countries, or regional non-oil countries on the other. The main purpose is the exploitation of investment opportunities in basically complementary economies. An oil producer may seek partnership with an advanced country or another developing country because it needs skills and technology, markets, or labor resources. Several Arab countries, with the oil producers being the principal capital contributors, often collaborate in the exploitation of promising regional investment opportunities in the field of oil and gas transmission, agricultural development, and energy-based industries. Similarly, in the financial field, joint ventures are initiated by regional investment companies and banks and in many cases with significant European and Japanese participation. The explicit aim is to further various banking and investment activities, particularly the distribution of surplus capital resources on a global basis. In all types of joint ventures, the West plays a key role, as it is the major source of advanced technology for the region and the developing world at large. There is a growing realization on the part of the oil producers in particular that Western participation, Western technology and expertise, and possibly also Western markets are indeed indispensable for the establishment and operation of large and complex industrial plants.

From January 1973 to July 1975, total capital committed to multicountry joint ventures by the Arab countries amounted to $5,720 million. The contribution of the Arab non-oil countries to this sum is minor. The major multicountry joint ventures include investment schemes in all phases of the petroleum and petroelum-related industries (exploration, production, transportation, and petrochemicals); establishment of an Arab company for mining potash in Jordan; construction of a dry dock in Bahrain; the initiation of a modern Arab weapons industry; and implementation of projects in the area of agricultural development including animal husbandry, particularly in the Sudan and in the area of tourism and housing in Egypt.

Capital committed to multicountry financial joint ventures, including investment banks and other financial institutions, amounted to about $2,374 million. In most cases the time frame of these arrangements is not indicated.

Table 4.11 shows joint ventures between one major oil producer and in most cases one partner, either in the region, the industrialized countries, or the developing world. These joint ventures cover a very wide range of projects and aim foremost at developing and transforming the domestic economy of the respective oil-producing states and other Arab countries in the region.

The major oil producers involved in joint ventures are Saudi Arabia, Iran, and Kuwait. They alone account for $6,505 million out of a total of $7,317 million. The Arab countries predictably have most of their joint ventures with the region, whereas Iran's partners are mainly OECD countries. The total of

TABLE 4.11

Joint Ventures of Selected Major Oil-Producing Countries (millions of dollars)

Country	Region	OECD	Developing World	Total
Saudi Arabia	1,900.0	722	—	2,622
Iran	—	2,462	—	2,462
Kuwait	1,357.0	—	64	1,421
Abu Dhabi	2.3	338	68	408
Iraq	350.0	—	10	360
Libya	—	44	—	44
Total	3,609.3	3,566	142	7,317

Source: Calculations made by the ICEED staff utilizing selected issues of *Middle East Economic Digest* and *Middle East Economic Survey.*

$7,317 million is almost equally divided between the region and the OECD countries, with the developing world receiving only $142 million. Thus, the contribution of joint ventures to the economic development of Third World countries so far is limited.

Joint ventures, even when they are between two regional countries or between an oil-producing state and a developing country outside the region, have significant implications for the industrial West. For one thing, the needed technology and skills usually come from the OECD countries. The reliance on Western technology and know-how is becoming increasingly clear even in such states as Iraq and Syria which are normally considered of leftist inclination. The general present policy of Iraq and Syria is veering away from ideological disputes and following more or less a pragmatic path, especially in the economic sphere. There is a growing realization of the necessity to tap Western know-how and resources in implementing extensive and complex programs of industrialization and agricultural development in the region. Shunning Western cooperation would retard significantly the pace of national and regional economic development and might even bring the whole process to a standstill. This is essentially the lesson drawn from more than a decade of close Egyptian and Iraqi economic relations with the Soviet Union.

Joint ventures with OECD countries generally involve some capital inflow into the oil-producing countries themselves because the projects agreed upon are often located in the oil-producing states. Some of these ventures are predicated upon detailed economic and feasibility studies, thus satisfying the criterion of allocative efficiency. Their positive welfare implications for both parties are therefore obvious. However, the majority of these ventures still await the results of further technical and economic analysis.

During 1974, it is estimated that the Arab oil producers provided about $1.5 billion to the Arab non-oil economies for development purposes.[7] The analysis presented here indicates that the capital flow committed by the Arab oil producers for regional development in 1975-80 is in the neighborhood of $11 billion or an average of $1.833 billion annually. This means that the average committed annual capital flow during 1975-80 is only $333 million larger than the 1974 level. However, the net additional capital flow to the non-oil economies required for a 10 percent rate of economic growth was estimated to be about $5.2 billion annually. The ensuing capital gap is, therefore, $4.867 billion annually. Unless the Arab oil producers step in to fill this gap, the Arab non-oil economies will exhibit only moderate rates of economic growth and will be grossly unable to realize their developmental potential.

The commitment of the Arab oil producers to the developing countries outside the region is estimated at $7.44 billion during 1975-80 or about $1.24 billion annually. Although such a volume of capital transfer is by no means insignificant, it is, nevertheless, small in relation to the immense capital requirements of these countries. The World Bank program for 1974-78 envisages an average of about $4.4 billion a year in loans to the developing countries. The present level of economic assistance is inadequate and there is need for a substantial increase in capital flows to the developing countries.[8] There are indications, however, that the current level of capital flows from the major Arab oil producers to the developing countries may be stepped up, as the OPEC countries recently agreed in their Paris meeting of January 1976 to channel some $800 million in interest-free loans this year alone to developing countries seriously affected by the high oil prices.

SUMMARY OF THE RESULTS

Tables 4.12 and 4.13 summarize the results of this chapter. The analysis clearly shows that the size of the capital surplus, even with the most optimistic forecasts of domestic absorptive capacity of the major oil producers, is considerable, averaging about $30.5 billion during 1975-80. The present commitment to regional cooperation and assistance to developing countries outside the region would reduce the volume of capital available for investment in the West to a

TABLE 4.12

Capital Surplus and Its Uses, Assuming High Level of Regional Cooperation (billions of dollars)

	1975	1980	Annual Average 1975–80
Capital surplus			
Maximum	42.57	35.19	38.90
Minimum	38.24	22.79	30.50
Regional requirements*	5.301	8.342	6.80
Regional debt repatriation (maximum)	1.00	1.00	1.00
Capital flows to the developing countries	1.24	1.24	1.24
Residual			
Maximum	35.00	24.60	29.80
Minimum	30.70	12.20	21.50

*Regional requirement is defined as the sum of actual flow in 1974 plus additional capital transfer necessary for a 10 percent rate of economic growth in the regional non-oil economies.

Source: Calculations made by the ICEED staff.

TABLE 4.13

Capital Surplus and Its Uses, Assuming Continuation of Current Level of Regional Cooperation
(billions of dollars)

	1975	1980	Annual Average 1975–80
Capital surplus			
Maximum	42.570	35.190	38.900
Minimum	38.240	22.790	30.500
Committed Capital Flows to			
Regional Non-Oil Countries*	1.833	1.833	1.833
Committed Capital Flows to			
the Developing Countries*	1.240	1.240	1.240
Residual			
Maximum	39.500	32.120	35.800
Minimum	35.170	19.720	27.500

*Annual averages.
Source: Calculations made by the ICEED staff.

yearly average of about $27.5 billion. A substantially larger regional capital flow would diminish the minimum size of the residual to $21.5 billion annually. Thus a higher commitment to regionalism would involve only a minor redirection of capital flows from the West to the region, amounting to an annual average of $6 billion during 1975-80.

The analysis also indicates that the proportion of the capital surplus that has to be channeled to the region diminishes as the size of the surplus increases. Therefore, ceteris paribus, the oil producers' willingness to commit funds to regional development is likely to vary inversely with the size of their capital surplus. This explains in part the current leading role played in regional cooperation by countries with enormous surplus, such as Saudi Arabia and Kuwait. It also elucidates the reason for the slow pace of regional cooperation historically.

It must be emphasized that a greater commitment to regionalism and assistance to other developing countries, though reducing the direct flow of capital channeled into various investment outlets in the West, does not necessarily affect adversely the total flow of petrodollars—direct and indirect—into Western economies. Whether or not, and to what extent, funds provided for regional development and assistance to the developing countries are recycled to OECD countries in the form of higher import levels depends principally on the patterns of trade of recipient countries. However, since the OECD countries are by far the leading exporters to the majority of recipient countries, the leakage effect must indeed be small. This does not mean, of course, that regional cooperation in the Middle East has little bearing on Western economies. Rather, it points out that the impact of greater regional cooperation must be sought, not so much in the magnitude of capital flowing from the major oil producers to the West, as in the composition of these capital flows. The implications of regional development in the Middle East on the relevant aspects of the U.S. economy will be outlined and briefly discussed in the final chapter of this study.

NOTES

1. Constantine Fliakos and Ronald D. Lewison, "Prospects for International Oil Supply and Demand: 1975, 1980, 1985," *Journal of Energy and Development* 1, no. 1 (Autumn 1975): 73-74.

2. Historical rates of growth of GNP in 1965-71 in the region ranged between –0.1 percent in Jordan and 6.4 percent in Syria. See International Bank for Reconstruction and Development, *The World Bank Atlas, 1973* (New York: IBRD, 1974).

3. See F. Abdul-Rasool, *The Role of Arab Monetary Reserves in Arab Economic Integration* (memo in Arabic, 1974).

4. *Al Ahram*, December 30, 1975, p. 1.

5. *Middle East Economic Survey; Middle East Economic Digest;* Organization for Economic Cooperation and Development, *Flow of Resources from OPEC Members to Developing Countries*, December 6, 1974, and the *Addendum* dated April 23, 1975; United Nations Economic and Social Council, *Multilateral Institutions for Providing Financial and Technical Assistance to Developing Countries*, E/AC.54/L.75 (New York: United Nations, March 28, 1975).

6. United Nations Economic and Social Council, *Multilateral Institutions*, op. cit., p. 32. A new addition may be the Libyan-United Arab Emirates Fund.

7. Antoine Ayoub, "Demand for Capital of the Non-Oil Producing Arab Countries and the Constraints of Supply," paper presented to the Second International Conference on Energy, Surplus Funds, and Absorptive Capacity, The International Research Center for Energy and Economic Development, University of Colorado, November 6-7, 1975, p. 7.

8. OECD, *Development Cooperation, 1974 Review* (Paris: OECD Publications, 1974).

CHAPTER

5

REGIONAL CAPITAL FLOWS
AND PATTERNS OF
DEVELOPMENT

Apart from the important economic factors outlined earlier, the long history of Arab culture articulates a protest against the divisive and exclusive sovereignties of the modern Arab world. Moreover, the imperatives of global and regional politics, especially the desire to contain Israel and to confront her with a united and powerful Arab front, call for greater cooperation and cohesiveness among Arab countries.* Thus, the dictates of economics, culture, and politics point in the direction of regional cooperation. The analysis presented in Chapter 4 evinces a recent acceleration in the pace of regional cooperation among Arab countries, and a greater recognition of the importance of regionalism as a vehicle of economic development and military might. This awareness is likely to receive added impetus from the implementation of already initiated regional schemes, particularly those in the fields of transport and communications, which tend to strengthen the linkages and cohesiveness of Arab economies and society. The steps that have been already taken in the area of regional cooperation were necessarily the most obdurate because of the absence of close and extensive economic ties and thus the lack of a strong community of interest among the variout Arab states. As economic relations are gradually forged, developed, and strengthened, they act as powerful stimuli for further economic cooperation. Nevertheless, when our estimates of regional capital requirements are juxtaposed to anticipated levels of capital transfer, the disparity between the two hampers the observer's optimism regarding the future pace and scope of regional cooperation.

---

*The close association between military and economic power and bigness is too obvious in the modern world to require any documentation.

94

Obviously, it may be too sanguine to assume, at least for the next five years, that the annual capital transfer of $1.833 billion will approach the projected yearly average capital requirements of $6.8 billion. Given the internal and external obstacles facing extensive cooperation, it may be self-defeating to view regional integration as an automatic process that will evolve naturally over time; rather, regionalism should be correctly perceived as a vehicle of accelerated growth and efficient development patterns that must be energetically sought, nurtured, and carefully cultivated. This calls for examining and outlining policies capable of enhancing and improving present regional cooperation. Three areas that appear to have direct bearing on the scope and efficiency of regional cooperation— proliferation of development funds, shortcomings of the financing method, and climate of investment in recipient countries—will be analyzed in sequence.

REGIONAL CAPITAL FLOWS: AN APPRAISAL OF POLICIES

Proliferation of Development Funds

The proliferation of development lending agencies appears to encourage the diffusion of scarce manpower—planners, economists, administrators, engineers, and technicians—into small units that are less capable and efficient in the prompt evaluation of submitted projects in a reasonably professional manner. A small lending agency, moreover, has little weight and leverage in effecting the transfer of Western technology because it lacks the bargaining power usually derived from a large financial base. Amalgamation of the existing lending institutions into one large development bank similar to the World Bank would yield diverse benefits, not the least of which would be the capacity to promote the transfer of modern Western technology and the opening up of Western markets for Middle East products.

The proliferation of agencies prevents the application of uniform criteria for project appraisal both among and within sectors and countries. The establishment of such criteria would greatly enhance the prospects of regional development and economic integration, as the flow of aid would be channeled to countries and sectors with the explicit goal of securing such an outcome.

The large number of lending agencies militates against the formulation of integrated programs of aid to individual recipient countries, and increases the costs of aid administration and surveillance. These costs may be substantially reduced and the effectiveness of aid supervision considerably strengthened if the lending agency is large enough to permit the establishment of country or regional and subregional representative offices in the recipient countries.

Increasing numbers of lending agencies reduce the capability of individual lending agencies to carry out substantive and comprehensive research concerning the economies of recipient countries, the promising avenues of investment, and possibly the preparation of a list of bankable projects.

And finally, the proliferation increases the donor's nondevelopment considerations, since a national lending institution is more likely to be subject to narrow political pressures than a multinational agency. Moreover, multinational aid agencies, which include the recipient countries even if on a modest scale, increase the sense of involvement and participation of the latter in the aid program, to the benefit of all concerned.

It is, therefore, in the interest of donor and recipient alike that the proliferation of Arab non-specialized-development lending institutions be restrained and a move toward consolidation, or at least coordination, of their various lending activities and policies be initiated. The growing awareness of this need prompted the Economic Commission for Western Asia (ECWA), a U.N. body based in Beirut, to hold a meeting with representatives of the KFAED, AFESD, and the ADFAED to discuss methods and procedures of initiating cooperation among them. As a result, the following decisions were adopted:[1] (1) to achieve the maximum degree of cooperation and coordination between the Arab funds and the ECWA and to hold regular meetings; (2) to exchange specific information concerning projects undertaken by each organization; (3) to study a framework for cooperation within the work programs of each agency for 1975-77; and (4) to invite the Iraq Fund for External Development (IFED) and the Saudi Development Fund (SDF) to attend these regular meetings.

A coordinating meeting took place in Abu Dhabi January 10-12, 1976. Representatives of the following institutions were present: AFESD, KFAED, SDF, Arab Bank for Economic Development in Africa, and the AFAED.[2] The discussions focused on exploring the possibilities for cooperation and coordination among the various funds themselves, and among them and other regional funds and organizations such as ECWA and the Arab League. The possible participation of the funds in issuing a specialized newsletter to disseminate information pertaining to the funds' activities was also addressed. No concrete decisions, however, have yet been taken.

A higher level of cooperation and coordination among the various Arab development funds may eventually lead to their consolidation or perhaps specialization in well-defined activities and sectors, such as an industrial bank or an agricultural bank. A larger organization would operate with greater efficiency and effectiveness in many areas, such as the handling of aid requests, the provision of technical services, the supervision of supported projects, the capacity to augment and channel capital resources, the security of loaned capital, and the lower administration costs of the aid program. The benefits of consolidation, cooperation and coordination are not only immense and diverse, but also accrue to donors and recipients alike.

Shortcomings of the Financing Method

In evaluating Arab developmental aid the following observations are pertinent. First it must be recalled that Arab aid is generally provided on a project-by-project basis. Plan or program aid is seldom extended. However, if a country does operate on the basis of a tightly knit plan, in which everything depends appreciably on everything else and where the timing of projects is, therefore, of importance, extending aid for projects only may be harmful for a number of reasons.[3] If support on an aided project is delayed due to unforeseen circumstances, the funds cannot be transferred to another project that may be wilting for lack of money. Also, where there are many donors, it may prove very difficult to wed the projects in the plan to donors' preferences. Moreover, if aid is restricted to projects only, the result may be that either the aid cannot be absorbed within the prescribed period or that too many projects get started at a time when there is a high demand for replacements and minor extensions of capacity throughout the economy. These considerations presently are not very serious, however, for most developing countries fail to produce tightly knit plans. Thus, project aid retains its distinct advantage as a means of surveillance without the disadvantage of being too restrictive. As the art of planning improves, however, Arab development lending institutions might reassess their policy of extending loans directed toward projects only.

The second point concerns the policy of financing exclusively the foreign exchange cost of projects. Arab development funds generally shun even the partial financing of domestic costs of projects. On a priori grounds this policy tends to create distortion in the optimum ratio of domestic to foreign exchange costs of projects for which aid is requested, since recipient countries may be unable or unwilling to use their fiscal powers to marshal additional domestic resources to finance these projects. They would, therefore, tend to maximize the foreign exchange component in proposed projects or neglect the development of sectors such as education and technical training, in which import costs tend to be low. This partly explains the conspicuous absence of any loans extended in support of educational projects, a fact that constitutes a major weakness at the present stage of development.

Third, currently the bulk of Arab aid is not channeled through development lending institutions, but is provided according to bilateral agreements between individual states. This has accentuated the importance of political considerations in aid-extending activities and has discriminated against small projects and private investment. For any given level of investment, large projects normally require major engineering and technical inputs which are at present extremely scarce in the Middle East. Such projects, moreover, are characterized by a high capital-labor ratio, thus lessening their contribution to the reduction of unemployment in such countries as Egypt.

The practice of extending finance only to public enterprises is regrettable in the light of the disproportionate size of the public sector and the inefficiency of the government machinery in most Middle East countries. In fact, the encouragement of public enterprises, especially in the industrial sector, may create serious obstacles for future economic integration schemes because these enterprises often enjoy monopolistic status or follow irrational pricing policies, relying on government support and subsidies. Free from the stringent market criterion of profitability, the price structure of public enterprises does not necessarily mirror true cost differentials and thus cannot be taken as an appropriate guide for regional resources allocation. It is not advocated that the Arab development lending agencies should muddle in the sensitive issue of the appropriate size of the public versus the private sector. However, one can question the rationale for discriminating against private investment which is potentially more efficient, and which poses less of a problem for future economic integrative schemes. The pace of economic growth in the individual Arab countries and the region as a whole may accelerate significantly if the Arab lending institutions, cognizant of the critical role of private enterprise in the economic development of the region, pursue imaginative policies capable of promoting private investment activities.

Climate of Investment in Recipient Countries

The gap between the capital requirements of the non-oil Arab countries and the anticipated or committed capital flow from the oil producers during 1975-80 is considerable, averaging, it is calculated, some $4.867 billion annually. Despite the recent serious interest the major Arab oil producers are exhibiting in regionalism and the calls for "an Arab Marshall Plan" to aid Egypt, it is improbable that such a vast capital inflow will take place unless the recipient countries undertake to improve the climate for investment in their economies.[4] The oil producers, while still committed to the provision of aid and grants on a relatively large scale to a few Arab countries, are making it clear that their long-run interest lies not in aid but in remunerative investment opportunities in the region. Moreover, in most oil-producing countries a significant portion of oil revenues are usually percolated to the private sector by means of various government spending schemes such as the purchase and resale of private land.[5] This, along with the dramatic increase in trade activities, has created a wealthy and prosperous class which due to limited domestic investment avenues is constantly scouting profitable investment outlets for their considerable liquid assets in the region and elsewhere. The non-oil countries must tap this source if they are to receive a greater proportion of the petrodollar surplus.

Currently, the investment climate in the non-oil Arab countries is less favorable and attractive than its counterpart in the West, though this picture is gradually changing and the situation may soon turn around, provided both parties—the oil producers and the non-oil producers—resolve to alleviate the obstacles hindering more extensive cooperation. Some of the major impediments facing greater regional capital mobility are discussed below.

The political situation in most non-oil producing countries may act as a deterrent to regional investment. For one thing, Saudi Arabia, Kuwait, the United Arab Emirates, and Qatar are committed to a philosophy of free enterprise, while most non-oil producers and even some of the oil producers themselves, for example, Iraq, pursue policies emphasizing state ownership and control of the economy. Sequestration of foreign investments and the nationalization of private indigenous enterprises have not been isolated and rare phenomena in the Arab Middle East. Sequestration and nationalization, especially in the field of industry, tend to impact adversely on the economy and therefore must be justified, if at all, in terms of noneconomic considerations. The major drawbacks of nationalization of private industry are[6]

1. Reduction in general industrial efficiency due to the practical elimination of competition, the prevalence of administered prices, and the lack of the profit motive as an allocative device for society's scarce resources.

2. The misdirection of private capital from industry to other less desirable investment activities. Moreover, the role of the private sector as a training background for entrepreneurs and managerial talents is substantially diminished. Consequently, private investment or at least its rate of growth may suffer.

3. Even where public investment compensates for the possible decline in private investment or deceleration in its rate of growth, this tends to limit expansion in employment because private investment generally is less capital-intensive and thus is capable of creating more jobs per unit of capital invested.

4. In an atmosphere of insecurity and vast governmental control, foreign investment and entrepreneurial talents are severely discouraged.

This explains at least in part the inadequate performance of certain Middle East economies that have practiced nationalization on an extensive scale.

But more importantly, drastic economic reorganization measures such as nationalization further increase political instability which is generally inimical to regional investment. Also, frequent changes of governments or of planning and other strategic ministers within the cabinet have prevented in most countries the adoption of consistent policies toward the private sector. As a result, the demarcation lines between the public and private sectors have constantly shifted. The private sector has been dealt with primarily outside the plans and its role in the development process remained ambiguous and ill-defined. Evidently, such an uncertain and insecure environment is incapable of attracting sizable regional private investment which, unlike public funds, is motivated exclusively by profitability and adequate pecuniary return. Recognition of these aspects has led the Arab countries to form the Arab Investment Guarantee Organization capitalized at $33.8 million and entrusted with the task of protecting Arab regional investment against confiscation, nationalization, and other noneconomic risks. Aside from the apparent inadequacy of the capital of this insurance agency in relation to the required flow of regional investment, this route should not be conceived of as a viable substitute for creating an atmosphere of mutual trust and confidence in the intentions—and respect for the basic interests—of the parties involved, donors and recipients alike.[7]

Despite the prevalence of extensive government involvement in the economy in practically all Middle East countries, the scope and character of this involvement varies considerably, depending on the nature of the economic and political system embraced by the respective governments. The most successful economies in the region, however, have been those that displayed sustained political stability and pragmatism in internal socioeconomic policies, irrespective of ideological persuasion.[8] Obviously, political stability and economic success can act as powerful stimuli for the regional inflow of funds, especially private capital. One possibility for accelerating the capital transfer process is for all Arab countries suffering from capital shortages to enter into a treaty whereby they jointly resolve to offer similar incentives and guarantees for regional investment. The treaty must stipulate severe and collective penalties against any member that subsequent to ratification violates any of its articles. Furthermore, the security of regional loans and investment may be greatly enhanced if the Arab oil producers acquiesce in amalgamating their diverse aid and investment programs by establishing a multinational Arab development agency capitalized at $10 billion or more, and entrusted with the mobilization of capital resources and the administration of aid and investment on a regional basis. Apart from the advantages of a large-sized multinational agency mentioned earlier, an arrangement of this sort would effectively deter a recipient country from undertaking measures that expose regional loans and investments to noneconomic risks, because the suggested agency may then immediately retaliate by canceling or suspending all existing and future capital flows to that country.

The notorious inefficiency of government institutions and the bureaucratic complications, unnecessary delays, and pervasive obstructions are major obstacles facing potential private investors, whether local, regional or foreign. The local investor may be constrained in his options and is therefore less discouraged by these practices. His regional or foreign counterpart, however, is not. Thus, regional and foreign investment tend to be especially sensitive to the attractiveness of the business environment and government regulations in the host country.

The inadequacy of information concerning investment opportunities in the region is one of the most crucial hindrances limiting the scope of intraregional investments. Information in the broadest sense is not restricted to awareness of procedures, regulations, and conditions prevailing in the host country, but includes the search for and the establishment of a list of bankable projects, that is, concrete propositions based on detailed economic studies and articulated into feasible blueprints ready for implementation.[9]

The attractiveness of regional investment vis-a-vis investment in the West is reduced by "the absence of or at best the extreme weakness and vulnerability of locally organized financial markets in the Middle East."[10] This is a factor of considerable significance because the existence of well-organized markets offering multifarious financial instruments greatly enlarges investors' choice and enhances the liquidity of the committed capital, thus permitting the potential investor to exercise greater control and latitude in selecting his optimal portfolio. It should be noted, however, that the development of an efficient regional capital market in the Middle East may not proceed smoothly, due at least in part to the excessive government control of economic activities in certain countries. If these countries, namely, Sudan, Syria, Algeria, and Iraq, decide to follow Egypt's open policy and gradual liberalization of the economy, the prospects for the emergence of an integrated regional capital market will be considerably brighter.

The oil producers view regional cooperation as a two-way street; they express willingness to help capital-deficit countries in the area, but wish to do so in a manner that assures the simultaneous development and prosperity of their own economies. This sentiment is forcibly aired by Abdlatif Y. Al-Hamad, the prominent Kuwaiti general director of the KFAED.

> Another obstacle which to my mind could prove even more important in the longer run is the fact that, in the consideration of joint investment ventures, attention in the non-surplus countries of the Middle East has been almost exclusively directed to projects hosted by these countries themselves. The need of the surplus-countries—especially in the Gulf area—to restructure their economies and build up viable branches of production catering to markets larger than their own local ones, have hardly been a joint concern. In other words, interest has hitherto been concentrated on a one-way flow of funds to the neglect of an issue which from our own point of view is at least as important: namely, the necessity of creating an industrial base in countries which are almost wholly dependent on one depletable resource. Such a task should not be viewed solely as a local problem or at best as an issue between the oil exporting countries and the Western world. It should indeed be considered as an integral aspect of economic and financial co-operation within the Middle East itself.[11]

These considerations emphasize the necessity for each Arab country to structure its own economy within the context of a broader regional development framework. Consequently, the distribution of economic activities in the area must reflect closely regional factor endowment, locational advantage, and other pertinent elements.

REGIONAL DEVELOPMENT PATTERNS

In order to delineate potentially efficient patterns of development for the countries in the area, it is essential first to survey regional factor proportions and the degree of utilization of existing resources. Generally, economic growth hinges not only on the quantity and quality of the factors of production, whether natural or human, but also on their proportions. Factor proportions are important primarily because of the limited factor substitutability in most production functions. Alternatively stated, a given commodity is normally produced using a finite set of similar production processes, each with fixed factor requirements. Thus, a country extremely well endowed with a specific resource, but lacking other cooperant factors of production, may face tremendous difficulties in its development efforts. Adopting a regional approach to development may not only help the countries in the Middle East overcome the conspicuous geographic skew of resources distribution, but possibly also turn the local unfavorable factor proportions into a distinct economic advantage.

Resource Endowment of the Arab World

Human Resources

The total population of the Arab world is probably about 148 million. About two-thirds of this total is concentrated in four Arab African countries, namely, Egypt, Sudan, Morocco, and Algeria. Egypt alone has some 40 million inhabitants. Other Arab countries with a population in excess of five million are Iraq, Syria, North Yemen, Tunisia, and Saudi Arabia.

Average population density in the Arab world is about 10.8 persons per square kilometer. However, population density varies considerably throughout the region with a minimum of 1.4 persons per square kilometer in Libya and a maximum of 317.3 persons in Lebanon.

The population of the Arab world may be classified into three groups: nomads and semi-nomads, the rural population, and urban and city dwellers. The nomadic population is small and constitutes presently less than seven percent of the total. It is mainly found in the Arabian Peninsula, the desert areas of Iraq, Syria, and Jordan, and in the Sudan and Libya.[12] This portion is, moreover, consistently and rapidly declining under the pressures of development and the emerging labor shortages in many oil-producing countries. The rural population makes up about 63 percent of the total and this portion is also diminishing for reasons similar to those indicated above. The urban population constitutes about 30 percent of the total, is increasing at a higher rate than the rest, and is concentrated in such huge metropolises as Cairo (more than eight million), Alexandria, Baghdad, Casablanca, Beirut, and Damascus—all with a population well in excess of one million.

The birth rate is very high, ranging generally between forty and fifty persons per thousand population.[13] The death rate is moderate and ranges between 14.9 and 22.7 persons per thousand population.[14] Consequently, the rate of population growth is one of the highest in the world, averaging recently about 3.24 percent for the Arab world as a whole.[15]

The net effect of population growth on the economy depends not only on the magnitude of the increase, but more importantly, on the particular pattern of population growth and on the context in which it occurs. The pattern of population growth is very important, since different patterns produce different age structures. In the Arab world, fertility is high and mortality is moderate and steadily declining, indicating not only that the rate of population growth is high, but also that the age structure is dominated by the unproductive age cohorts; as a result the dependency load is high and generally exceeds 50 percent in most Arab countries.[16] A high dependency load implies a low labor participation rate,[17] and thus represents a real drag on the productive effort of the economy. Consequently, the margin between production and consumption is low, which limits the possibility of capital accumulation. Moreover, resources not only have to be diverted from capital formation to the maintenance of a larger population, but, due to the high infant mortality rate, are wasted. This and the fact that the great majority of the active population is engaged in subsistence farming explain the clear inability of Arab economies, with the notable exception of the oil producers, to generate sufficient indigenous savings.

Another adverse effect of a high dependency ratio is a low and undifferentiated demand structure. Since consumption does vary with age, and since the Arab world has a very large proportion of young people, the bulk of aggregate demand is directed toward food and social welfare services. As a result, the income elasticity of demand for food tends to be high and food expenditures generally absorb a large percentage of income. However, price elasticities of supply of agricultural products are low, mainly because of the prevalence of primitive agriculture. Thus, rising incomes necessitate a diversion of foreign exchange earnings from the importation of capital goods to the importation of food. Also, the combination of a high demand for food and a low level of income restrains the demand for industrial products, thus retarding the process of industrialization.

The high proportion of income spent on food should not be construed, however, as an indication of adequate nutritional standards. Low income levels and faulty dietary habits are responsible for the prevalence of undernourishment and nutritional deficiencies in many parts of the Arab world. Malnutrition and adverse health conditions may then explain in part the general low levels of labor productivity observed in the region.[18]

In the Arab world where the percentage of literacy is very low (in many cases well below 40 percent),[19] the rapid increase in the size of the school age population makes it very difficult to achieve the cherished goal of universal literacy within a reasonable time span. But literacy is an important vehicle for modernization, since it determines to a large extent the capacity of the labor force to acquire modern skills and knowledge. Thus, large investment outlays in basic education are required despite the scarcity of capital resources in the densely populated countries of the region. Consequently, the expenditures per child are meager and children are very much handicapped in the matter of preparation for future employment. What is worse, an effort is made to relieve the dependency load, represented mainly by the large proportion of children, by employing them at any early age and making them contribute what little they can to the family income. As a result, there is overt and disguised unemployment in the economy as a whole at low productivity levels. Also, the premature employment of young people has serious social and economic consequences. Denying the young people opportunities to build up their mental and physical endowments amounts to wasteful exploitation of the oncoming generation of laborers. Indeed, "The position is rather like that of peasants compelled by hunger to harvest their wheat every year before it has ripened."[20]

It may also be argued that if a rapid population growth is to be fully exploited, some necessary preconditions are currently lacking in many parts of the Arab world. Population growth can be a stimulus to increased activity only if the social attitudes and values of the people are conducive to a favorable reaction. The will and preparedness to face and surmount economic difficulties and turn seeming obstacles into opportunities are characteristic of people in a developed economy. The absence of such qualities among the majority of the Arab people is precisely what keeps them underdeveloped.

Although labor is in abundant supply in Algeria, Egypt, Lebanon, Morocco, Sudan, Syria, Tunisia, and even perhaps Iraq, technical skills and scientifically trained manpower are generally scarce and unevenly distributed. The overall enrollment ratios in the educational systems of Egypt, Syria, and Iraq are comparable to West European standards; however, the enrollment ratios in technical and vocational education represent on the average only ten percent of those of their European counterparts.[21] According to a recent study by an agency of the United Nations,[22] acute labor shortages exist in middle management and middle level professionals, while clerical skills and office workers are generally in over supply. Imbalances also extend to university education which is not directly geared to satisfy the requirements of development; greater emphasis is placed on the humanities and social sciences than on the physical sciences, technical training, and professional education. Several social and cultural factors also coalesce to make the supply of labor, especially in blue-collar categories, relatively inelastic. These include the virtual exclusion of females from the labor force, the dim relationship between effort and reward, and the social disdain of manual labor and the low status and prestige associated with industrial occupations.

While the region as a whole may not be deficient in the overall labor supply, the regional pool of skilled labor is extremely limited. Indeed, trained manpower and skill shortages may prove to be the overriding bottleneck in economic growth in the Middle East. The present pattern of population growth constitutes an obvious impediment to development throughout the region; in the densely populated states, it tends to worsen the proportions between human and other resources, thus accentuating the existing structural disequilibrium. In the sparsely populated oil countries, its immediate impact is greater diversion of personnel to education and other social services, thus intensifying the existing labor shortage.

The contribution of regional cooperation to the amelioration of manpower shortages in the Arab world is two-fold. First, regional cooperation permits the efficient utilization of existing labor resources. Increased labor mobility promotes allocative efficiency thus tending to rectify unfavorable factor proportions. This is basically a short-run remedy. Second, in the long run, regional cooperation may contribute, albeit indirectly, to the augmentation of regional manpower resources, particularly skilled labor. The inflow of capital to the regional non-oil economies will permit these countries to achieve a higher rate of investment, including investment in human resources. As a result, the pool of industrial workers and skills tends to rise. Some countries in the region, particularly Egypt, are becoming increasingly sensitive about losing a significant proportion of their highly skilled manpower to the oil-based economies which offer considerably higher remuneration. Thus, Egypt is planning to request Saudi Arabia to reimburse her for part of the past expenses that went into the education and training of Egyptian university graduates serving currently in Saudi Arabia. Given the general shortage of skills throughout the region, a policy of skills dispersion and mobility is a short-run measure and thus appears to command little merit. The new Egyptian attitudes toward exportation of skilled and highly trained manpower are therefore understandable.

Agricultural Resources

The total area of the Arab world is about 2.4 million square miles or 1,200 million hectares, of which about three percent or 40 million hectares are currently under cultivation.[23] The potentially cultivable area however is at least double that, permitting in the future a considerable increase in the land-labor ratio.[24] It must be borne in mind, however, that although the Arab world might be regarded as sparsely populated in terms of population per square mile, population density is relatively high when presently cultivated area alone is considered. Moreover, population density per arable square mile varies substantially throughout the region; in 1970, it ranged between a high of 3,027 per square mile in Egypt and a low of 199 in Libya, with the majority of countries having an average of between 241 and 573.[25] The present high labor intensity of Arab agriculture may be explained by the relatively limited area under cultivation and the fact that about 60 percent of the population is engaged directly or indirectly in agriculture. Agricultural value-added per worker is generally low; in 1970 it ranged between $389 and $549 in most Arab countries with the exception of Algeria and Morocco (around $300) and the Sudan ($163). Agricultural value-added per square mile of arable cropped and pasture land was, however, very high in Egypt ($194,697) and to a lesser extent in Lebanon ($107,228), but was very low in all the rest. Regional yield variation per hectare is attributable principally to soil quality and weather conditions, and to a lesser extent to the human factor and the use of scientific farming techniques and methods. Because of a combination of factors, including aridity, the nature of parent materials, and topography, the soils in the region have acquired characteristics that impact adversely on soil productivty. These comprise high content of sand and thus high degree of porosity, low content of organic matters and high concentration of calcium carbonate and salts.[26] Soil salinity is the most pervasive and critical problem in the whole area, especially in countries relying heavily on perennial irrigation systems, such as Iraq, Egypt, and Syria. The problem of salinization is also compounded by the absence of adequate drainage facilities and inefficient water use.

In a generally arid or semi-arid area, water resources are scarce and water availability in many cases represents a binding constraint on agricultural expansion. Water in the Arab world is derived from rainfall, rivers, aquifers, and desalinization of sea water. The latter source is not yet important for agricultural production, though its potential—depending on cost-reducing technological developments—is obviously vast and revolutionary. The winter rain-fed agricultural area of the Arab world encompasses the Mediterranean coast from Syria in the northeast to Morocco in the west, the northeastern part of El Gazierah in Syria, and northern Iraq. Winter precipitation in most of these areas exceeds 16 inches, thus permitting the cultivation of wheat. Rain generally decreases as one moves away from the coast, and it diminishes in El Gazierah and Iraq as one moves to the south. In those areas where precipitation is about 12 to 16 inches, barley is grown.[27] Summer rain-fed areas include North Yemen and the vast areas of central and southern Sudan. About 30 million hectares in central Sudan and 2.4 million hectares in southern Sudan receive rainfall above 16 inches and precipitation increases to 40 inches in the south. These areas could produce a variety of summer crops such as sugar and corn.

The main rivers in the Arab world are the Nile, the Tigris, and the Euphrates. The region also contains several other smaller and less important rivers such as Al-Khaboor in Syria, Al-Litany in Lebanon, El-Shaloof in Algeria, and the Jordan River. The discharge of the Tigris is about 100 cubic meters per second and rises to an average of 3,000 cubic meters per second during the flood season, March to May. Similarly, the discharge of the Euphrates is about 100 cubic meters per second and increases to an average of 2000 in its flood period.[28] The total amount of water brought by the Nile at its entry into Egypt is about 84 billion cubic meters which is divided between Egypt (55.5 billion cubic meters) and the Sudan (18.5 billion cubic meters). About 10 billion cubic meters are lost by evaporation. Moreover, the Nile's water supply may be significantly increased if the evaporation in the marshy area south of the Sudan can be restrained.

The considerable variations in the discharge of these rivers both during the year and between years necessitate substantial investments in irrigation and storage facilities. Many important dams and irrigation facilities have been built or are being constructed or planned in Iraq, Syria, and Egypt. The Aswan High Dam in Egypt, the Euphrates High Dam in Syria, and the several dams and barrages in Iraq, including Dokan, Derbandikhan, Tharthar, and Feloogah, are but a few prominent examples. The completion of storage and irrigation facilities already in progress or in the planning stage, the construction of adequate drainage systems, and the rationalization of the present archaic patterns of water use would no doubt permit a substantial increase in the agricultural area especially in Iraq. Similar efforts in the North African Arab states—Tunisia, Algeria, and Morocco—particularly with respect to improving drainage facilities to combat increasing soil salinization, would also augment agricultural land and enhance land productivity.

Ground water is also available in most parts of the Arab region with concentration in the Egyptian Nile Valley, the northeastern part of El Gezierah and the Deir El Zor area in Syria, and the Al Hassa region of Saudi Arabia. Vast reserves of ground water have also been struck recently at Kufra in Libya, Jizan in Saudi Arabia, and the Egyptian New Valley.[29] The implications of these new discoveries for future agricultural expansion are obvious.

The scarcity of productive land and the adequacy of water resources, important as they are, are not the only major factors constraining agricultural production. Archaic agricultural practices mirrored in the extensive adoption of the fallow farming system, the limited use of machinery, fertilizers, pesticides, herbicides, improved seeds and crop rotation, are perhaps as important, if not even more critical. Moreover, specialization in producing a few crops most suitable for the type of soil and weather conditions is not widely practiced.[30] There are certain notable exceptions, however: cotton in Egypt, Sudan, and Syria, citrus fruits in Morocco and Lebanon, wine in Algeria, and dates in Iraq.

The animal wealth of the Arab world is sizable and important especially with respect to the sheep population, and to a lesser extent cattle. In 1968, total sheep population of the Arab world exceeded 100 million with significant concentration in Morocco (21.8 million), Sudan (19.4 million), Iraq (12.8 million), and Algeria (10 million). In the same year, the cattle population numbered over 21 million mainly concentrated in the Sudan (11.2 million), Morrocco (3.4 million), Egypt (1.7 million), Iraq (1.4 million), and North Yemen (1.3 million).[31] However, the importance of livestock as an integral part of the agricultural sector is not fully recognized. Livestock is generally raised with no medical attention or proper feeding and breeding; as a result, quality is poor and disease is prevalent.

The lack of an integrative, well-defined and consistent agricultural strategy in most Arab countries has been responsible for the generally sluggish response of production to heavy public investment in agriculture and to the variety of policy measures applied. Basically four different approaches have been followed in dealing with the problems of agriculture:[32] construction of an adequate infrastructure—dams, irrigation and drainage networks, roads, and so on—hoping that these will furnish the farmer (and the commercial community) with a basis on which to build his own future prosperity; land reform and social development which in theory should give the farmer, as a miniature capitalist, sufficient incentive to increase his output and improve his own standard of living; direct assistance to the farmer, with instruction on scientific farming techniques and small capital investments, assuming that he is too conservative to respond on his own to incentives created by the first two approaches; and if everything else fails, leaving the farmer to make slow progress at his own pace, and directing the thrust of policy to the establishment of agrobusinesses run by large corporations in the California style. Unfortunately, however, no serious attempt has been made, except perhaps in Egypt, to integrate these approaches or to follow consistent agricultural policy. Policy measures have not been carefully selected to suit the requirements of the situation and when a given policy has shown little immediate success, it has quickly been abandoned and substituted for by a drastically different approach. This continuous experimentation has created confusion and insecurity in the agricultural community, thus causing private decision makers to conduct their activities on a day-to-day basis and to refrain from medium-term or long-range planning. But, without such planning, substantial improvement in agricultural production is practically impossible.

It appears from this brief discussion of agricultural resources that there exists considerable room for h   on   and vertical expansion in agriculture in practically all the Arab   untries. Thus, the rational exploitation of the agricultural potential of the Arab world may prove to be indispensable to a genuine economic and social development of the whole region.

Mineral Resources

The Arab world is rich in mineral resources, especially oil, natural gas, sulphur, and phosphate. Import   concentrations of other minerals are also found, but in most cases, they are still not extensively exploited. It must be

TABLE 5.1

Oil and Natural Gas: a Global Overview

Area	Proved Reserves January 1, 1976		Oil Production				Refining b/cd January 1, 1976 (barrels per day)		
	Oil (thousands of barrels)	Gas 10^9 ft^3	Producing Wells, July 1, 1975	Estimated 1975 (thousands of barrels per day)	Percent Change from 1974	No.	Crude	Cracking	Reforming
Asia-Pacific	21,234,230	111,560	7,156	2,197.2	-4.9	108	9,868,344	539,125	921,835
Europe	25,487,700	180,875	5,981	540.4	41.1	161	19,972,306	959,690	2,350,630
Middle East	368,410,570	538,648	3,919	20,332.0	-6.5	33	3,284,951	119,253	196,935
The Arab world	342,237,220	366,392	5,356	17,242.7	-4.6	39	2,501,301	57,653	129,390
Africa, excluding African Arab countries	26,650,000	49,350	1,468	2,208.0	-14.8	21	835,350	64,900	114,040
Western hemisphere	75,468,000	358,887	540,885	14,167.3	-7.3	390	24,943,093	5,303,336	3,805,125
Total noncommunist	555,685,720	1,397,122	561,640	42,100.6	-6.6	730	59,396,894	6,990,304	7,434,965
Communist world	103,000,000	835,000	—	11,750.0	9.0	—	—	—	—
Total world	658,684,720	2,232,122	—	53,850.6	-3.6	730	59,396,894	6,990,304	7,434,965
Arab world as percent of total noncommunist	61.6	24.1	0.95	40.9	—	5.3	4.2	0.82	1.7

Source: *Oil & Gas Journal*, December 29, 1975, pp. 86-87.

stressed, however, that little is known about the exact mineral wealth of practically all Arab countries, due to the lack and inadequacy of geological studies and surveys.[33] A complete regional industrial strategy must, therefore, await the availability of pertinent and urgently needed information about the total mineral wealth of the area. Nevertheless, the existing mineral wealth should be the basis for an efficient pattern of specialization, and could support a rather diversified industrial development.

Table 5.1 portrays the global distribution of oil and natural gas resources and refining output. It will be seen from the table that the Arab world contains more than 60 percent of the total noncommunist world reserves and about one-fourth of total gas reserves. However, Arab oil production is only 40.9 percent of total noncommunist world production. If this trend continues, the dominance of the Arab world in oil reserves will evidently grow and not diminish.

The number of producing wells in the Arab world is less than one percent of that for the noncommunist world, while the Arab world produces more than 40 percent of noncommunist-world oil. In fact, average well productivity in the Arab world is 3,220 barrels per day, while the average for the noncommunist world outside the Arab region is 45 barrels per day. Such a dramatic disparity in average well productivity gives Arab oil a tremendous competitive cost structure, thus affording the Arab producers greater flexibility in setting crude oil prices. This is a factor that must be reckoned with in the West when suggestions or plans are advanced or initiated for the production of alternative energy sources.

Contrary to what is commonly but erroneously believed, the behavior of the Arab oil producers since 1974 has been relatively less protective of the new oil prices. The recent decline in the quantity of oil demanded as a reponse to the combined effects of higher prices and the deceleration of economic activities in the West has been significantly offset by production programming, which has been practiced elsewhere on a larger scale than in the Arab world. Arab oil production decreased in 1975 from its 1974 level at a rate of 4.6 percent, well below the 6.6 percent reduction in noncommunist world production. This behavior may be explained at least in part by the limited oil reserves of the non-Arab producers; thus the desire to maximize benefits derived from these reserves by conserving and lengthening their expected life span.

Oil generally is not refined where it is produced; the Arab world refines only about 10 percent of its oil production and this proportion grows considerably smaller when further processing (that is, cracking and reforming) is considered. The reasons for this are multifarious and complex. First, very little of the oil production is consumed in the Arab world itself, mirroring the limited extent of industrialization and development in the area. Second, the refining industry is subject to economies of scale with per unit cost declining precipitously as the size of plant expands and output level rises. Thus when European product markets expanded subsequent to World War II,

> . . . it became economical to transport the crude oil and refine it
> close to the product markets since crude was cheaper to transport
> than products. In addition, many consuming countries considered
> that the security of their product supplies was greater when refin-
> eries were located outside the main areas of crude oil production. In
> the event of interruptions from any one area, other sources of
> crude could be substituted.[34]

It must be pointed out that while such a policy has served Western economies admirably well in the past, its long-run consequences may not have been all
beneficial. In fact, the economic benefits reflected in higher levels of value-
added and employment that the West reaped from processing crude domestically
have been at least partially eroded and may even be fully nullified in the future
by the mounting adverse environmental impact, and more recently the enhanced
flexibility of OPEC countries with respect to production programming. The
latter point is extremely important and has to be spelled out in greater detail.
In a period of falling demand for oil, OPEC countries could successfully resist
pressures on crude prices by simply reducing their output levels. Although
certain friction and strain have developed among OPEC members regarding
the apportionment of production cutbacks,* the matter so far has been resolved
peacefully, probably because the costs involved in shifting production to future
periods are comparatively small. Moreover, countries with tremendous production potential, such as Saudi Arabia and Kuwait, have been willing to shoulder
the brunt of production reduction necessary to preserve oil prices, mainly
because of their limited domestic absorptive capacities and the uncertain outlook for their investments in the international money and financial markets.

Assume for the moment that all crude is produced and refined upstream,
that is, in the OPEC countries themselves. Further assume for simplicity that
each oil-producing country owns and operates either directly or indirectly one
or more plants that refine all its crude production.† Evidently, each country
would be keenly interested in operating its refinery units at or near capacity,
for to do otherwise in an industry characterized by economies of scale would
mean higher per unit cost and, ceteris paribus, lower profit margin. Should the
demand for refined oil products fall, an oil-producing country could not easily
reduce its crude production, for this necessarily leaves some of its refining

---

*If current demand trends for oil continue, admittedly an unlikely possibility,
friction may be exacerbated, thus subjecting the unity of OPEC to greater strain. It must be
emphasized, however, that the sluggish demand for oil is not the only source of friction
in OPEC. The development of the domestic absorptive capacity of the member countries
is at least as important, as has been explained earlier.

† The number obviously depends on the country's crude production in relation to
the efficient size of plant.

capacity idle. In an industry with a very high fixed cost component, lower capacity utilization must increase per unit cost of final products, thus lowering the profit margin or possibly even turning continued production uneconomical. The oil producer is forced to perceive crude extraction and crude processing as one integral operation and not two distinct activities. Thus, the costs of reducing crude output would not be confined to the small cost associated with the intertemporal allocation of crude production, but would encompass the sizable and immediate costs of operating refining units at less than optimal levels. This by itself could increase friction, tension, and strain among OPEC members, making it very difficult to reach collective decisions and to preserve unity. The problem is further compounded, however, because, under the above assumptions, Saudi Arabia and Kuwait would not concede reducing their crude output proportionately more than the other OPEC members, for if they do, they would be incurring considerably greater losses on their refining units due to the large amount of capital sunk in these facilities. One possible solution is to decrease output of all members by a uniform percentage; but such a solution would leave considerably less resources at the disposal of countries with large domestic absorption—such as Indonesia, Iran, and Nigeria—and relatively more for the low absorbers, thus creating additional incentives for the high absorbers to break away from OPEC.

In conclusion, our analysis clearly shows that OPEC's shell has proved difficult to crack in the face of falling demand, at least in part because of the historical spatial separation of crude extraction from crude processing and refining. It follows that the gradual relocation of crude refining and processing activities in the oil producing countries themselves would tend to make prices of oil products more sensitive to market conditions.

A number of other significant mineral deposits exist in the Arab world, including phosphate, iron ore, sulphur, and others.

The Arab world is a major phosphate producer with total production comprising about 35 percent of total world output.[35] Phosphate deposits are concentrated in Morocco, Tunisia, and Egypt. Recently, significant phosphate deposits were discovered in the western desert of Iraq, in Al-Akashat. Iraq announced subsequently that a West European firm will develop these deposits under a $94 million contract, with production scheduled to commence in 1979 at 3.4 million tons annually.[36] Moreover, the phosphate production potential of the Arab world is due to increase substantially as a result of the annexation of the phospahate-rich Spanish Sahara territory by Morocco and Mauritania, both members of the Arab League.

About 85 percent of total Arab current production is destined for export, due to the absence of a well-developed phosphate fertilizer industry.[37] The growing need to expand agricultural production, and consequently the shift to intensive farming with its considerable use of fertilizers in the region and in many other developing countries, should improve the prospects of an already lucrative phosphate mining and processing industry.

Total iron ore reserves of the Arab world amount to an estimated 7,000 million tons. Production, however, has been very low, amounting to under 15 million tons in 1973. Moreover, less than two million tons, that is, about 13.5 percent of the iron ore produced in the region, are used by the existing integrated steel plants in Algeria, Tunisia, and Egypt.[38]

Iron ore reserves are concentrated in Algeria, Mauritania, Libya, Tunisia, Morocco and Egypt. Important reserves are also found in northern Iraq (Benjaween), Syria (Rajoo), and Saudi Arabia (near Jeddah).[39] Libya's iron ore reserves located in the southernmost province of Fezzan in the region of Wadi Shatti are substantial.

It is estimated that the deposit extends to some 3,600 million tons—equivalent to about 5 percent of total world resources. The quality of the ore is high with an estimated 2,000 million tons, thought to contain 50 percent of iron.[40]

Total Arab consumption of iron and steel amounted to 5,891 million tons in 1974 against a domestic production of 4,482 million tons. Historically, the development of the Arab iron and steel industry has been slow despite the availability of a key raw material, iron ore. This may be attributed to a number of factors, including the limited financial resources, the lack of suitable technology, the lack of an industrial structure, the scarcity of trained and skilled labor, and the lack of what may be termed the industrial mentality, that is, the willingness to assume risks, to organize, and to invest with a view to long-term objectives. Recently, however, some of these obstacles have been effectively overcome, and others may gradually ease in the course of development. Thanks to the recent surge in oil revenues, capital is no longer an important constraint for the oil producers, and provided extensive regional cooperation takes place, for the non-oil economies as well. Moreover recent advances in steel-making technology have considerably improved the prospects for the establishment of this industry in the major oil-producing countries, especially those that are simultaneously endowed with rich iron ore deposits.

Traditionally, steelmaking·has been based on the blast furnace route and the basic oxygen system (BOS). The blast furnace and the BOS require high grade coking coal as well as iron ore, and the lack of suitable supplies of coking coal locally would clearly be a major constraint on effective and efficient production by Middle East countries.

But the development of the direct reduction (DR) process, particularly when allied to the electric arc furnace, has now brought steelmaking within the grasp of almost any country. Even in the established steelmaking areas, the development of new plants centered on the DR process and the electric arc, is becoming increasingly attractive. Reformed natural gas is used to remove oxygen from iron ore. This leaves a product known as sponge iron which can be then melted and refined in electric arc furnaces to produce steel. Similarly, scrap can be fed directly into an electric arc in order to make steel. With ample supplies of natural gas—wastefully flared off over many years—the Middle East now has an opportunity to harness that valuable natural resource for the production of steel and launch the region into an era of industrialization.[41]

Capital availability, access to technology, the growth of domestic steel demand, and the desire to diversify the economic base have rekindled Arab enthusiasm and interest in the iron and steel industry. Several bold and imaginative plans have been initiated or are currently under study. It is improbable, however, that all the envisaged blueprints will materialize, given the scarcity of trained labor, the inefficiency of the government bureaucracy, and the notorious implementation gap.

Table 5.2 shows the pertinent data on iron and steel in the Arab world for the period 1971-80. Sulphur can be extracted from natural gas or from heavy oil with high sulphur content. In a pollution conscious world, petroleum with low sulphur content commands a premium. Thus, the Arab oil producers could reap substantial economic benefits from expanding petroleum-refining and gas-processing facilities. These advantages include higher value for processed raw materials, greater integration of the petroleum sector into the rest of the economy, and the recovery of pure sulphur as a by-product, which could then be locally utilized in various industries or exported abroad. Iraq possesses one of the world's largest sulphur deposits, which is currently being exploited on a modest scale. The sulphur reserves at Mishraq are estimated at several hundred million tons,[42] and the rate of production could be stepped up, depending on world market demand, mitigating certain logistic problems, and increasing sulphur utilization both locally and regionally.

Other minerals[43] include copper in Jordan, Syria, and other Arab countries; manganese in Morocco, Algeria, Egypt, and Syria; lead in Morocco, Algeria, and Egypt; zinc in Morocco, Tunisia, and Egypt; potash in Jordan; and glass sand and ceramic clay in Iraq and other Arab countries. In addition, almost all Arab countries possess sizable quantities of clay and sand suitable for cement and other construction industries.

Most of these minerals are being exploited, but their production could be further expanded, provided regional demand is stimulated, logistic problems are solved, and the necessary finance is secured.

Regional Comparative Advantage

Generally speaking, all the countries in the region can expand and rationalize their agriculture and some of their existing industries, or perhaps initiate

TABLE 5.2

Iron and Steel Production, Consumption, and Trade of Arab Countries to 1980
(thousands of metric tons)

Country	Production			Imports			Exports			Consumption			Consumption per capita (kilograms)		
	1971	1975	1980	1971	1975	1980	1971	1975	1980	1971	1975	1980	1971	1975	1980
Algeria	128	980	2,050	466	170	–	–	250	950	648	900	1,100	43	50.5	51
Egypt	666	1,691	2,025	485	–	–	100	310	522	1,051	1,381	1,503	29.8	35	34
Iraq	–	210	430	486	445	470	–	–	–	442	655	900	49	59	70
Jordan	65	185	290	87	155	270	–	105	145	101	235	415	44	91	134
Kuwait	–	–	–	159	180	205	–	–	–	159	180	205	265	225	170
Lebanon	188	295	390	363	370	480	55	30	100	496	635	770	200	235	256
Libya	24	125	405	236	270	75	–	–	135	232	395	345	122	188	142
Morocco	9	371	460	136	5	10	–	145	155	145	231	315	8.9	12.3	14.4
Saudi Arabia	12.5	160	265	288	280	80	–	–	–	300	448	345	31.6	42	27.5
Sudan	–	–	–	81	140	130	–	20	35	81	120	95	5.4	7.2	5.5
Syria	–	135	245	293	120	90	–	20	45	293	235	290	44	31.5	33.4
Tunisia	104	330	405	52	–	–	–	264	325	200	366	325	40	66	54
Yemen (N)	–	–	–	–	–	–	–	–	–	–	–	–	–	–	–
Yemen (S)	–	–	–	–	–	–	–	–	–	85	110	158	53	61	79
Total	1,196.5	4,482	6,965	3,132	2,135	1,810	225	1,144	2,412	4,277	5,891	6,766	33.3	40.6	40.5

Source: *Middle East Economic Digest*, March 19, 1976, p. 36.

new ones that utilize available natural resources and cater primarily to local demand. Transportation costs and the natural characteristics of certain goods may require their being produced exclusively for the domestic market. But the majority of commodities could be produced more efficiently on a larger scale to serve the regional and/or the world market. Four broad categories of industries fall into the latter group. These include capital- and energy-intensive industries, labor-intensive industries, certain agricultural products, and services— including banking and finance, shipping, repair yards, and tourism. The rest of this secion analyzes these industries and suggests a general optimal spatial distribution for them.

Energy- and Capital-Intensive Industries

Aside from gas liquefaction, which has become commercially feasible due to recent technical progress in processing and transportation of liquefied natural gas, the prime example of a capital- and energy-intensive industry is petrochemicals. Obviously, countries with tremendous natural gas reserves, namely, Algeria and Abu Dhabi, would do well in establishing gas liquefaction plants, provided long-term marketing arrangements could be secured with major gas-consuming countries. But the major industry that would be established in the oil-based economies is refining and petrochemicals. Traditionally, petroleum has been used as a source of energy, but increasingly petroleum is being used in the manufacture of petrochemicals. Although less than 5 percent of the world's oil is used in petrochemical manufacture, the industry is growing rapidly with total world sales of petrochemicals and petrochemical products exceeding $100 billion in 1974.[44] The products of this industry consist of basic or first generation petrochemicals, and intermediate and end products or second generation petrochemicals.[45] There are several characteristics of the petrochemical industry that make it attractive for most oil-based economies, especially the Arab states of the Gulf and Libya.

Capital intensity. The petrochemical industry enjoys one of the highest capital-labor ratios in the world. In fact, investment per new job created is estimated at $20,000 to $100,000.[46] Moreover, basic products and intermediates entail larger and larger investments as they advance from the stage of transformation to the state of finished products and then to consumer goods.[47] Investment required for the transportation of finished products into consumer or industrial goods (third manufacturing phase) is two to three times higher than that necessary for the production of intermediate products (second manufacturing phase), and five times higher than that necessary for the production of basic products (first manufacturing phase).[48]

Availability of raw materials—natural gas and oil. The Arab states of the Gulf completely dominate the world's oil picture.[49] Total oil reserves of these states account for 89 percent of total Arab reserves and 55.5 percent of total non-communist world reserves. The corresponding figures for oil production are 85 percent and 35 percent. Gas reserves of these countries, though not so substantial, are nevertheless significant; they stand at 20 percent of total non-communist world reserves.

The mere availability of raw materials is, of course, not a sufficient argument for industrialization. Whether or not industries based on local raw materials should be established must be determined by analyzing prospective production costs "to find out how much of the cost of the product is attributable to the raw material, and how the cost of the raw material locally compares to its cost elsewhere."[50] However, given that most of the associated gas, which cannot be reinjected, is presently flared off for lack of gas processing and utilization facilities, there is prima facie evidence that failure to establish industries utilizing natural and associated gas results in these resources being economically wasted.

Existence of economies of scale.

[Indeed], investments do not vary in proportion to the capacity, but rather according to a power factor generally lying between 0.6 and 0.85. This is the reason why it is advantageous to build large capacity units which cost proportionally less than small or medium capacity units. The same observation can be made for the manpower as well as the general and plant overhead, all of which are proportionally lower expenditures in large capacity units.[51]

High degree of vertical industrial integration. Petrochemical plants involve the production of a number of joint products or by-products, and it is generally not economically sound to build a plant unless a secure market outlet exists for all or most of these products.[52] Moreover, if integration is carried out to a maximum degree, that is, if a petrochemical complex is built in the neighborhood of a refinery so that it may utilize the latter's by-products, profitability is increased substantially provided the bulk of the products is marketed.[53]

Other features of the petrochemical industry may pose some difficulties, at least in the immediate future, and are related basically to two factors. First, the industry is characterized by a very high and sophisticated technology and competition. Extremely complex installations utilizing the most modern technological developments and a highly specialized and extensively trained manpower are required.[54] Moreover, the industry is exceedingly dynamic and research into new processes and products plays a vital role. Competition is intense, in part because of the availability of various substitutes. "Different products have comparable uses. For example, cellophane, waxed paper, aluminum foil, polyethylene sheets and acetate film are all competing with each other."[55] The Arab countries, however, currently lack both the necessary technology and the extensively trained manpower required for the establishment of such an industry and would, therefore, have to resort to importation of these imputs.

The second factor militating against the establishment of such an industry lies in the fact that at the present stage this industry must cater primarily— and in the case of the smaller states of the Gulf almost exclusively—to the export market, thus making market surveys of critical importance. Moreover, the marketing of petrochemicals assumes added significance because of the large overhead costs that render per unit total costs highly sensitive to variations in capacity utilization. It has been argued that:

> . . . despite the apparently favorable aspects of a determined project, if the outlets have been badly calculated and the plant can operate at no more than 50% of its capacity, it will obviously have difficulties competing with another plant which may be less advantageously conceived but which is able to operate at maximum or almost maximum nominal capacity.[56]

It must be emphasized that regional cooperation is here essential, not only as a means for securing access to the wider regional market for the growing petrochemical industries, but also as a vehicle for coordination and harmonization of the oil producers' plans for the development of petrochemicals and other energy- and capital-intensive industries, thus preventing duplication, waste, and harmful competition.

The consideration above calls for a carefully designed strategy in developing petrochemical industries in the oil-based Arab countries. Although an identical strategy for petrochemical development is unlikely to be optimal for all energy-rich nations, the following general principles constitute a useful guide.[57] First, only mature petrochemical products should initially be developed. The identifying characteristics of a mature petrochemical product are large worldwide markets, large volume of world trade, many buyers and sellers, relatively low unit prices, dominant raw materials costs, and readily available and stable technology. Examples of such products are methanol, benzene, ammonia, and mature plastics including PVC, polystyrene, and polyethylene. Evidently, the energy-rich nations have a competitive edge in such standardized and thus price-sensitive products which, moreover, use considerable amounts of raw materials and possess large and diversified outlets, as well as relatively stable technology. The new and more glamorous petrochemicals such as terephthalic acid or polyurethane use comparatively less hydrocarbons, more skills and scientific knowledge, and are characterized by highly dynamic processes of production. The energy-rich nations should therefore refrain from competing with the multinational chemical companies in these lines of production, at least for the next decade or so.

Second, the availability of a secure source of raw materials plus capital calls for building very large integrated plants to harness the benefits of economies of scale and to minimize the costs of production. Thus, the products may be offered at very competitive prices thereby practically guaranteeing a market for the plant.

Third, in order further to reduce risks in building and operating petro-chemical complexes, it may be advantageous for the energy-rich nations of the Gulf to seek the active participation of a foreign partner with considerable technical, distributional, and sales experience in the field. The host country should retain majority interest and control, but must actively involve the foreign partner in the project so as to guarantee success.

The strategy of development in the oil-based economies in the region must also emphasize industries and techniques of production that make maximum use of available energy, other raw materials, and/or capital resources. Aluminum, cement, iron and steel using the direct reduction method, glass, and phosphates are examples of such industries. Currently several of these industries are well established in the region, such as aluminum in Bahrain, cement in practically all the Arab countries, and phosphates in Morocco and Tunisia. Production in these lines could be, however, considerably expanded with an eye to exports to regional and/or world markets.

In Iraq, plans are under way to build an aluminum complex, to mine available phosphate deposits, to produce superphosphate fertilizers, and to expand sulphur mining and processing. Also, a glass factory is being envisaged that will utilize domestic glass sand as raw material. Furthermore, in Iraq as well as in Saudi Arabia, existing contracts call for the construction of iron and steel complexes, using the plentiful supplies of natural gas as a reducing agent and imported Brazilian ore to produce a variety of products such as reinforcing bars, billets, tinplate, galvanized sheets, and pipes. Presently, however, Egypt is the leading steel producer in the Arab world with four major producing firms for crude steel together with one unit producing steel tubes. The Egyptian steel industry has featured in the country's development plans since the 1960s, and the plans called for the annual production of a total of 2.5 million tons of crude steel by 1970. "But financial and technical difficulties and the Middle East hostilities have set these plans considerably back."[58] The revised target calls for the production of 2.8 million tons yearly by 1978, but due to further constraints, crude steel production may not exceed two million tons annually, provided no major difficulty is encountered. It must be emphasized that although Egypt is an important consumer of steel and steel products, the pros-pects for expanding steel production are not particularly good. The iron ore deposits around the Bahria Oasis are limited; the reserves are estimated at 120 million tons with an iron content of 48-61 percent.[59] Although the country is relatively well endowed with skilled labor, finance is in short supply and proven natural gas reserves are modest (4,000 billion cubic feet in January 1976). Thus, allocative efficiency would not encourage further expansion of Egyptian steel production capacity. The two Arab countries most suited for the production of iron and steel are Algeria and Libya. Finance, natural gas, con-siderable iron ore deposits, and in the case of Algeria, adequate labor supply, especially Algerians working in France and other European countries, are con-spicuous assets for the establishment and expansion of the steel industry. In fact,

Algeria already possesses one integrated plant at Al-Hadjar near Annaba. Projected development for the complex envisages raising crude steel production to about 2.2 million tons annually by 1980. In addition the government is seriously considering the construction of a new complex with a production capacity of 11 million tons annually. Nippon Steel has expressed willingness to cooperate in the promotion of that venture.[60] In Libya, the government has engaged consultants from West Germany and India to draw up plans for the building of the country's first steel complex with an initial capacity of 0.5 to 1 million tons, rising to 5 million tons annually by 1986, at Misrata on the Mediterranean Sea. The steel works would be using Libyan ore from the Fezzan area which means that considerable investment must be made in transportation facilities. The total cost of the project which again is based on the direct reduction route is presently estimated at $1,000 million. Furthermore, Libya is building a tube works with assistance from the Spanish firm of Arrasate at Benghazi, and has asked the Japanese Marubeni Group to help in construction of a 150,000-ton-a-year pipe mill near Benghazi.[61]

It appears from these and other potential developments that Algeria and to a much lesser extent Libya might emerge in the 1980s as important centers for heavy industry in the Arab world.

Labor-Intensive Industries

Countries like Egypt, Syria, Sudan, and Morocco have obvious advantages relative to other countries in the region in such labor-intensive lines of production as textiles, cottage and traditional industries, and electronics. In the area of textiles, Egypt and Syria already possess an established and flourishing industry. Egypt, Syria, and the Sudan could develop into major world producers of cotton textiles, provided their potential in this area is fully exploited. In all the three countries raw cotton features as a major foreign exchange earner. Moreover, labor is abundant and cheap, and textiles technology is simple and could be easily procured. If the necessary finance could be obtained and captive markets in the region secured, the expansion of this industry would not only increase value-added and export earnings, but also contribute significantly to the alleviation of acute labor unemployment and underemployment, especially in Egypt.

Morocco's animal wealth is substantial, particularly with respect to the sheep population, thus guaranteeing a plenteous supply of wool and hides. Moreover, the country has an abundant supply of labor and a well-established tradition in cottage and handicraft industries. Therefore, Morocco could expand its output of wool textiles and leather products to cater to a larger regional market. Excellent opportunities also exist for expanding the traditional handicraft industries, especially wood carving and leather products, in both Syria and Egypt.

Labor-abundant countries would also benefit from the establishment or expansion of plants designed to produce various electronic products. Similarly, assembly plants for electric appliances and other engineering products hold promise. The region spends very large sums on imports of such items as TV sets, radios, wire and wireless equipment, air conditioning units, refrigerators, deep freezers, ovens, heating equipment, and cars, all of which could be assembled domestically in the labor-abundant countries, particularly in Egypt. Such a policy of starting with the "finishing touches" in order to enhance labor's skill and experience and to widen the existing market has been advocated by many economists as a successful strategy for industrialization.[62] This policy may be perceived as phased import substitution; the initial stage starts with assembling certain parts and progresses to complete assemblage, and the final stage commences with the production of a few parts and advances to complete manufacture. Of course, all these ventures require additional capital resources which are in short supply in most non-oil Arab countries. Thus, increasing regional cooperation and interdependence is bound not only to accelerate economic growth in the labor abundant countries, but also to diminish the egregious current regional income inequality in the Arab world.

Agricultural Production

As stated earlier, almost all countries in the region can and should expand their agricultural areas and improve and rationalize prevailing agricultural practices. The region is presently a major importer of agricultural products, and the rate of growth in the demand for food is accelerating, due mainly to rising population and income. Thus, to attain a higher measure of self-sufficiency or at least to prevent greater reliance on foreign food sources, the supply of agricultural products must be increased. The countries with the greatest agricultural potential are, in order of importance, the Sudan, Iraq, and Syria. Heavy agricultural investments, particularly in drainage facilities in Iraq and Syria, would not only permit intensive agriculture, but also increase the potentially cultivable area in those countries about threefold. Similarly, investments in land reclamation and in mechanization could bring new parts of the vast rain-fed area of the Sudan into cultivation. Given the currently limited area under cultivation and the very low yields per acre for most crops, the practice of scientific agriculture, including soil analysis and preparation, efficient water usage, proper irrigation and drainage practices, crop rotation, improved seeds and saplings, the use of fertilizers, pesticides and herbicides, proper grading and marketing of agricultural products, and so on, would increase output sufficiently to cover the regional requirements and leave sizable surplus for export to other food-deficit countries outside the Arab world.

Agricultural expansion would involve export of a few specialized crops: for example, cotton, rice, onions, and citrus fruits in Egypt;[63] cotton, sugar, and corn in the Sudan; cotton, wheat and barley, and grapes in Syria; wheat and barley, and dates in Iraq; wheat, grapes, olives, tobacco, and citrus fruits in Algeria; wheat, citrus fruits, and olives in Morocco; olives in Tunisia; vegetables and citrus fruits in the West Bank and Lebanon; and coffee in Yemen.[64]

The development of agriculture must also pay increasing attention to the rational exploitation of the animal resources of the Arab world. As indicated above, the animal resources of the Arab world are considerable, and provided scientific measures are practiced with respect to feeding and breeding, veterinary care, and epidemic control, some of the Arab countries, particularly the Sudan, Morocco, Algeria, and Iraq could become important exporters of meat, dairy, and other animal products. Furthermore, the Arab world's potential in the area of fishing remains insufficiently exploited. With vast sea water spaces in the Gulf, the Arabian Sea, the Red Sea, the Mediterranean Sea, and the Atlantic Ocean, in addition to inland river systems including the Nile, the Tigris, and the Euphrates, the current consumption per capita of fish in the Arab world of about 9 lbs. annually, compared to more than seven times as much in Japan seems very low.[65] This conclusion is reinforced when it is realized that the waters of the Gulf, the Arabian Sea, and the Red Sea teem with substantial quantities of fish and shrimp. The quality of the shrimp in the Gulf is, moreover, excellent by world standards. This has enticed Japanese fishing boats to come all the way from Japan to fish in the Gulf and Arabian Sea waters. But aside from a few modern fishing companies primarily in Kuwait and Qatar, fishing methods are generally primitive, and fishing activities are not scientifically planned.* It follows that appropriate investments in modern fishing fleets, scientific fishing, shrimp farming, fish and shrimp processing and refrigerating plants, are likely to increase substantially the present low level of output, and yield a high rate of return on invested capital. However, the distribution of fishing rights in the Gulf currently poses some problems, but, provided these were solved, fishing could prove an extremely viable diversification activity for most oil-based littoral states of the Gulf.

It must be emphasized that what is urgently needed in the Arab world is an integrative approach to agricultural development, one that would involve, in addition to the expansion of plant and animal output, improvement in such measures as provision of efficient transportation, marketing techniques, including grading and packaging, and the establishment or expansion of food-processing and canning industries. Without adequate recognition of the inter-relationships among various agricultural activities, heavy investment in one area alone is less likely to show significant positive return.

---

*Recently, Iraq entered into a joint venture with South Yemen whereby the former would provide the finance necessary for the establishment of a modern fishing fleet to exploit the fishing potential in the area.

Services and Tourism

With respect to services, many Gulf countries could profitably specialize in shipping and repair facilities for oil tankers and other ships. Moreover, the small littoral Gulf states have traditionally led in the transit trade serving Saudi Arabia, Iraq, and Iran, among others. With excellent port facilities and new dry-dock harbors being constructed in Bahrain and in Dubai, these states could expand their activities as depot trade centers.

Many perceptive observers also believe that the combination of a mercantile community dating back to the nineteenth century and earlier and the availability of surplus petrodollars is particularly opportune for the establishment and expansion of banking and finance in the littoral states of the Gulf. Dr. Al-Awadi, for example, advocates this when he states:

> In a nutshell, this author believes that Kuwait's comparative advantage, after oil export of course, is in the service sector, particularly banking and investment. Therefore, the money and capital markets in Kuwait should be carefully expanded in order to decrease the near total reliance of the economy on the oil sector. To fulfill this objective, technical, administrative and legal changes and improvements regarding the financial activities in Kuwait should be soon undertaken.[66]

Until recently Beirut, Lebanon, with its advantageous geographic location, pleasant climate, excellent infrastructure, well-established and agile business community, and open and free enterprise economy, has been unquestionably the financial and commercial center of the Middle East. Beirut has attracted considerable regional investment, especially in real estate, and has served as the Middle East headquarters for a number of major transnational companies doing business in the area. However, the bloody civil war that started in 1975 and continued into 1976 brought all relevant commercial activities virtually to a standstill. The flight of capital and entrepreneurial talents from Lebanon has been almost complete, and it may be years before the country can regain its recent outstanding position as the hub of commerce and the haven for foreign investment in the region.

Meanwhile, the Gulf states, Jordan, Syria, and Egypt are exhibiting keen interest in becoming major financial and commercial centers in the region. Egypt in particular is pursuing aggressive policies, such as the gradual decontrol of her economy, the offering of ample and lucrative incentives for foreign enterprise, and the adoption of a decidedly reconciliatory attitude toward the West especially vis-a-vis the United States, with the aim of luring a larger volume of regional and foreign capital, and of enticing greater flow of entrepreneurial talents into the country, realizing that these ingredients are sorely needed for the reconstruction and the rapid development of the Egyptian economy. However, due to a variety of factors including infrastructural constraints, location and climate, and other sociopolitical elements, the attempt on the part of some Arab countries to substitute for Beirut's ideal position is likely to be only partially successful.

Furthermore, other Arab countries, particularly Egypt, Lebanon, Jordan, Syria, Iraq, Saudi Arabia, Tunisia, and Morocco, could expand and modernize their tourist industry, which is already a major foreign exchange earner in many of them. The Arab world is reowned for its richness in tourist attraction. As the cradle of human civilization and the crossroads of diverse distinctive ancient peoples and cultures, countries like Egypt, Jordan, Saudi Arabia, and Iraq enjoy an unusual wealth of archaeological remains and/or religious shrines. Other Arab countries, including Lebanon, Syria, and the North African states of Tunisia, Algeria, and Morocco offer pleasant climate, varied and interesting landscape, and excellent beaches. Investments in hotels, restaurants, recreational facilities, communications and general infrastructure, handicraft and traditional industries, and tourist advertising campaigns promise to increase the influx of tourists into these countries both from the region and outside, thus generating additional income and augmenting the supply of valuable foreign exchange.

NOTES

1. *Middle East Economic Survey* 18, no. 14 (February 24, 1975).
2. KFAED, News Release, January 1976.
3. I.M.D. Little and J.M. Clifford, *International Aid: An Introduction to the Problem of the Flow of Public Resources from Rich to Poor Countries* (Chicago, Ill.: Aldine, 1966), pp. 188-89.
4. "Oil Lands Pledge Millions to Cairo," New York *Times*, March 1, 1976, pp. 1, 4.
5. See Ragaei El Mallakh, *Economic Development and Regional Co-operation: Kuwait* (Chicago: University of Chicago Press, 1968), pp. 75-76.
6. Mihssen Kadhim, "The 1964 Nationalization of Private Industry in Iraq," *American Journal of Arabic Studies*, 4, 1976.
7. A.Y. Al-Hamad, *Towards an Arab Financial Market* (Kuwait: KFAED, 1974), (In Arabic), pp. 8-10.
8. Jahangir Amuzegar, "Ideology and Economic Growth in the Middle East," *Middle East Journal* 28, no. 1, (Winter 1974), p. 9.
9. A.Y. Al-Hamad, *Towards Closer Economic Cooperation in the Middle East* (Kuwait: KFAED, 1975), p. 7.
10. Ibid.
11. Ibid., pp. 7-8.
12. S. Abdelhakim, "Population Trends in the Arab World," *Journal of the Middle East* 2, 1975, p. 7. (in Arabic)
13. Ibid., p. 18. Lebanon with 26.5 and Egypt with 38.7 per thousand population are notable exceptions, however.
14. Ibid. Lebanon with 4.5 and Kuwait with 7.4 per thousand population obviously do not conform to the norm.
15. Ibid., p. 15.
16. Ibid., p. 20.

17. The labor participation rate, defined here as the proportion of economically active population to total population, ranges generally between 22 and 30 percent. Such a low rate is traceable to the virtual exclusion of females from the labor force, which is explained by cultural and traditional factors especially in highly conservative Arab countries such as Saudi Arabia, the littoral states of the Gulf, and Libya. See Ibid., p. 21. It is also interesting to observe that, under the pressure of high population growth, the proportion of the economically active population appears to have declined in the 1960s in all Arab countries. See Kuwait Fund for Arab Economic Development (KFAED), *The Arab World: Key Indicators* (Kuwait: Press Advertising Agency, 1975), p. 12.

18. United Nations Food and Agriculture Organization, *Production Yearbook, 1966.* (Rome: Food and Agriculture Organization, 1967). Population per physician and per hospital bed is generally low. See KFAED, *Key Indicators*, op. cit., p. 57.

19. Abdelhakim, op. cit., p. 22, and KFAED, *Key Indicators*, op. cit., p. 58. Note that the literacy rate varies considerably between the sexes. The females literacy rate is substantially lower than the corresponding rate for males.

20. United Nations, Department of Social Affairs, *The Determinants and Consequences of Population Trends* (New York: United Nations, 1953), p. 265.

21. Republic of Iraq, Ministry of Planning, *The Preliminary Detailed Framework for the National Development Plan, 1970-74* (Baghdad: Ministry of Planning, 1970), p. 75 (in Arabic.) In caluclating the average for Egypt, Syria, and Iraq, the ratios are weighted by the respective populations. Note that these ratios are much smaller in other, less developed Arab countries.

22. United Nations Economic and Social Office in Beirut, "Some Aspects of the Development of Human Resources in Various Countries of the Middle East," in *Studies on Selected Development Problems in Various Countries in the Middle East, 1968* (New York: United Nations, 1968), pp. 35-45.

23. A.E. Balbaa, "An Outline of Soil, Water and Agriculture in the Arab Countries," *Journal of the Middle East* 2, 1975, p. 75. (In Arabic.)

24. "Agriculture in the Middle East, A Special Report," *Middle East Economic Digest*, (MEED), June 25, 1971, p. 712. Here it is estimated that because of the water constraint not more than 8 to 10 percent of the region as a whole may be brought under cultivation.

25. United Nations Food and Agricultural Organization, *Production Yearbook 1973* (Rome: United Nations, 1973); and United Nations, *Yearbook of National Accounts Statistics 1973* (New York: United Nations).

26. Balbaa, op. cit., p. 60.

27. Ibid., p. 72.

28. Ibid., p. 73.

29. MEED, op. cit., p. 713.

30. Balbaa, op. cit., p. 77.

31. MEED, op. cit., p. 718.

32. Ibid., pp. 715-716.

33. M.S. Abdul-Hakim et al., *The Economic Resources in the Arab World*, 2nd ed. (Cairo: Dar al-Qalam, 1966). (in Arabic)

34. Edith Penrose, "International Oil Companies and Governments in the Middle East," in *The Middle East: Oil, Politics and Development*, ed. John D. Anthony (Washington, D.C.: American Enterprise Institute, 1975), p. 6, for footnote.

35. Y. Arodky, *The Arab Common Market* (Damascus: Ministry of Culture Press, 1970), p. 105 (in Arabic).

36. CACI, Inc.–Federal, *Medium Term Ability of Oil Producing Countries to Absorb Real Goods and Services*, Vol. II (Arlington, Va.: CACI, Inc.–Federal, 1976), pp. 9-12.

37. Arodky, op. cit.

38. Peter Hill, "Middle East Industrial Development Rests on Iron and Steel," *Middle East Economic Digest*, March 19, 1976, pp. 3-6, 36-37.

39. See also Arodky, op. cit., pp. 105-106.

40. Peter Hill, op. cit., p. 36.

41. Ibid., p. 5.

42. Albert Y. Badre, "Economic Development of Iraq," in *Economic Development and Population Growth in the Middle East*, ed. Charles A. Cooper and Sidney S. Alexander (New York: American Elsevier, 1972), p. 301. Cf. also *Middle East Economic Survey* 14 no. 50, (October 8, 1971), and 15, no. 12, (January 14, 1972).

43. See Arodky, op. cit., pp. 106-107.

44. Robert B. Stobauch, "The Economics of Energy vs. Non-Energy Uses of Petroleum: The Case of Petrochemicals," paper presented at the Seminar on Administration of the Oil Resources of Arab Countries, Tripoli, Libya, April, 1974, p. 1.

45. Claude Mercier, *Petrochemical Industry and the Possibilities of Its Establishment in the Developing Countries* (Paris: Editions Technip, 1966), Chs. IV, V. Basic or first generation petrochemicals include the following: olefin, acetylene, butadiene, aromatic hydrocarbon, ammonia, and methanol. End products or second generation petrochemicals include the following: plastics (polyolefins, vinyls, polystyrene), synthetic rubbers (styrene-butadiene rubber, streo-regular rubbers), detergents, nitrogen fertilizers.

46. United Nations, *The Petrochemical Industry* (New York: United Nations, 1973), p. 3.

47. Claude Mercier, op. cit., p. 8.

48. Ibid., p. 11.

49. These countries include: Bahrain, Iraq, Kuwait, Oman, Qatar, Saudi Arabia, and the United Arab Emirates. Percentages are calculated from *Oil & Gas Journal*, December 1974, pp. 108-109.

50. Murray D. Bryce, *Industrial Development: A Guide for Accelerating Economic Growth* (New York: McGraw-Hill, 1960), p. 12.

51. Claude Mercier, op. cit., pp. 17-20.

52. Arthur D. Little, Inc., *A Plan for Industrial Development in Iraq* (Cambridge, Mass.: Arthur D. Little, 1956).

53. Claude Mercier, op. cit., pp. 13, 17.

54. Ibid., p. 18.

55. Ibid., p. 19ff.

56. Ibid., p. 23.

57. Robert B. Stobauch, op. cit., pp. 20-24. Differences among the oil-based economies in reserves, in production and characteristics of oil and gas, in distance to foreign markets, and in size of local markets preclude the applicability of a unique strategy for petrochemical development.

58. Peter Hill, op. cit., p. 5.

59. Ibid.

60. Ibid., p. 36.

61. Ibid., p. 37.

62. Albert Hirschman, *The Strategy of Economic Development* (New Haven: Yale University Press, paperback ed., 1972).

63. Cotton is by far the major export commodity in Egypt; in 1973, it accounted for 75 per cent of agricultural exports and 42.5 percent of total visible exports. See Central Bank of Egypt, *Economic Review* 14, no. 3, 1974, p. 109.

64. See Arodky, op. cit., p. 110.

65. Ibid., p. 112.

66. Yousef A. Al-Awadi, "OPEC Surplus Funds and the Investment Strategy of Kuwait" (Ph.D. Diss., University of Colorado, 1975), p. 252.

6

PROSPECTS FOR
REGIONAL INTEGRATION
IN THE MIDDLE EAST

The discussion in this chapter is organized into two parts. The first summarizes the treatment of regional integration in the Middle East, focusing on the current scope and potential of economic coordination measures among the various Arab states of the region. The second addresses some of the critical issues that have recently arisen in the context of oil and development in the Middle East, concentrating on the broad implications of these for prospective economic and political relationships between the Arab world and the West. The next and final chapter analyzes some of the specific implications in the area of trade and capital flows of regional development and cooperation in the Middle East for the United States.

REGIONAL INTEGRATION IN THE MIDDLE EAST:
SCOPE AND POTENTIAL

The preceding analysis leads to a number of conclusions, which are summarized below:

1. Economic cooperation in the Middle East is most visible among the Arab countries, particularly among the Arab oil producers themselves and between them and other non-oil-exporting Arab states. For this reason the focus of the analysis has been consistently on economic cooperation in the Arab world. However, significant cooperation is taking place between Iran and a few Arab countries, Egypt and Syria, though the volume of transaction and the extent of cooperation are comparatively small. Nevertheless, it is perfectly conceivable that toward the end of this century, Iran, Turkey, and possibly

other states will join with the Arab countries to form a customs union or even
a common market.

2. Historically, the aggregate trade volume among Arab countries has
been rather limited. This conclusion may not stand up, or stand up unequally,
against detailed analysis involving subregions and trade in specific products. If
a few subregions are identified—for example, the Gulf area, Egypt and the Gulf,
the Fertile Crescent, the Northwest African Coastal states—the analysis may
reveal considerable variation and perhaps even opposite results in certain cases.
Similar considerations pertain to disaggregation according to type of commodity—
agricultural versus nonagricultural commodities, commodities versus services,
including tourism. Much could be learned from such an analysis regarding the
relevant factors involved in regional trade, their relative weight, and the latent
opportunities and obstacles in the broad field of regional economic cooperation.
Here is, then, an area where further research is indicated.

3. The regional variation in factor proportions is pronounced and pervasive;
capital, labor, land, and other natural resources are unevenly distributed among
the various states of the region. The recognition of this fact by leading Arab
economists and policy decision makers is undoubtedly a prime driving force for
greater regional cooperation. The basic idea is that regional specialization and
higher factor mobility would, by creating complementary and larger economies, enhance the growth prospects and improve allocative efficiency throughout the region. These dynamic and static benefits of economic cooperation are,
of course, nothing new; the history of European economic cooperation via the
European Coal and Steel Community and later the European Common Market
have demonstrated the positive contribution of such cooperation to the economic development of the participating countries. The scope of economic
cooperation in the Middle East prior to the 1970s was, nonetheless, limited. The
majority of the states were actively engaged either in infrastructural development, using whatever meager amount of capital could be mobilized, or in nation
building. The question of industrialization on a significant scale did not arise.
Thus, intraregional transactions remained small in value and restricted in composition. The bulk of trade was mainly conducted with the West and consisted
of the importation of capital goods and various manufactures, and the exportation of minerals and to a much lesser extent a few agricultural products. The
path of economic blocs as a means of rapid economic development began to
attract greater emphasis in the 1970s for a number of important factors,
including the accumulation of surplus capital in a few oil-producing nations,
the maintenence of greater military and political coordination among the Arab
states vis-a-vis Israel, and the progress accomplished in the basic tasks of
building the necessary infrastructure and the promotion of nation cohesion.

4. The differential contribution of regional cooperation with respect to
capital mobility as distinct from labor mobility must be stressed. Greater capital
mobility and the development of an Arab money and financial market, rich in
terms not only of volume of capital traded, but also in the varieties of financial

and debt instruments exchanged, are unequivocally a most important factor in achieving the economic potential of the region. As has been repeatedly emphasized, the capital-deficit countries in the region cannot realize appreciably higher rates of economic growth without substantial increment in the current net capital inflow from the major oil producers. Furthermore, such capital mobility serves not only the interests of recipients but those of the donors as well. Donors find remunerative and diverse outlets for their surplus capital, secure an efficient regional pattern of economic activities, and promote political harmony and orderly development in the region.

Labor mobility is similarly a potent force in accelerating the pace of economic development in the region, but its contribution is greatest in the category of unskilled labor. Given the general shortage of trained manpower and skills throughout the region, a policy of intraregional skills dispersion and mobility tends to possess modest positive allocative effects. Like capital mobility, unskilled labor movements generate significant dividends to both parties—the labor importer and the labor exporter. In addition to the obvious amelioration of the opposite structural disequilibrium in the two groups of countries, the labor exporter gains from the repatriation of part of the earnings of the exported labor. Thus, regional labor mobility serves to promote and enhance capital inflows to the labor exporting country. Such capital inflows are likely to rise significantly in the future, given the current acute labor shortages in the major oil-producing states and their ambitious national programs for development and industrialization.

It must be stressed, however, that the positive effects of labor mobility generally transcend the realm of economics. Labor mobility augments the existing social and cultural ties among Arabs, thus tending to strengthen the fabric of Arab society and the sentiment for broad and extensive cooperation.

5. One of the most important factors impeding the development of an integrated regional market is the lack of extensive and modern regional communications and transportation systems in the Arab world. As a result, not only are national markets isolated and fragmented, but also the typical Arab state has been, until recently, developing with a few and largely ineffective linkages with the rest of the Arab world. This has preserved existing heterogeneity, limited social contacts, and fostered parochial and local political leadership. The new oil era seems to be gradually but surely eroding isolationism and disintegration. Prompted by logistic needs, Iraq, for example, has recently underwritten the cost of a modern highway linking the Jordanian port of Aqaba on the Red Sea to the Iraqi-Jordanian borders. Moreover, work has started on a 360-mile segment linking Baghdad with Turkey.[1] Throughout the Arab world, moreover, a number of projects with regional ramifications in the area of transportation and communications are either being implemented or are in the planning stage. In May 1976, five U.S. and European firms were reported to be competing for contracts to set up a planned $200-$400 million pan-Arab satellite communications network for the Arab Satellite Organization. The

establishment of the latter organization was agreed on earlier by the communications ministers of the member states of the Arab League.[2]

Radio and television programs are transmitted to and exchanged with neighboring Arab countries, possibly paving the way for the future establishment of regional radio and television broadcasting networks similar to the national U.S. broadcasting networks, ABC, CBS, and NBC.

The potential impact of these developments for future regional economic integration cannot be overemphasized, for a high level of economic coordination and cooperation must be based on a reasonable degree of political and social cohesion. The latter is evidently fostered by the new regional projects in the transportation and communications fields.

6. Formal economic integration among the Arab states still remains a cherished objective, which, however, is quite often paid only lip service by Arab politicians and government officials. The various attempts at serious economic integration and/or political unification among a number of Arab states have so far been unsuccessful. The reasons for this failure are multifarious and complex. Recognition of the difficultties involved seem to have convinced the Arab states that the most fruitful approach to eventual economic integration lies in pursuing a high measure of cooperation, coordination, and policy harmonization on the sectoral level. In other words, the path of joint regional ventures and growing cooperation and coordination on the sectoral level is presently the most feasible and attractive avenue for possible future economic integration and/or political unification.

The petroleum sector has been one of the first and perhaps most important areas of cooperation. Aside from the successful use of the "oil weapon" to achieve certain political ends, the Arab oil-producing countries have established through OAPEC several joint companies, namely, the Arab Maritime Petroleum Transport Company (AMPTC), the Arab Shipbuilding & Repair Yard Company (ASRY), the Arab Petroleum Investments Company (APIC), and the Arab Petroleum Services Company (APSC). Two more schemes will probably follow soon—an Arab Petroleum Training Institute and an Arab Energy Research Center. The eventual aim of the latter will be research into sources of energy other than oil, but initially it will serve as a data bank.[3] The thrust of these endeavors is to involve the Arab states in the different phases of the oil industry, including exploration, transportation, and marketing, thus increasing their control over their petroleum resources. A second goal may be the channeling of funds into remunerative employment and the creation of nonfinancial linkages between the oil sector and the respective domestic economies of the participating Arab states.

Another promising area of cooperation is the field of energy- and capital-intensive industries, including petrochemicals, oil refineries, iron and steel, and aluminum smelting. As has been emphasized earlier, technology and economics in these industries make extensive regional cooperation an essential ingredient for success. This has been increasingly recognized by the various Arab states, but the steps taken in this direction are so far limited and fragile, consisting chiefly of sponsoring two Arab petrochemical conferences (the first convened in March 1971 in Kuwait and the second in March 1976 in Abu Dhabi), and some technical training and consulting cooperation in the industrial utilization and liquefaction of natural gas between the leading Arab states in this industry— Algeria, Saudi Arabia, Iraq, Qatar, and Abu Dhabi.[4] Nevertheless, Arab countries seem to be committed at least in principle to effective planning and coordination in the field of petrochemicals. It remains to be seen how and when this apparent commitment is translated into concrete actions.

Cooperation in the agricultural sector has been largely confined to the establishment of a few joint-venture Arab agricultural and livestock companies, and the exportation of surplus agricultural labor from Egypt to Iraq. The most prominent of these joint-venture firms are the Arab Company for Agriculture and Food Production capitalized at $345 million and headquartered in Cairo, and the Arab Company for Livestock Resources capitalized at $207 million and headquartered in Damascus.[5] These companies have been established only recently; thus it is premature to assess their impact on agricultural production in the Arab world.

The scope for agricultural cooperation in the Arab world is substantial indeed; however, the realization of this potential faces at least three major obstacles: the regional shortage of agricultural experts, technicians, and skilled labor; the necessity of extensive regional labor movements; and the relatively long gestation period of most agricultural projects. Nevertheless, the vast agricultural potential of the Sudan, the rapidly rising demand for food in the Arab world, and the emerging planetary scarcity of food supplies are potent stimuli for cooperation. A most important project in this area is the Arab Institute for Investment in Agricultural Development (AIIAD), which is to have an initial capital of $510 million.[6] Delegates from 11 Arab countries to the first organizational meeting of the Institute met in Khartoum on May 29, 1976, and prepared plans for a six-year agricultural investment program in the Sudan estimated to cost up to $2,800 million. The Institute is being set up with the eventual aim of achieving self-sufficiency in food production by the member states. However, even if this big investment program materializes during the envisaged time frame, it is improbable that full self-sufficiency can be attained before the end of this century, given current estimates of food needs which foresee a doubling of food imports over the next decade. More realistically, the probable impact of this program could be the creation of an "Arab bread basket to help reduce shortages and lessen dependency on the costlier food imports."[7]

Except in Iraq, Oman, and a few scattered pockets, the agricultural sector in the Arab Gulf states has been either nonexistent or largely restricted to greenhouse development and hydroponics. Abu Dhabi has been a pioneer in this regard. At the Arid Land Research Center at Sadiyat, not far from Abu Dhabi City, horticultural experiments are conducted that aim at providing an economical means of agricultural production in the desert environment. Plants are grown indoors with irrigation furnished from desalinated sea water. The Center is testing different varieties of vegetables for possible commercial use. The year-round growing season combined with warm temperatures provides an atmosphere of high crop yields in comparison with conventional farming. At Sadiyat one acre can produce 71 tons annually versus a conventionally farmed acre which could produce 31 tons. The Center is funded jointly by the Abu Dhabi government and the Rockefeller Foundation and is under the direction of a team from the University of Arizona.[8] Similar efforts are going on in Kuwait and Qatar. However, most of these ventures are still heavily subsidized and thus uneconomical. Moreover, research in arid land development is small-scale, uncoordinated, and fragmented, tending to augment costs and reduce effectiveness. There is, therefore, considerable merit in establishing a large regional center devoted to such research, especially in view of the similarity of problems confronting the highly arid Gulf region.

Similarly, in the area of fishing, cooperation among the Gulf countries has been so far limited, though there is much to be gained from a joint and coordinated approach to the exploitation of the vast fishing potential of the Gulf, the Arabian Sea and the adjoining waters.

In conclusion, it appears that the possibilities for agricultural cooperation among the Arab states are diverse, the potential is vast, but apart from the recent establishment of a few joint-venture firms, particularly the Arab Institute for Investment in Agricultural Development, little has been done to exploit this untapped potential.

A most dynamic area of inter-Arab economic relations has been the field of money and finance. The emerging capital surplus in the major Arab oil-exporting states and the concatenation of economic and political factors—such as the worldwide inflationary tendencies, the constant fluctuations in the value of major currencies, the displayed anxieties in many Western quarters regarding the impact and consequences of OPEC and Arab investments in the major industrialized economies, and the existing political tension between the West and the Arabs concerning the Middle East crisis in particular and the new world economic order in general—have all played an important role in the growing attention paid by the Arab oil producers to regional investment and finance. Several national and regional development funds, financial institutions, and investment companies have been marching across the Middle East stage. Most of these institutions presently suffer from a multiplicity of deficiencies, including inexperience, shortage of trained manpower and financial experts, excessive reliance on rather modest paid-in capital, and conservative practices in lending operations. The borrower must come to the lending agency with a proposal involving a project for which initial economic and engineering feasibility studies have been carried out. The lending agency is seldom involved in identifying such bankable projects. But, given the dearth of already studied and economically sound projects in practically all developing countries, the volume of loans extended by Arab lending institutions must necessarily be small.

Recognizing this weakness, Kuwait and Morocco recently agreed to set up a joint company for feasibility studies capitalized at $4.66 million, whose main purpose will be to conduct feasibility studies of economic projects in which the two countries can cooperate. It is understood "that once a project is deemed feasible by the company and is approved by the two governments, a special agreement will be concluded to provide the necessary finance and other facilities for the project."[9] It remains to be seen whether this will be an isolated bilateral agreement or the beginning of similar agreements between the major oil states and other Arab countries, thus paving the way for the eventual establishment of a multinational Arab company entrusted with the identification of technically feasible and economically sound projects on a regional basis. However, it should be clearly recognized that unless the lender actively participates in the search for viable economic projects in the region, his lending operations are bound to be limited in volume and scope.

It must also be emphasized that the proliferation of Arab lending agencies has impaired the efficiency and effectiveness of these institutions in many areas such as the handling of aid requests, the provision of technical services, the supervision of supported projects, the capacity to augment and channel capital resources, the security of loaned capital, and the administrative costs of the aid program. Moreover, this fragmentation has decreased the potential leverage that these institutions could exercise in the critical process of the transfer of Western technology to the region. It follows that unless the various Arab lending institutions can be consolidated or at least their diverse activities effectively coordinated in well-defined sectors, their positive contribution to the economic development of the region will be diminished.

The formation of an Arab regional money and financial market will depend to a significant extent on the willingness of the Arab development funds and banks to pursue an imaginative, aggressive, and coordinated approach to the mobilization of capital resources on a regional basis. This approach must accord the private sector in the Arab countries at least an equal access to loanable funds. In addition, it must encompass other policies such as the sales of the institutions' own obligations, portfolio sales, underwriting of securities, and active participation in proposed projects.[10] This will not only increase the resources at the disposal of the lending institutions beyond the current paid-in capital, but also foster the creation of a regional money and financial market with breadth and depth. In other words, the volume and variety of debt instruments can be enhanced and private funds more effectively mobilized, provided the lending institutions go beyond their current practice of merely lending mostly their own capital resources.

It must be concluded that the greatest contribution of these lending institutions to the economic development of the Arab world may perhaps lie in the creation of a well-developed and organized regional capital market that can reinforce economic integration measures in other sectors.

Another regional move with potentially far-reaching ramifications for closer economic ties among Arab states was the establishment on April 27, 1976 of the Arab Monetary Fund with a capital of 250 million Arab dinars—a unit of account equal to 3 Supplemental Drawing Rights in the International Monetary Fund.[11] It is believed that the main function of the fund would be to assist member Arab states in managing their balance of payments. The fund would probably operate along lines similar to those followed by the IMF.

There are considerable opportunities for inter-Arab cooperation in the field of tourism with a view to promoting intraregional tourism and attracting a greater number of tourists from outside the area through coordinated programs, package deals, and tourism campaigns. Package deals involving the North African countries or the East Mediterranean countries or the Gulf countries may be more enticing to the average European or U.S. tourist than visiting a single country.

Recently, Egypt and Morocco agreed among other things to cooperate in the field of tourism by setting up joint tourism projects, activating tourist exchanges, and settling tourist expenses between them through negotiable currencies.[12] Also, the Council of Arab Economic Unity in its June 5, 1976 meeting in Cairo discussed the possibility of establishing a number of joint Arab ventures, including a company for tourism with a capital of $500 million.[13] No information is as yet available as to the specific activities for this company.

7. Cooperation among the Arab states is not restricted to the areas discussed above; it encompasses, in fact, many other fields: military, education, and government at varying levels. Recently, a resolution to establish an Arab Educational Fund with contributions from all Arab states was drafted by the Arab Educational Scientific Cultural Organization. The fund is to finance domestic education and set up education centers for Arabs abroad. It is also reported that an Arab bank to finance housing development was proposed on May 12, 1976 by a committee of housing ministry officials from five Arab states meeting in Abu Dhabi.[14] There are a number of federations of trade unions and professional societies such as the federations of Arab students, teachers, physicians, engineers, writers, and so on. Inter-Arab student and teacher exchanges have always been important and they are steadily growing in recent years with respect to both scope and number. While these aspects lie outside the immediate interest of this study, their significance and implications for enhancing Arab economic cooperation and trade ties should not be overlooked.

8. Regional cooperation in the Arab world is not taking place in an atmosphere of political accord and harmony. On the contrary, political dissonance, conflict, and rivalry abound among the various groups within each state, as well as among the various Arab governments. In fact, many observers usually known for their acumen, perception, and foresight tend to be overwhelmed by the apparent political discord and the intensity of competition and rivalry among some Arab states to the point of dismissing the idea that economic factors constitute an independent force drawing the region together as being merely an academic exercise. The Arab governments, they contend, fashion their relations with each other on the basis of political issues, and economics is always subordinated to considerations of power play, alliances, and divergent political philosophies. This view must be rejected for the following reasons.

` First, whereas political dissension and conflict are visible in inter-Arab relations, they stem mainly from differences regarding means and methods rather than ends and goals. There are no fundamental and basic differences among the states such as those between India and Pakistan. Indeed, the intensity of the political conflict may be to some extent symptomatic of the genuine concern and solicitude for the welfare of the Arab nation. All Arab governments, at least in principle, profess unrelenting faith in the common destiny of the Arabs, and for many of them the eventual unification of the Arab countries remains a cherished, albeit a distant and somewhat vaguely defined goal. We have to emphasize that although the hindrances confronting Arab political unity may be extremely obdurate—judging by existing national variations, political differences and vested interests—economic integration, and certainly economic cooperation, face no such obstacles. In fact, a measure of economic cooperation and planning on the sectoral level is increasingly becoming a necessity and not an option particularly for those small and similarly endowed Arab states.

Second, the considerable attention paid to political factors by students of the Middle East and the Arab world must at least in part be explained by the fact that politics makes the news and captures the headlines, whereas developments in the economic sphere are of a more quiet, subtle, and sober nature. Moreover, the full consequences of many economic policies, especially those related to growth, integration, and cooperation, normally take a long time to materialize. In other words, the proclivity of people to be moved more easily by what is immediate and dramatic accounts in part for the underrating of economic factors and the insufficient effort directed toward economic analysis.

Those who are cynical about the prospects of economic cooperation and integration among Arab states ususally cite the existing considerable gap between talk and action in inter-Arab relations and the frequent reversal of economic policies in response to shifting political attitudes and interests. However, it is well to remember that in the field of economic policy there is almost always a substantial lag between the time a problem is perceived and recognized, the time when policies are designed and implemented, and the time when respective policies have perceptible impact. In recent years there has been much awareness of the necessity of greater inter-Arab economic cooperation, which is mirrored in the number and scope of the various initiatives undertaken in the field of oil, labor movements, and finance. Most of these initiatives, however, will bear fruit only in the long term, but this should not be discouraging because, whereas individuals may be dead in the long run, nations will not. The second charge that economics mixes with politics, or for that matter vice versa, is not unique to the Arab world. Moreover, it appears to have been recently abating somewhat, considering the sizable number of Egyptian workers still in Libya despite the prevalence of severe political tension between the two neighbors.

Third, even in the political field, there is a new sense of compromise and accomodation emerging between the major Arab states—witness the excellent relations developing between Saudi Arabia and Egypt and the Saudi-Iraqi rapprochement. The splinter group, though vociferous, is markedly less important economically, strategically, and culturally.

It is misleading and naive to dismiss regional developments and cooperation in the Arab world and to discard the long-term trend they signify, merely on the basis of prevailing political rivalry and dissension. The existence of diverse and divergent opinion as to how the goal of economic integration or eventual economic unification is to be accomplished is not tantamount to the denial of the goal itself. More realistically, it may be that the achievement of extensive inter-Arab cooperation or possibly economic integration will be relatively slow and painful, but given current developments, it is probably bound to come. It may also be the case that if the movement toward greater economic ties is forced into a rigid pattern out of primarily political considerations, the whole effort will backfire, creating unnecessary tension and strain among the Arab countries and setting back the process of economic integration. Economic integration must indeed be viewed as either the final stage in inter-Arab economic relations or an intermediate phase preceding the ultimate goal of economic union. However, a prerequisite for the realization of economic integration, and a fortiori, economic union, is a period of extensive and intense economic cooperation. Without such a period during which interdependence is enhanced and strengthened and national economic policies are harmonized, the forces of division and the special interest groups in the national Arab states would be extremely difficult to overcome.

It is appropriate to conclude this section with the apt statement of a perceptive Middle East observer:[15]

> The Arab world is a mosaic of countries with boundaries arbitrarily dictated by history, but the States which have emerged have developed a personality and special interests of their own. The odds are, however, that the greater cohesion achieved over the past few years and especially since the October War will be maintained and with the injection of oil wealth, strengthened.

CONTROVERSIAL ISSUES

Three issues directly related to regional development and cooperation in the Middle East will be examined in this section. These are: oil versus money, OPEC's future, and asymmetry in Arab-West economic relations. The reader must be warned that the issues discussed here are intertwined and, moreover, that they overlap with parts of the analysis presented in the next section. A separate treatment was, nevertheless, preferred because it offers greater insight and sharper focus.

Oil versus Money

The typical oil-exporting country must make a fundamental decision as to the optimal rate of oil production, or alternatively, the time span during which its proven oil reserves are to be depleted. The decision, to be sure, will not be dictated by economic criteria alone, for oil, being a strategic commodity, possesses palpable political dimensions.[16] Nevertheless, economic considerations loom large in any production and pricing decisions. Moreover, deviation from basic economic principles entails some costs that should be weighed against any potential political gains. Focusing on the economics, the question of the optimal rate at which oil reserves should be depleted lies basically in the field of the general theory of portfolio analysis. More specifically, the rate of conversion of oil into other types of assets depends on the comparative yield, security, and liquidity of all assets including oil in the ground, available to the investing unit—in this case, the government of the oil-exporting country. The more oil currently recovered and sold, the less will be available for future sale. Economic rationality implies maximization of the present value of the oil exporting country's known reserves. This requires an intertemporal allocation of oil reserves such that "the present value from extracting an additional unit of petroleum, net of recovery cost, be the same in all periods."[17] Unfortunately, this formula is deceptively simple; its application demands extensive and rigorous information concerning the evolution of recovery costs, including marginal cost, the development of oil prices, and the appropriate rate of discount. Given the problem of imperfect foresight, most of this information becomes virtually untractable. Nevertheless, one often encounters the statement that given current oil prices, a faster rate of depletion of petroleum reserves is economically justified. Such a conclusion is arrived at using the compound interest rate formula. Table 6.1 displays various future values of a sum of $10, approximately equal to the current price of a barrel of oil, invested at rates of 8 and 4 percent compounded semi-annually. The 8 percent rate is on the lower end of interest rates prevailing in the Eurocurrency market.

The oil reserves of major Arab producers would last at current rates of production some 50 to 70 years. Even in the case of Venezuela, the ratio of reserves to current annual production is in the neighborhood of 14. The following question is then posited: what is the likelihood of a barrel of oil selling 50 years hence at $505, and 70 years hence at $2,425? The answer is hardly surprising—very remote and practically nil. It is on the basis of such evidence that conservation policies of major Arab oil producers are often characterized as irrational. However, such a conclusion, which incidentally implies that present oil prices are excessively high—thus warranting a higher rate of production—is probably wrong for a number of reasons. First, it assumes away inflation in the West; since inflation is still high in the West, the real rate of return on financial investment may be low or possibly negative. In other words, if current inflationary trends continue in the future, and if oil values keep up with inflation,

TABLE 6.1

Hypothetical Future Values of Oil Proceeds

Number of Years	Future Value (dollars at 8 percent)	Future Value (dollars at 4 percent)
10	21.9	14.9
20	48.0	22.1
30	105.2	32.8
40	230.5	48.8
50	505.1	72.5
60	1106.6	107.7
70	2424.8	160.0

Note: Initial fixed investment is $10 compounded semi-annually.
Source: Calculations made by the ICEED staff.

projected oil prices may not be too high. Second, investment abroad is fraught with many dangers that generally stem from the loss of control over committed funds. These risks include changes in tax rates and laws governing foreign investment, nationalization and sequestration, default, currency fluctuations and devaluations. Third, the present value formula assumes a constant rate of interest which guarantees that proceeds could always be reinvested at, say, 8 percent. But while such an assumption might be realistic for a period covering a few years, it is generally untenable in the long run because economic conditions are expected to oscillate and economies to undergo fundamental structural changes. In fact, the fiction involved in such long-run projections can easily be exposed by observing that $10 invested 500 years ago at 8 percent compounded semi-annually would have an astronomical value of 1.07979×10^{18}. Evidently, such calculations, which are based on the assumption of certainty, are meaningless for a truly uncertain world.

While investment and discounting considerations lurk in the background of decisions to conserve oil resources, most oil-producing countries base their decisions regarding oil-production levels on largely practical factors. These include four major elements: the absorptive capacity of the domestic economy, the desirable size of the foreign aid and investment program especially in countries within the oil producer's own region, the desire to conserve petroleum to serve as the base for future industrialization in an otherwise resource-poor country, and the so-called international obligations of the country. Many Arab countries, producing oil in excess of their need for capital to satisfy domestic and some regional and other aid requirements, rationalize their behavior as being a service performed in the interest of the West. This is merely "a euphemism for the awareness of the political and military pressures to which these countries are so clearly vulnerable given their weakness militarily."[18] But there must be a limit to the use of political maneuvering by the West as a means of maintaining oil supplies beyond levels considered necessary and desirable by the oil producers themselves, given the popular resentment toward the channeling of a significant proportion of oil revenues into largely financial investments abroad. Thus, unless the domestic capital absorptive capacity of the Arab oil producers increases precipitously, the commitment to the regional transfer of resources expands, or the climate, prospects, and security for investment in the West improve, the Arab oil countries will probably resist further political pressures to increase their oil production beyond the current levels.

The Survival of OPEC

When OPEC was founded in September 1960, in direct response to the unilateral reduction of oil prices in 1959 and 1960 by the multinational oil companies, it was generally believed that the organization would attain very limited success, if any. These predictions proved initially to be correct. Under the shadows of surplus productive capacity and the palpable reluctance of member countries to jointly manipulate supply, the accomplishments of the organization in the first decade of its life were modest indeed. They consisted principally of halting the further erosion of oil prices, the partial settlement of the royalties and marketing expenses issues, and some general valuable services.[19] In retrospect, it appears that the precipitance and severity of the energy crisis of the 1970s must be traced at least in part to the limited initial success of OPEC policies. Specifically, a crude price of about $2 per barrel to Western consumers encouraged the rapid displacement of coal, restricted the development of non-OPEC oil reserves, and promoted greater energy-intensive technology and the cultivation of wasterful energy consumption habits and lifestyle.

However, what is bewildering seems to be the longevity of OPEC rather than its recent successes. Currently, some economists are leading the camp of those sceptical of the survival prospects of OPEC. They contend that the cartel structure involves inherent elements of instability that cannot be suppressed successfully in the long run. Demand elasticity being an increasing function of time, one cannot expect market conditions to continue favoring a cartel arrangement in the long term. Inevitably, one or a combination of factors will lead to the demise of OPEC: new petroleum reserves outside OPEC will be discovered and developed, the consumers will counteract with potent strategies of their own such as conservation, and technological breakthroughs will eventually usher the world again into an era of cheap and abundant energy. There is no wish to question the validity of this line of reasoning; however, it is important to observe that the term "the long run" is obviously and perhaps deliberately vague. Indeed, as indicated earlier, in the long run a more competitive market structure could emerge for at least one reason: the increasing involvement of the oil producers in downstream activities, particularly refining. If the time horizon, is, however, explicitly and accurately specified—for example, the period until 1985— one cannot persuasively argue that OPEC will disintegrate because of the external factors mentioned above. Specifically, oil from fringe areas is very expensive, conservation as a means of reducing demand is of limited effectiveness in Western Europe where such efforts have been practiced for a long time and on a large scale, and revolutionary technological breakthroughs necessitate immediate and enormous investments with long gestation periods. Moreover, even when the technology becomes available and economically feasible, the conversion of the present industrial structure to a new source of energy is bound to be a slow and protracted process. Indeed, the development and implementation of a national comprehensive energy policy in the West requires a prevailing sense of urgency and crisis—a condition that seems to be rapidly dissipating, in part because of the restraint and caution that have characterized OPEC oil-pricing policies since 1974.

Having ruled out exogenous economic factors as a plausible source of OPEC's disintegration at least until 1985, one is left with the external politico-military elements as well as the politico-economic competition and rivalry within OPEC which could possibly lead to its eventual demise. As stated earlier, Western political pressures within tolerable limits cannot effect a sizable change in production and pricing policy of the typical oil-exporting country, and by extension, cannot result in the breakup of OPEC. Similarly, a policy of military intervention is not only ineffective, but also damaging to the basic interests of the West.

> However, apart from the moral calculus involved, there are tech-
> nical obstacles to employing modern variants of gunboat diplo-
> macy in cases where delicate machinery and instruments control
> the resource flow, as in petroleum. It was not clear in 1974 what
> military countermeasures were in fact available even to the most
> powerful country in the world in the face of threats by Arabian
> countries to blow up their portside installations. Logic argues that
> a Western military attack on Gulf oil installations is virtually the
> only way the Soviet Union could get a strong foothold there,
> hardly something we ought to facilitate.[20]

One observer suggests that the immediate sources of disintegration of OPEC are endogenous and that they stem from divergent political and economic interests of member states. In the economic realm, three factors are considered as contributing to a varying degree to the alleged strain and tension that are bound to exacerbate within OPEC. These include divergent costs of production for individual exporters, the lack of "similarity in ways and rates of discounting future profits," and the absence of "a compatible valuation framework by which sellers seek to maximize profits and buyers seek to minimize the cost of goods purchased."[21] The issue of production costs is correctly assessed as being of little relevance in the case of petroleum, "since costs constitute a small proportion of price for all the producer states."[22] The second factor, that is, the existing dissimilarity in ways and rates of discounting future profits, contributes, in fact, to the present cohesion and solidarity of the organization and not to its supposed internal instability. It is precisely this factor, which is closely related to the question of differential absorptive capacities of OPEC members, that has enabled the organization to accomodate successfully the recent decline in world demand for oil. The structural differences among OPEC members in terms of population size, the extent and diversity of the resources base, and the subjective valuations of risks associated with investment abroad, give rise to the adopted dissimilar discount rates which, in turn, bear heavily on the intertemporal allocation of oil reserves. It appears that at present this dissimilarity has been a source of compatibility of the divergent economic interests of OPEC members.* Choucri is fully cognizant of this, but she contends that:

> It is ironic that the sources of the strength of OPEC can be found in structural differences among its members and that these differences also harbor the roots of its weakness.[23]

What seems to be implied here is that the existence of these structural differences bestows considerable economic power on certain oil producers, particularly Saudi Arabia, thus permitting her in the future to pursue narrow nationalistic objectives that may be at odds with the political aspirations of one or more OPEC members. Four scenarios leading to the breakup of OPEC appear, according to Choucri, probable from both economic and political perspectives. Two scenarios involve basically potential political disputes developing between Saudi Arabia and Iran on the one hand and the former and Algeria on the other. The other two envision the erosion of OPEC solidarity as a result of either Kuwait or Iraq following disruptive unilateral moves with respect to production and pricing of petroleum. Choucri implies that such behavior could be motivated by either economic or political considerations or possibly both. For these scenarios to be realistic, at least one of the ensuing two conditions must obtain.

First, the capacity of OPEC to absorb internal friction, whether of a political or economic nature, must be severely constrained. This, Choucri admits, is not the case.

> To a large extent OPEC has been successful so far primarily because of the diversity of interests of its members. As a result, the persistence of different and sometimes conflicting interests has become a source of bargaining and negotiation, and possibly of mutual accomodation. The hypothesis that structural, economic, and

---

*As emphasized earlier, the low absorbers have been reducing their oil production levels proportionately more than the high absorbers, and this has served the cause of OPEC's unity.

cultural diversity among the members provide the basis for cohesion appears increasingly plausible. OPEC seems to be organized as a loose coalition in which any subgroup may align on a specific issue but is free to align differently others. The bounds of permissible behavior appear to be broad and the degree of formal cohesion low. This feature provides a means of adjusting to differences and may well be an important source of strength for the cartel.[24]

Second, and this seems what Choucri has in mind, an intolerable degree of tension, perhaps even war, could prevail in the Gulf, thus making any measure of cooperation among the combatants virtually impossible. Anything short of this does not appear to rule out limited cooperation between member states on matters of common concern—witness the history of Iranian-Iraqi cooperation within OPEC throughout the 1960s. The breaking out of a large-scale war in the Gulf is admittedly possible, but, given its disastrous aftermath for all parties directly involved as well as for the international community, appears highly remote. Mindful of the dire consequences of war to their peoples and economies and the probable outside intervention in such an event, the states of the area are actively seeking accomodation, compromise, and cooperation among themselves.[25]

The possibility of a political rift developing between Algeria, portrayed by Choucri as the leader of the radical Arab camp, and conservative Saudi Arabia, which could lead to the disintegration of OPEC, must be judged in view of at least geography and the limited Algerian oil reserves as exceedingly speculative and unconvincing.

Finally, Choucri's contention that another Arab-Israeli war "would almost inevitably destroy OPEC"[26] is questionable at best. A new Middle East war would recreate an extremely tight oil market, thus tending to strengthen rather than weaken OPEC. It is well to keep in mind that OPEC scored its recent dramatic successes primarily during a period of tight market conditions that were further exacerbated by the October War of 1973.

The statement that "The oil exporting countries are not simply seeking to maximize economic profits; they are maximizing some composite goal of which profit is an important, and perhaps the most critical, factor but it is not the only one"[27] is accurate, but it is more descriptive of the behavior of the Arab members of OPEC for obvious reasons. Moreover, such a behavior has contributed and still does to a greater measure of flexibility and room for negotiation, compromise, and accomodation within OPEC, thus serving to sinew rather than debilitate the organization.

Every member of OPEC, now and in the future, seems to value the benefits that OPEC provides more than the dubious gains that it could possibly reap by following an independent course of action. Thus, it appears that neither external factors nor internal dissension and conflict within OPEC are likely to jeopardize the solidarity and cohesion of the organization, at least until 1985.

However, it must be pointed out that even if OPEC could be destroyed, this by itself would not vitiate the influence that the Arab oil producers, through OAPEC or perhaps individually as in the case of Saudi Arabia, could exercise on the West including the United States regarding West European and U.S. policy in the Middle East crisis. A new Arab oil embargo in a period of crisis is still likely and it would be equally effective if not even more consequential than the one in 1973-74, considering the greater current U.S. reliance on imported oil.[28]

Economic Dependence and Independence:
The West vis-a-vis the Arab World

Economic dependence is generally resented by sovereign states. The statement that economic independence is necessary to the pursuit of a national policy that aims at safeguarding the vital national interests has been repeatedly reiterated by politicians and officials in the United States and was epitomized in Nixon's, now largely derelict, "Project Independence." The recent oil embargo vividly demonstrated an old truth: Foreign trade has a political dimension that could be used as an instrument of national power. The most prominent aspect of foreign trade as a political instrument derives from the fact that:

> . . . trade conducted between country A, on the one hand, and countries B, C, D, etc., on the other, is worth *something* to B, C, D, etc., and that they would therefore consent to grant A certain advantages—military, political, economic—in order to retain the possibility of trading with A. If A wants to increase its hold on B, C, D, etc., it must create a situation in which these countries would do *anything* in order to retain their foreign trade with A. Such a situation arises when it is extremely difficult and onerous for these countries:
>   1) to dispense entirely with the trade they conduct with A, or
>   2) to replace A as a market and a source of supply with other countries.
> The principles of a power policy relying on the influence effect of foreign trade are in their essence extremely simple: *They are all designed to bring about this 'ideal' situation.*[29]

If OAPEC is substituted for country A, and B, C, D for OECD countries, the above statement fits closely the current oil situation save that the influence in non-oil trade runs exactly in the opposite direction. It should be emphasized, however, that a U.S. policy of self-sufficiency in energy, and ipso facto a significantly smaller volume of trade with the Middle East, is not a panacea. In addition to the possible adverse economic repercussions on the U.S. economy in terms of reduction in efficiency and underutilization of industrial capacity, such a policy could not absolve the United States from its responsibility as a major world power to contribute positively to peace and stability in the Middle East. In other words, the long-run goal of achieving self-sufficiency in energy, invariably at a high cost, would entail depriving the Arabs of whatever influence they could marshal to support their views regarding the Middle East crisis. Some may find this prospect encouraging and appealing, but a sober analysis reveals that it is not in the best interests of the United States.

> Proponents of a close `American-Israeli alignment assert that Israel's proven military effectiveness together with the democratic nature of its political institutions makes Israel America's natural and reliable ally. As an alternative in United States policy this line has been frequently espoused, implicitly or explicitly, by aspiring leaders running for public office. Pushed to its logical conclusion, such a policy would mean alienation of the Arab world from the United States and a strategic situation in which American interests in the Eastern Mediterranean—or what would be left of them— would have to be exposed to sustained hostility of the majority of nations in the area.
>
> In practice, no such drastic choice may be necessary, some scholars suggest, if the United States were to adopt a policy of strict neutrality. Such a policy would call for (a) a clear indication that the United States does not support Israel's security at the expense of the independence and territorial integrity of the neighboring Arab states; (b) an equally clear indication that Israel as a state recognized by most of the other states and as a member of the United Nations has the right to secure existence free of threats to its survival; (c) condemnation of violent methods either by Israel or the Arab states to achieve their objectives and support for peaceful procedures, especially those under the auspices of the United Nations.[30]

It must be kept in mind that self-sufficiency is costly to procure, entails considerable economic dislocation, and is politically a dubious course to adopt for at least two important reasons. First, self-sufficiency in energy for the United States alone, if it could be achieved in the next decade, would still leave other OECD countries heavily dependent on outside oil supplies, thereby tending to fuel centrifugal forces within the Western alliance. Second, the severance and/or weakening of trade ties with the Arab world would be accompanied by a precipitous diminution of U.S. influence in the area, thus contributing to greater instability and radicalization of many Arab governments. In the final analysis:

> It remains true that complete autarky can hardly be considered as an element of an intelligent power policy. And if the nations which have proclaimed autarky as their ultimate goal have remained far off the mark, this may be due not only to the economic difficulties which they have experienced in trying to dispense with

foreign trade, but also because they have found it politically inexpedient to do without trade relations.[31]

The pursuit of greater U.S. and Western energy security can, moreover, be accomplished by means other than the weakening of trade ties and the reducing of the volume of imports from and exports to the Arab world. In this respect three possible routes suggest themselves. First is the achievement of closer cooperation in energy among the major consuming nations. The creation of the International Energy Agency, which in a relatively short span succeeded in developing some basic rules and regulations regarding a common oil policy for its members, is certainly a step in the right direction. However, this agency should not adopt a belligerent posture vis-a-vis the oil producers, which could lead to polarization and confrontation to the detriment of both sides. Rather, in its attempt to articulate the legitimate interests of the consumers it must show sensitivity to the equally valid concerns of the producers. Its efforts must be focused on devising long- and short-term solutions to the global energy problem. It may even solicit the cooperation and participation of the oil producers in its research and development activities. Nevertheless, the mere existence of close cooperation and coordination in energy among consumers could act as a deterrent against any potential excesses on the part of OPEC or OAPEC. In other words, countervailing power would not have to be used to be effective, but it must be there.

Second, the United States could enhance its short-run maneuverability by emulating European policy of strategic oil stockpiles. The U.S. Congress has recently mandated a program to store up to one billion barrels of crude by 1982 to "protect the nation in event of a future embargo."[32] At present, this is the equivalent of one year's imports of Arab oil.[33] However, if current oil import trends continue, oil stored as a percentage of total oil imports from Arab sources will certainly decline.

The idea of stockpiling as a means of reducing the risk factor in oil supply is undoubtedly valid but one must not overlook its drawbacks and limitations.[34] Specifically, the proposed plan is costly and would be effective, if at all, in the 1980s. The Federal Energy Administration envisages the creation of "a national 150-million-barrel crude reserves by 1978 at an initial cost of about $850 million."[35] While such a level of stockpiling may be significant as a bargaining tool against possible excessive or unwarranted demands by the oil producers, it is a grave mistake to view this measure as a *cordon sanitaire*, permitting the United States to destabilize OPEC and/or to display insensitivity toward the economic and political aspirations of the oil producers in general and the Arab world in particular.

Many distinguished scholars seem to believe that the energy problem is real, mirroring to a large extent the increasing planetary resource scarcity.[36] Thus, to rely principally on tactical weapons in combating a genuine problem is not only difficult, but is probably self-defeating. Unless this point is clearly recognized and appreciated, little progress can be made in solving the thorny issues between the oil produers and the oil consuming nations.

Third, and somewhat ironically, the West and the United States could effectively safeguard their interests by more and not less economic and political involvement in the region. The route to greater Western security lies, in fact, in creating and promoting what might be termed as offsetting dependencies. Several of these already exist and could be expanded. And the potential for exploiting the full range of latent economic opportunities capable of cementing a healthy and symmetrical relationship between the West and the Arab oil producers is considerable. This point needs further elaboration.

The West is dependent on the Arabs in basically one commodity, oil. Admittedly, oil is a sensitive and strategic commodity, but to view this dependency in isolation is definitely misleading. Indeed, Western dependency on Arab oil is counterbalanced by a multitude of important and constantly growing trade, investment, cultural, and political relations. Arab imports from the West are growing, since 1973, by leaps and bounds, involving such strategic commodities as food, high technology capital goods, and sophisticated weaponry, among others. The percentage of total import growth in 1973-74 ranged for the Arab oil producers from over 100 percent for the United Arab Emirates to about 47 percent for Kuwait. The major suppliers were OECD countries. This trend accelerated in 1974 with the rate of growth exceeding the 100 percent mark in most cases.[37] Investment, whether financial or in directly productive facilities, of major world oil exporters in the West is similarly expanding, registering a total of $49 billion in 1974 and $28 billion in 1975. Most of this investment reflects the growing capital surpluses of key Arab oil-producing countries. The Arab countries in general and the oil producers in particular are currently implementing ambitious development plans, the various requirements of which in terms of engineering, contracting, and above all the transfer of technology are derived principally from the West. The interruption of these established channels could seriously jeopardize these plans and inflict severe setbacks to the economic development process itself. Moreover, most Arab countries depend heavily on the West in the field of education and manpower training, which is one of the most critical bottlenecks hindering rapid economic growth. The elite in the Arab world, especially the increasingly important group of technocrats, consists almost entirely of individuals either educated in the West or visibly influenced by Western culture. These ties are obviously of extreme importance in assessing the nature and significance of Arab-West relationships.[38]

In addition, Arab governments recognize that a just settlement of the Arab-Israeli problem depends crucially on U.S. attitudes, and that the United States is, indeed, the key to a lasting peace in the region.

We may conclude that the web of intricate Arab dependencies on the West, if juxtaposed to Western reliance on Arab oil, appears to dispute the contention of those who argue that current Arab-West relationship is dominated by structural asymmetries in favor of the Arabs.[39] Stated differently, the oil card in

Arab hands, though undeniably potent, is nevertheless countervailed by a multitude of Western cards, each of which may not be as effective as oil, but their combined weight certainly equals if not transcends the power of oil. This becomes especially clear if one remembers that the Arabs are restrained even in the use of their only significant card, oil, by a plentitude of economic and political constraints including ultimately the vast military power of the West.

There are, moreover, a number of as yet largely unexploited channels that can further strengthen Arab-West relationships. These include but are not confined to the following: cooperation in the area of recycling of surplus funds into different outlets (the Middle East region, Third World, and Western economies), cooperation in the financing of and research into alternative energy sources that could potentially replace depletable oil reserves, and joint ventures particularly in the field of petrochemicals and other energy- and capital-intensive industries. The case of petrochemicals discussed below could serve as a model for potentially viable Arab-West cooperation.

As noted earlier the oil-based economies may profitably establish and expand energy- and capital-intensive industries, such as petrochemicals. However, the development of petrochemicals requires advanced technology and highly specialized skills that are presently unavailable domestically and therefore must be imported. One may legitimately ask the following question: Why should the West assist these countries to develop their petrochemical industries when such development might displace and compete with similar Western products? It will be shown that the assumed dichotomy of interests is more apparent than real, provided the energy-rich nations follow a strategy of development for petrochemicals that reflects objectively their true comparative advantage.

Contrary to what might be impressionistically suspected, the emergence of the Arab states of the Gulf as major world producers of mature petrochemicals is, in fact, in line with the basic interests of the West. Indeed, not only is Western interest served, but also the world's welfare is increased because of the ensuing greater efficiency in the allocation of global resources as each region specializes in those items in which it possesses distinct and clear comparative advantage. The West can contribute positively to the meritable development of petrochemicals in the Gulf area by facilitating the international transfer of technology and by adjusting the structure of its own petrochemical industry away from the class of mature petrochemicals and toward the more dynamic classes. Such a change in Western industrial structure is also desirable from the standpoint of environmental standards. To the extent that energy-intensive industries tend to generate high levels of pollution, the expansion of mature petrochemical output in the Gulf will increase levels of pollution there, while a concomitant reduction in Western production will decrease levels of pollution here.

It must be emphasized, however, that the detrimental effect of pollution on the environment in the Gulf is probably negligible for at least two reasons. First, the Gulf countries, being capital-suplus, can afford the most advanced plants with built-in pollution control devices, which are normally costlier to introduce in old plants. Second, petrochemical complexes may be located in areas remote from population centers, thus minimizing their adverse environmental impact.

The reciprocity of interests between the West and the Gulf in particular and the Middle East in general is not confined to the petrochemical field. Western contribution to the process of economic and social development, whether on the individual state level or the regional level, is essential and practically indispensable. The limitations on absorptive capacities of the Gulf countries can be substantially ameliorated with significant Western help, which may include technical assistance, the transfer of modern technology, higher exports of goods and services, and the provision of markets for mature petrochemical products. The kind of interdependence thus created would serve not only to reduce the danger of another oil embargo but also to bolster the responsible forces of stability and orderly development in the region. Free international trade would become once again the true engine of economic growth to the satisfaction of all concerned.

The energy-rich nations and the West are becoming increasingly aware of the necessity of forging mutually advantageous economic relationships between themselves. However, this awareness still awaits translation into concrete, constructive, and imaginative policies fully capable of exploiting the impressive potential of extensive cooperation.

NOTES

1. U.S. Department of State, *Foreign Economic Trends and Their Implications for the Untied States, IRAQ* (Washington, D.C.: Government Printing Office, April 1976) p. 14.

2. *Middle East Economic Digest* (MEED) 20, no. 20, (May 21, 1976): 10.

3. *MEED*, Vol. 20, no. 20 (May 4, 1976): 14. A second OAPEC-sponsored dry-dock, this time in the Mediterranean, is being discussed with either ASRY or a new company taking the responsibility for the scheme.

4. *OAPEC Bulletin* 2, no. 3 (March 1976): 8-9 (in Arabic). ASRY is responsible for the OAPEC-sponsored dry-dock in Bahrain.

5. *Middle East Economic Survey* (MEES) 19 no. 30 (May 17, 1976): p. 11.

6. *MEED* 20, no. 20 (May 14, 1976): 15; and *MEES* 19, no. 30 (May 17, 1976): 10.

7. *MEED* 20, no. 20 (May 14, 1976): 15.

8. *London Times*, Dec. 21, 1971, p. VIII.

9. *MEES* 19, no. 30 (May 17, 1976): 10.

10. Hikmat Nashashibi, "The Domestication of Arab Funds: Its Necessity and the Means of Accomplishments," *Petroleum and Arab Cooperation* 2, no. 1 (Winter, 1976): 27-29.

11. *MEED* 20, no. 20 (May 14, 1976): 14; and *MEES* 19, no. 30 (May 17, 1976).

12. Ibid., p. 29.

13. *Al-Ahram*, May 27, 1976, p. 6.

14. *MEED* 20, no. 21 (May 21, 1976): p. 31.

15. Richard Johns, "Arab Unity and Cooperation," *Financial Times*, November 21, 1974, p. 34.

16. The political ramifications of oil production decisions by OPEC nations are discussed in detail in the following two volumes: Nazli Choucri, *International Politics of Energy Interdependence* (Lexington, Mass.: D.C. Heath, 1976), and Stockholm International Peace Research Institute, *Oil and Security* (Stockholm: Almquist & Wicksell International, 1974).

17. Dwight Lee, "Pricing of Oil and the Immediacy of the Future," *Journal of Energy and Development* 1, no. 2 (Spring, 1976): 294.

18. Nazli Choucri, op. cit., p. 118.

19. Abdul Amir Kubbah, *OPEC: Past and Present* (Vienna: Petro-Economic Research Center, 1974), Ch. IV.

20. U.S. Department of State, Bureau of Public Affairs, Office of Media Services, *Toward a Strategy of Interdependence* (Washington, D.C.: Government Printing Office, July 1975), pp. 17, 18.

21. N. Choucri, op. cit., pp. 176, 182. These arguments are critically addressed here because they surface from time to time in the perennial debate over Western policy options vis-a-vis OPEC, and not because they were espoused by a particular individual.

22. Ibid., p. 177.

23. N. Choucri, op. cit., p. 169.

24. Ibid., p. 173.

25. Rouhollah R. Ramazani, "Iran's Search for Regional Cooperation," *Middle East Journal* 30, no. 2 (Spring, 1976): 173-186.

26. N. Choucri, op. cit., p. 183. Apparently, Choucri predicates the continued existence of OPEC at least in part on Israeli tolerance and restraint. If this were true, the West could effectively dispose of OPEC by encouraging Israel to wage another war against the Arabs.

27. Ibid., p. 181.

28. "King Khalid Hints at Re-employment of Oil Weapon," *MEES* 19, no. 30 (May 17, 1976): 4.

29. Albert O. Hirschman, *National Power and the Structure of Foreign Trade* (Berkeley, Calif.: University of California Press, 1945), p. 17. Emphasis in original.

30. American Enterprise Institute, *United States Interests in the Middle East* (Washington, D.C.: A.E.I., 1968), p. 112.

31. Albert O. Hirschman, op. cit., p. 19, fn. 8.

32. *Platt's Oilgram* 54, no. 78, Houston Edition (April 23, 1976): 1.

33. *MEES* 19, no. 34 (June 14, 1976): 4.

34. Ragaei El Mallakh, "Oil Stockpiling: The False Hope," New York *Times*, Saturday, March 27, 1976, p. 24C.

35. *Platt's Oilgram*, op. cit.

36. Hollis B. Chenery, "Restructuring the World Economy," *Foreign Affairs* 53 (January, 1975): 242-63. Also OAPEC, *A Report on the Energy Crisis and the Development of Alternatives to Petroleum* (Kuwait: OAPEC, 1974). (In Arabic.)

37. Mitchell Hutchins Inc., *OPEC Expenditures: Size, Timing, Nature and Beneficiaries*, New York, August, 1975, p. 26.

38. Already in 1962, one perceptive Western observer remarked that education and training are perhaps the most effective and lasting legacy of the United States in the Arab World. See Robert Littell, "Our Best Investment in the Arab World," *Reader's Digest*, February 1963, pp. 1-5.

39. Choucri seems to advocate this line. See, N. Choucri, op. cit., Ch. 9.

7

IMPLICATIONS OF
REGIONAL DEVELOPMENT
IN THE MIDDLE
EAST FOR THE
UNITED STATES

U.S. ENERGY OUTLOOK AND THE MIDDLE EAST
THROUGH 1985

Figures 7.1 through 7.7 taken from the Federal Energy Administration's report provide a capsule overview of the U.S. energy outlook through 1985.[1] The main points of the report are summarized below.

The United States relies on its least abundant energy resources, oil and gas, to supply the bulk of its energy demand. This has been the result of the long-term displacement of coal by oil and natural gas, especially in the post-World War II period.

> The availability of inexpensive imported oil served as a disincentive to domestic production which peaked at 9.6 million barrels per day (MMB/D) in 1970, has been declining ever since, and now stands at 8.2 MMB/D. The combination of declining domestic production and rising demand led to a rapid growth in imports:
> —From 1.8 million barrels per day (MMB/D), or 19 percent of consumption in 1960.
> —To 3.4 MMB/D, or 23 percent of consumption, in 1970.
> —To a high of 6.0 MMB/D, or 37 percent of consumption in 1975. Today, the United States spends about $37 billion, or $125 per person, for imported oil; as compared to about $3 billion, or $15 per person, in 1970.[2]

Energy consumption is closely associated with economic expansion. In the 20 years preceding the Arab oil embargo of 1973, energy consumption in the United States has been growing at an annual rate of 3.6 percent. Given

FIGURE 7.1

What Are the Roots of Our Energy Problem?

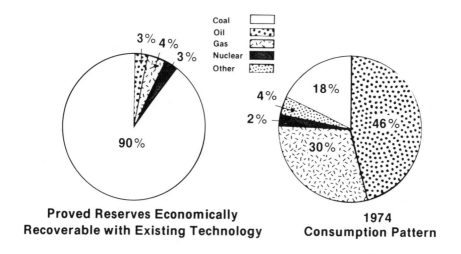

**Proved Reserves Economically
Recoverable with Existing Technology**

**1974
Consumption Pattern**

Source: U.S. Federal Energy Administration, *National Energy Outlook* (Washington, D.C.: U.S. Government Printing Office, February 1976).

current oil prices and assuming extensive conservation, this historical growth rate is expected to decelerate to 2.2 percent. The various sectors of the economy, however, exhibit differential responses to higher oil prices with the largest reductions being concentrated in the household, commercial and transportation sectors.

Total domestic supply is forecast to increase by 40 percent between now and 1985, with all major fuels playing a large role:

—*Coal production could increase to over one billion tons*, from current levels of 640 million tons.

—*Oil production could reach 13.9 MMB/D*, if Outer Continental Shelf leasing is strongly pursued and market prices prevail.

—*Natural gas production could reach 22.3 trillion cubic feet* (Tcf) if new gas prices are deregulated, but will be 17.9 Tcf under current regulations.

FIGURE 7.2

How Did We Become So Vulnerable to Oil Imports?

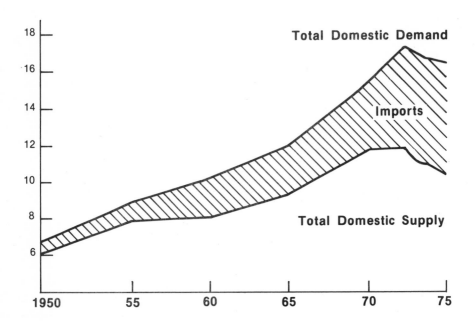

Source: U.S. Federal Energy Administration, *National Energy Outlook* (Washington, D.C.: U.S. Government Printing Office, February 1976).

—Although *nuclear power* has experienced significant delays, it *could grow from current levels of 8.6 percent to about 26 percent of electricity generation.*

—Emerging technologies such as the conversion of coal into oil or gas, solar, and geothermal energy, will be important in the post-1985 period, but will not produce much energy in the next ten years.

Each of these supply increases, while technically and economically feasible, requires significant growth of the energy producing sectors

FIGURE 7.3

How Much Energy Will the Nation Consume?

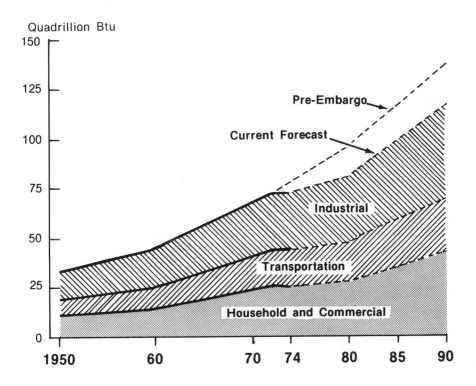

Source: U.S. Federal Energy Administration, *National Energy Outlook* (Washington, D.C.: U.S. Government Printing Office, February 1976).

and will not be forthcoming unless pricing and government regula-
tory policies encourage it. Institutional barriers and policy uncertainty will also delay development. *If one or more domestic energy
sources do not achieve these projected levels, imports will make up
the shortage because other domestic fuel sources could not compensate for the loss.*[3]

Until Alaskan oil comes on stream sometime in 1978, oil imports will
steadily rise and could only be moderated through determined and significant

FIGURE 7.4

How Will the United States Meet Its Growing Energy Demands by 1985?

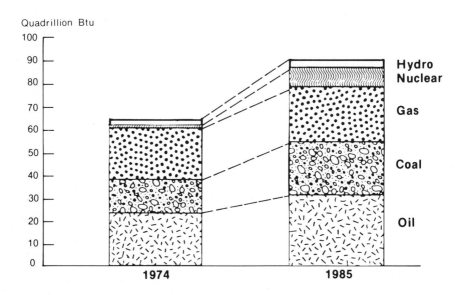

Source: U.S. Federal Energy Administration, *National Energy Outlook* (Washington, D.C.: U.S. Government Printing Office, February 1976).

energy conservation efforts and improvement in oil recovery from existing fields. The United States has, however, more latitude in reducing oil imports by 1985, provided certain policies are promptly adopted and implemented. These pertain basically to deregulation of oil and gas prices, greater conservation, the development of outer continental shelf oil reserves, and finding acceptable compromises to the often conflicting claims of the environment and energy growth, especially in the areas of strip mining of coal, uranium mining, and nuclear power generation. The Federal Energy Administration envisons three different outcomes with

FIGURE 7.5

What Will Oil Imports Be by 1985?

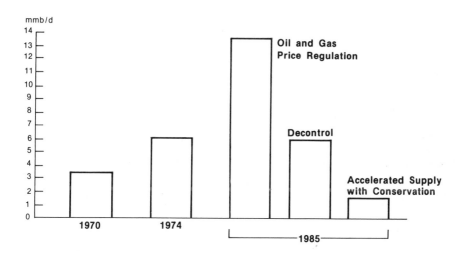

Source: U.S. Federal Energy Administration, *National Energy Outlook* (Washington, D.C.: U.S. Government Printing Office, February 1976).

respect to energy self-sufficiency, depending on which of the various policy options is pursued.

> —*If oil and gas prices are regulated at low levels, imports could reach 13.5 MMB/D in 1985.*
> —*With gradual deregulation of oil and gas prices, and a continuation of current world oil prices, imports could drop to 5.9 MMB/D,* slightly below today's level.
> —A maximum effort to increase supply and cut demand could reduce imports to about 1.0 MMB/D, making the United States invulnerable by 1985.

FIGURE 7.6

U.S. Proved Reserves of Crude Oil

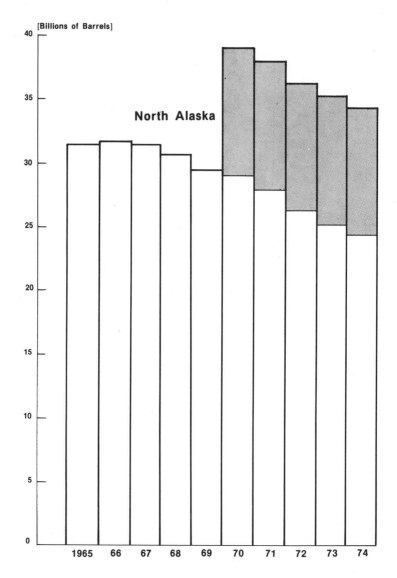

Source: American Petroleum Institute in U.S. Federal Energy Administration, *National Energy Outlook* (Washington, D.C.: U.S. Government Printing Office, February 1976).

FIGURE 7.7

Total U.S. Petroleum Imports by Regional and Organizational Sources

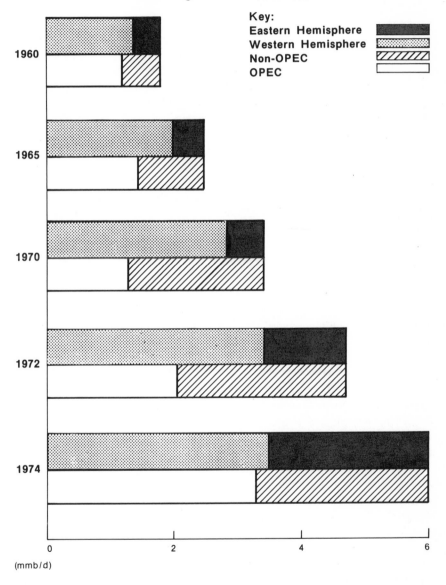

Key:
Eastern Hemisphere
Western Hemisphere
Non-OPEC
OPEC

(mmb/d)

Source: U.S. Bureau of Mines in U.S. Federal Energy Administration, *National Energy Outlook* (Washington, D.C.: U.S. Government Printing Office, February 1976).

By 1990, however, imports could increase as domestic production from older fields again declines. This decline will need to be offset by the growing use of nuclear power, synthetic fuels, solar and other emerging technologies.[4]

The development of these additional energy supplies entails huge investment outlays, probably totaling some $580 billion in constant 1975 dollars during the next decade. This is equivalent to about 30 percent of total business fixed investment which comports with energy's historical share. This, however, neither includes the sizable investment estimated at $250 billion through 1985 required to increase energy efficiency nor conservation investments "which are difficult to separate from non-energy investments and will be spread throughout the economy."[5]

While the analysis presented above is undoubtedly illuminating, the following points must be kept in mind.

First, the scenario of maximum effort (accelerated supply with conservation, henceforth referred to as Scenario I) seems to be overly optimistic, given the recent downward revision of U.S. proven reserves, the current debate concerning deregulation, conservation, and the pace of development in outer continental shelf leasing and tertiary recovery techniques. In particular, there is little evidence of an impending evolution of a comprehensive and integrated U.S. energy policy, which must involve a multiplicity of complex and presently controversial legislation. In addition, the assumed growth in nuclear power generation is overly ambitious in view of the current controversy surrounding nuclear energy and the intense opposition it faces from concerned environmental groups advocating extreme care and caution in undertaking irreversable decisions with pervasive and potentially disastrous consequences. Nuclear power, according to this view, is neither economically justified nor environmentally safe. Furthermore, the rapid growth of commercial nuclear power facilities contributes directly to nuclear weapon proliferation.[6] The scenario, indeed, stipulates that everything must go right and on schedule for the outcome to be realized, a condition hardly ever satisfied in the real world. Otherwise, imports must increase to make up any emerging shortage. This scenario may therefore be safely dismissed as remote and unlikely.

Second, the gradual decontrol scenario (Scenario II) is relatively optimistic with respect to the effects of decontrol on domestic oil production. While decontrol is certainly necessary in the long term from the standpoints of both efficiency and equity, its positive impact on crude production should not be exaggerated because it affects primarily old wells with increasingly depleting reserves. This scenario, moreover, assumes significant conservation efforts and demand reduction generated by higher prices. However, there is no indication that conservation is currently proceeding at an acceptable pace. On the contrary, "The International Energy Agency disclosed earlier this year, that the

United States had the poorest record among its 18 member nations in energy conservation last year."[7]

Even under these generally favorable assumptions, this scenario predicts that at a price of $13 per barrel, which is close to the current price of delivered imported oil in the United States, imports will amount to about six million barrels per day in 1985, that is, 29 percent of the then projected total consumption of petroleum.[8]

Third, the volume of required investment in energy for the next decade is estimated at $830 billion ($580 billion for development costs and $250 billion for increased energy efficiency). This is obviously biased downward because conservation investment is excluded. On an annual basis, this amounts to at least $83 billion, about 2.25 times the payment of $37 billion that the United States made for oil imports in 1975. It is not clear how much of this projected investment would be forthcoming without governmental subsidies.[9] Such subsidies have obvious misallocation effects. The cost of the ensuing inefficiency must ultimately be born by the American consumers. It is, therefore, essential to recognize the price at which greater energy independence could be secured. The high opportunity costs involved in drastically and discretionary curtailing oil imports should motivate the policy maker to investigate alternative routes to greater energy security. One alternative has already been suggested and will be elaborated on shortly.

Fourth, the recent phasing out of the depletion allowance (The Tax Reduction Act of 1975) and the vehement and sustained attacks by a number of influential groups and politicians on the major oil companies, accusing them of a multiplicity of charges, including public exploitation through monopolistic practices, complicity in the energy crisis, deliberate procrastination in the development of new energy sources, and so on, cannot but trammel the private energy sector in making a sustained and maximum effort toward the goal of energy independence. The recent calls for divestitures of the oil congolmerates could depress their stocks, thereby jeopardizing their access to the vital capital market that serves as a vehicle for raising a great deal of the funds needed to finance prospective investment programs. Furthermore, it is doubtful that the oil companies will be disposed to make maximum investment efforts, involving lengthy gestation periods, when their future appears highly uncertain. It appears, therefore, that the goal of attaining energy independence in the next decade is incompatible with the present campaign directed against the oil companies, which, even if it does not succeed in dismantling these conglomerates, could nonetheless debilitate their financial strength and public image.

Fifth, the third scenario, the persistence of price control with little or no significant action on the energy front, however unfortunate, may be more likely than the two scenarios outlined above, given the degree of uncertainty surrounding many critical factors and the demonstrated inertia in energy legislation and policy. If this scenario proves to be correct, the United States will derive about 60 percent of its oil requirement from abroad in 1985, thus accentuating rather than moderating U.S. reliance on foreign petroleum sources. In fact, this is the assessment of many independent analysts in the field:

> While Mr. Zarb and some other Government and congressional figures believe that the United States can be made virtually embargo-proof by 1985, most energy experts appear to see a considerable amount of wishful thinking in this assessment. Indeed, many independent analysts believe that the United States will be importing from 50 to 60 percent of its oil needs by 1985, with almost all of it coming from OPEC and the Arab states.[10]

In the light of this discussion, it appears that the goal of energy self-sufficiency by 1985 is highly uncertain and probably unattainable, given the set of parameters involved in such a policy, including in particular the enormity of the costs of the program. Realistically, U.S. energy policy would find it quite challenging to arrest, let alone reverse, the present trend of rising dependency on foreign oil. Thus, future oil imports must not exceed 40 to 45 percent of total American demand. This ratio is the average of the dependency ratios forecasted in the second and third scenarios and corresponds, moreover, to the anticipated ratio for 1976.[11]

This strategy could be accomplished by active and imaginative legislation on the homefront. However, greater energy security can and perhaps should be pursued by means other than the elusive goal of self-sufficiency.* This involves structuring U.S. foreign and trade policies so that existing offsetting dependencies in the prospective oil-exporting states are fostered and new ones created. The prospective oil exporters are inevitably OPEC members, among which the Arab states figure prominently.

Eastern Hemisphere oil, particularly Arab oil, has been steadily replacing Western Hemisphere oil as the major source of imports into the United States. This trend is expected to continue in the next decade as the limited Venezuelan oil reserves are rapidly depleted and Canadian oil is increasingly withheld to satisfy domestic requirements. Canada recently substituted a policy of self-reliance for self-sufficiency as it sharply revised downward its probable reserves.[12] Canada, moreover, lately raised the price of natural gas exported to the United States from $1.50 to $1.94 per thousand cubic feet. Frank Zarb noted that "future U.S. energy policy decisions will have to take account of this

---

*While self-sufficiency provides energy security, it is generally wrong to equate the two. This confusion seems to be at the root of the current preoccupation with energy independence.

action" which underscores U.S. energy vulnerability because of continued dependence on foreign sources of supply.[13]

What are these "offsetting dependencies" and in what context do they emerge? The following brief discussion attempts to answer this question.

Arab oil revenues are flowing into domestic development projects in the oil-based economies and imports of consumptive products to sustain a higher standard of living; regional joint ventures both among the oil producers and between them and the group of regional non-oil economies; economic aid and investment in and military subsidies to the Arab non-oil economies; aid to and investment in other Third World countries; and investment, financial as well as direct, in Western markets. In the field of investment, sophisticated capital equipment and advanced technology and skills are required. In the area of consumption, food, especially wheat, and other high quality manufactured products, particularly consumer durables, are demanded. Obviously, the United States is competitive in most of these items, and it is, and has been for decades, one of the major trading partners of practically all Arab countries. This, along with the growing captive Arab investment in the U.S. economy, organically links the development prospects and prosperity of the Arab world to the prosperity and economic well-being of the United States. The greater the pace of development in the Arab oil economies, and the bigger the commitment of these countries to regional development, the larger and wider are the opportunities for U.S. participation and exports to the Arab world, and the more complete is Arab dependence on these well-established and vital channels of trade and economic cooperation.

Furthermore, the oil exporters can secure higher oil revenues only through expanding their production and sales of petroleum. Thus, a U.S. policy of strong trade ties and economic cooperation with the Arab world could entice the Arabs to step up oil production levels. Higher oil supplies and not higher prices would then be the route for greater oil revenues because Saudi Arabia would resist, and has already been opposing, higher oil prices for a variety of reasons, including concern about the possible too rapid development of substitutes. The position of Saudi Arabia and similarly minded countries within OPEC could receive added strength, if inflationary tendencies in the West were effectively controlled. Enhanced Western stability could, moreover, stimulate the flow of Arab investment into Western economies, thereby thoroughly interlocking Arab and Western interests.

It must also be emphasized that the development of the Middle East as a major petrochemical center would require, among other things, access to European and U.S. markets. If the United States and its allies restructure their own economies to permit greater imports of oil products and entergy-intensive commodities from the Middle East and less crude petroleum, their vulnerability to the possible interruption of crude supply lines could be significantly reduced, while the competition among Middle East countries for Western markets considerably intensified.

Finally, the sincere pursuit of a U.S. policy of evenhandedness in the Arab-Israeli dispute and the constructive quest for a lasting and just peace in the region are probably a sine qua non for protecting the essential economic and possibly also political interests of the United States in this strategically important region.

In conclusion, the Arab access to the channels of trade and technical cooperation with the West in general and the United States in particular is of extreme value to the economic development of the Arab countries. The severance of these ties could wreak havoc on ambitious development plans currently being implemented, predicated on extensive Western involvement and continued economic cooperation. These ties, together with the growing awareness of key Arab governments of the pivotal role of the United States in any political settlement of the Arab-Israeli dispute, constitute effective offsetting or countervailing dependencies to Western reliance on Arab oil.

However, in the absence of a common stand among the major Western powers vis-a-vis the oil exporters, the effectiveness of these ties as a bargaining tool is severely limited.*

Regional Cooperation in the Middle East and Oil Supplies

One of the major concerns of the West regarding international energy transactions is the adequacy of oil supplies. Interruption of oil flows from the Middle East could have serious consequences for economic growth and employment in all OECD countries including the United States. It is therefore crucial to assess the impact of regional cooperation in the Middle East on this vital issue.

We have repeatedly emphasized that the preponderant factor determining the need for oil revenues in the oil-based economies is domestic absorptive capacity. The higher this capacity, the greater is the need for oil revenues, and ceteris paribus, the willingness of the typical oil-producing country to produce

---

*The current lack of a common policy among OECD members vis-a-vis OPEC and OAPEC countries stems basically from the differential reliance of these countries on imported oil, and from their divergent political views concerning the Arab-Israeli problem. However, the oil weapon, being extremely sensitive, cannot be employed by militarily weak Arab governments to secure political concessions incompatible with official U.S. policy in the Arab-Israeli dispute. In the economic realm, Arab multifaceted ties to the West can still play a decisive role in protecting Western interests, even in the absence of a unified Western policy.

and export larger volumes of petroleum. The decision to produce the current levels of petroleum, however, has been largely historical. In fact, oil-production levels prevailing prior to the dramatic price hikes of 1973 have not been significantly altered. As a result, oil revenues surged to unprecedented magnitudes well above the immmediate domestic absorptive capacity of the oil-producing states, thus creating a sizable capital surplus. This surplus was by necessity recycled to various foreign outlets with a significant portion flowing into the region itself.

The oil-producing countries, however, seem to view surplus capital as a sign of disequilibrium because the bulk of it must be directed to Western outlets. These outlets do not figure high on their scale of priorities. Consequently, many oil-producing countries stress that, given the climate of investment in the West and the inherent uncertainites associated with international investment, oil proceeds must be increasingly abosorbed first at home and secondly in the region. In this connection, the level of domestic abosorptive capacity of the oil producers may be envisaged as setting the lower bound for the oil producers' demand for foreign exchange, and this minimum demand for capital would determine a corresponding minimum level of oil exports.

The contribution of regional cooperation in the Middle East is twofold: it increases the domestic capital absorption in the oil-based economies, and it stimulates significant capital outflows from the oil producers to the regional non-oil-exporting countries. In this way, then, it raises the lower bound of the foreign exchange requirements as perceived by the oil-exporting states. This, in turn, will raise the minimum level of oil exports that the oil consumers can definitely count on. It must be emphasized that the above analysis implies that regional cooperation will not affect the current levels of oil supplies; the additional capital required to satisfy regional demand will be secured through the redirection of the capital surplus from the West to regional outlets. This perception of the issue is based on the fact that oil supply basically responds to world demand for oil at given prices, the latter are being fixed collectively within OPEC.

However, if one is willing to assume that the current flows of capital from the oil exporters to outside sources are equilibrium flows, then it would be logical than any increase in the desired level of one of these flows, for example, a higher capital transfer to regional outlets, must disturb the initial equilibrium. The new equilibrium is likely to involve some reshuffling of funds among various outlets in favor of the region, and a greater need for oil revenues. Given the world demand for oil, higher oil revenues cannot be secured by all the oil producers merely by increasing oil supply at fixed prices. Oil revenues can only rise if prices are reduced, provided, of course, that the relevant demand is fairly elastic. If OPEC resists any price reduction, the member encountering a revenue constraint may decide to lower his price to exploit the highly elastic demand he faces. If he succeeds in cutting significantly into the market shares of other producers, there will be a strong motivation for the latter to follow suit, thereby increasing supply and lowering prices. While this analysis is logically consistent, its predictions may be questioned for two reasons. First, the assumption that the oil producers view the current distribution of their surplus capital as optimal is contradicted by a plentitude of statements of key policy makers and the declared structure of priorities of these states. More likely, the oil producers would prefer a lower volume of investment in the international financial and money markets and a higher volume in the region. To the extent that the forecasted additional regional capital transfers are larger than the volume of excessive investment in the West (excessive as viewed by the oil producers themselves), this will constitute a net increase in the demand for foreign exchange by the oil-producing states and ipso facto a possible increase in oil supplies. However, our estimate of the additional, potential, regional capital transfer is rather modest, about $5 billion annually during 1975-80. This comprises only about 16.5 percent of the projected annual capital surplus. It is, therefore, unlikely that such a magnitude of capital transfer would significantly exceed the level of excessive international investments by the Arab oil exporters. Second, even if all additional regional capital transfers are construed as augmenting the oil producers' demand for foreign exchange, this could at the prevailing oil prices result in an increase of about 1.5 million barrels per day in oil supplies. This level of additional supply represents only about 8.6 percent of total Arab production in 1976. The impact of such an increase in supply on oil prices and OPEC solidarity depends very much on its timing. Given the present situation characterized by significant excess production capacity and sluggish world demand for oil, such an increase could have potentially disruptive consequences. If, however, greater oil exports needed to finance additional regional investment are planned over the next five to ten years in consonance with the world demand-supply equation for oil, no serious disruptive effects may ensue.

Finally, there is the following possibility. Assume that the world demand for oil shifted to the right and that regional commitments remained substantially the same. Then the Arab oil exporters would, ceteris paribus, be disinclined to raise their output and exports of oil. Obviously, such behavior would put new pressures on oil prices. If, however, regional cooperation were rigorously pursued, leading to higher demand for foreign exchange, the increase in the world demand for oil could be easily accommodated without undue pressures on existing prices.

It appears from this discussion that in the context of oil supplies, regional cooperation in the Middle East plays basically the role of a safety valve, maintaining a minumum level of oil exports and ensuring greater responsiveness of supply to higher world demand for petroleum.

U.S. EXPORTS TO THE MIDDLE EAST

Volume of U.S. Exports

Table 7.1 projects U.S. exports to the Middle East through 1985, on the basis of the following assumptions.

First, total imports of the Arab oil exporters as well as Iran, including imports from the United States, will grow in line with the maximum expansion in absorptive capacity as projected in this study. This means an annual compound rate of growth of imports of about 15 percent for 1975-80 and 10

TABLE 7.1

U.S. Exports to the Middle East, 1975-85
(millions of 1975 U.S. dollars)a

	1975 (Actual)	1980 (Projected)	1985 (Projected)
Arab oil exportersb	3,627.6	7,001.3	11,412.0
Percent of total Arab imports from U.S.	68	72	75
Arab non-oil exportersc	1,708.8	2,734.1	3,827.7
Percent of total Arab imports from U.S.	32	28	25
Total Arab imports from U.S.	5,336.4	9,735.4	15,239.7
Iran	3,241.7	6,256.5	10,198.1
Total Middle East imports from U.S.	8,578.1	15,991.9	25,437.8
Percent Arab	62	61	60
Percent Iran	38	39	40
Middle East as percent of total U.S. exports	8	12.0	16.0
Arab countries as percent of total U.S. exports	5	7.4	9.6

aThe Middle East is defined here to include the following Arab countries and Iran: Bahrain, Iraq, Jordan, Kuwait, Lebanon, Oman, Peoples Democratic Republic of Yemen, Qatar, Saudi Arabia, Syria, United Arab Emirates. Yemen Arab Republic, Algeria, Libya, Morocco, Tunisia, and Egypt.

bBy far the most important country in this category is Saudi Arabia, accounting in 1975 for over $1.5 billion or 28 percent of the total for this group. Algeria is a distant second with $631.8 million followed by the United Arab Emirates ($371.5 million), Kuwait ($366.1 million), and Iraq ($309.7). The balance ($466.7 million) was contributed by Bahrain, Oman, Qatar, and Libya.

cThe most important country in this category is Egypt, accounting in 1975 for $682.7 million or about 40 percent of the total for this group. Lebanon with $402.3 million is second followed by Morocco ($199.5 million), Jordan ($195.4 million) and Syria ($127.8 million). The balance of $101.1 million was contributed by the two Yemens and Tunisia.

Note: All reported percentages are calculated.

Source: Actual data derived from U.S. Department of Commerce, April 26, 1976.

percent for 1980-85. It also assumes that the United States will maintain its 1975 market share of total imports.

Second, imports of the Arab non-oil exporters, including imports from the United States, will grow at an annual compound rate of 10 percent during 1975-80, which is equivalent to the maximum rate of growth of GNP projected for these countries. During 1980-85, however, the rate of import growth is expected to decline to about 7 percent, due principally to smaller capital transfers to these countries from their fellow oil exporters as the capacity of the latter countries to abosorb their oil revenues domestically rises significantly.

Third, evidently, the projection is predicated on a relatively high degree of regional cooperation among the various states of the area. Without rather significant labor and capital mobility across national boundaries, neither the oil-exporting countries nor the non-oil-based economies could fully realize their economic potential. Thus, in the absence of significant regional cooperation, total exports to the region will diminish, and in the case of the non-oil Arab countries, the decline may be substantial as the rate of growth of the economy is reduced by half. This underscores the importance of regional cooperation as a crucial determinant of the volume of imports into the Middle East.

Fourth, total U.S. exports are assumed to increase in real terms at about 4 percent through 1985, which is equivalent to the rate of growth of U.S. GNP in the 1960s. If GNP displays a similar rate of growth in the next decade, the proportion of U.S. exports to GNP will remain constant. Obviously, this stipulation is not necessary for the validity of the projection, but merely aids in ascertaining the relative importance of Middle East trade to the United States.

The projection above indicates the growing significance of U.S. export trade with the Middle East. The volume of exports is forecast to increase about threefold during the next decade, rising from $8.6 billion in 1975 to $25.4 billion in 1985. U.S. exports to the Middle East as a proportion of total U.S. exports will accordingly double from 8 percent in 1975 to 16 percent in 1985. Thus, in 1985, the Middle East is expected to be the third major export market for the United States, coming right after Canada and industrial Europe.[14] Furthermore, given the still relatively small current U.S. share in the import market of most Middle East countries (ranging generally between 10 and 16 percent, with the notable exception of Saudi Arabia in which U.S. share amounted to 25 percent), the United States should be able to improve its competitive position in future years. Undeniably, there are tremendous market opportunities in the Middle East for U.S. goods and services, and these could grow considerably, provided the United States capitalizes on its latent trade advantages with the area and continues to play a constructive role in bringing a just peace and enduring prosperity to all the nations of the area, including Israel.[15] We expect, therefore, that projected U.S. exports to the Middle East, substantial as they are, will be appreciably surpassed, given favorable commercial and political climate.

Commodity Composition of U.S. Exports
to the Middle East

The composition of U.S. exports to the Middle East mirrors largely the requirements of countries at once relatively wealthy and in a stage of rapid development. Some of the product categories offering the best future market are discussed below.

Infrastructure

Although there is some variation in degree among Middle East countries, all of the states place high spending priority on social and physical infrastructure development. The Arabian Peninsula states, with their relatively small populations and extremely limited manpower resources, cannot reasonably be expected to articulate their requirements for many individual capital equipment items. Therefore, opportunities exist in all countries for turnkey projects and sales of plant packages or manufacturing kits, and in Saudi Arabia, Iraq, and the littoral Gulf states, this is likely to be the only way in which most capital equipment will be purchased. In Egypt, Lebanon, and Iran, professional and managerial resources and government programs have evolved to the extent that many diverse capital items are marketable. Good sales prospects exist particularly in the fields of biomedical equipment, educational equipment and materials, power-generating machinery, desalination plants, and water-resource equipment.

Transportation

Massive expenditures will be allotted to transportation systems. As much as 35 percent of total transport purchases will be spent in the aviation sector and the funding will probably be equally divided between aircraft and ground facitities. All indications are that the market for civil aircraft in the Middle East and North Africa will expand even more rapidly than now with a growing tourist industry and increased air freight and business travel. Large expenditures will also be quickly made to expand port facilities. Railroads and major urban transit systems are other important projects. New highway construction is being undertaken. The rapidly expanding transportation sector has increased the demand for trucks and off-road vehicles for use in the petroleum industry and truck assembly plants. For all of these transportation needs U.S. products and standards have been favored; however, competition is keen and both Japanese and German exports are making inroads in the markets of the Middle East.

General Industrial Machinery

With economic diversification a primary goal of all the countries in the area, and with the problem of limited manpower resources and pressures for rapid industrialization, a market for package plants is gaining importance. Often these are turnkey projects with precise performance and completion guarantees that make bidding for them less attracitve. However, several countries have established sufficient basic industry to afford good sales prospects for industrial tools, metalworking and finishing machinery, packaging machinery, machinery for the manufacture of plastic products, and equipment for producing pharamceuticals, industrial chemicals, and building materials. Projects in which large sums will be spend for importation include petroleum refining and liquified natural gas (LNG) facilities, as well as several LNG cryogenic installations; plants to produce such downstream products as fertilizers; and other construction projects including prospective aluminum smelters in Saudi Arabia, Abu Dhabi, Iran, Iraq, and Kuwait, copper mining and smelting plants, cement plants, textile plants, paper mills and steel mills.

Agricultural Machinery and Food Processing Equipment

In Egypt, Lebanon, and Syria agricultural products account for substantial shares of export earnings and in Iran and Iraq concentration on agricultural development is receiving increased attention. First-rate equipment is sought with the United States setting the quality standards. Also included in this heading is fishery development which also requires important spending for equipment. The Gulf and the Red Sea teem with fish and shrimp to be harvested by Oman, the United Arab Emirates, Kuwait, Iran, Iraq, Saudi Arabia, Bahrain, and Egypt. Egypt is also pursuing plans for the development of a freshwater fishing industry in Lake Nasser, located behind the Aswan Dam.

Construction Machinery

A spectacular building boom is under way throughout the Middle East. Mounting tourism and business travel have strained hotel capacity. In Egypt, Suez Canal area reconstruction will require mobilization of vast machinery resources. The infrastructure needs of the Gulf littoral states will require buildings of every type. Sand and inclement weather cause most construction equipment to deteriorate much faster in the Middle East than in the United States and as a result, most heavy machinery is written off after a single, one- to two-year project. Industrial development in Iran, Iraq, Syria, and Egypt will also swell the demand for all types of construction equipment. The ruggedness and capacity of U.S. construction equipment give it a clear competitive edge in the Middle East, but other suppliers are trying hard to change this situation. Japanese equipment has won admiration mostly for the perseverance of its Japanese service technicians and the efficiency of parts distribution. Long delivery schedules for some U.S. machinery also has given a boost to Japanese suppliers.

Building Systems and Materials

The construction boom in the area is creating a rapidly escalating demand for new building materials and systems. Traditional construction methods have made maximum use of local materials and unskilled labor, but often have produced buildings below Western standards of appearance, utility, and durability. Where structural integrity remained sound, appearance and utility often failed in a few years. Construction of a few modern hotels and office buildings, and the desire of ambitious local architects to make creative use of the latest materials and techniques, already are having an impact. To some extent, the higher freight costs of importing from the United States are offset by the appeal of superior state-of-the-art and cost savings. In addition, the reopening of the Suez Canal should reduce freight rates substantially. Complete modular construction systems are ideally suited to the need for rapid expansion of popular housing and schools with a minimum influx of alien laborers, but effective demonstration of a versatile system will be needed to overcome traditional reservation in most countries.

Air Conditioning and Refrigeration Equipment

The climate of all of the Middle East countries is extremely hot. On the Arabian Peninsula summer temperatures reach 120 degrees Fahrenheit in the shade. Air conditioning assumes the character of a basic necessity, for in some circumstances the failure of just a few refrigeration units could result in losses of millions of dollars. In the punishing climates of this region, the durability and reliability of air conditioning and refrigeration equipment have justified the premium often paid. The U.S. market position has recently been strengthened by the scheduled completion of a joint-venture repair and reconditioning facility in Bahrain.

Oilfield Equipment and Supplies

To expand oil production on a large scale requires astronomical capital expenditures. Sources for products required in vast quantities, such as tools, pumps, valves, and steel pipe, usually are decided first by delivery time and second by price, once they fulfill the basic requirements. Any supplier competitive on these terms, regardless of size or exporting experience, can probably secure sales in the Middle East. Competition between U.S., Japanese, and European sellers is extremely keen in this area.

Food and Other Consumer Products, Including Manufactures

Imports of other products such as consumer goods and foodstuffs are steadily rising as both population and income increase. The United States has the most favorable commercial image in this area.

Armaments

Imports of armaments and other military equipment are substantial, especially in the case of Iran and to a lesser extent Saudi Arabia. However, these imports may vary widely from year to year, depending on many factors, including primarily the political situation in the Middle East. Information as to the precise content of this category is understandably lacking.

Appendix B exposes the content of the groupings above, and thus provides a workable portfolio for explaining areas for marketable commodities in the Middle East.

CAPITAL FLOWS FROM THE MIDDLE EAST INTO THE UNITED STATES

Foreign investment in the United States may be divided into two types: portfolio investment and direct investment. Foreign portfolio investment generally refers to foreign investment in U.S. securities that do not significantly influence the management of the enterprise. This "covers investments in the U.S. in voting stocks involving less than 10 percent ownership by the foreign investor, in non-voting stocks, and in debt instruments with maturities of more than one year by persons residing in foreign countries.[16] Direct investment on the other hand is primarily "the value of foreign parents' direct claims on the assests of their U.S. affiliates, net of claims of these affiliates on their parents' assests."[17]

The principal motivations for foreign portfolio investment in the United States include[18]

1. anticipation of long-term capital gains;
2. the relative economic and political stability of the United States, considered by foreigners as the bastion of free enterprise offering greater profit potential and smaller risk for nationalization than other countries;
3. the large size and liquidity of U.S. capital markets thus making it possible to place substantial amounts of fund in a relatively short time span;
4. well-organized and closely regulated U.S. securities markets offering safeguards against manipulation and fraud;
5. the existence of a wide range of investment choices;
6. the greater efficiency of U.S. markets where information is widely available and almost instantaneously reflected in the prices of stocks; and
7. salesmanship of U.S. brokers and dealers.

Foreign direct investment in the United States is motivated by two basic forces: first, the pull generated by the large size of the U.S. market, stable labor conditions, access to special technologies or relatively inexpensive raw materials; and second, "the push of overall economic conditions in other developed countries accompanied by the increased financial, technical and managerial capabilities of foreign firms for undertaking large-scale overseas investment."[19]

Evidently, foreign investment in the United States, whether portfolio or direct investment, is induced almost exclusively by market forces. The contention that OPEC investment in the United States, especially investment by the major Arab oil exporters, is directed toward the acquisition and/or control of major U.S. companies is unfounded and fallacious. Mr. Parksy, U.S. Assistant Secretary of the Treasury states;[20]

> The Saudi Arabian Government, for instance, has told me that they will not invest more than 5 percent in any particular company, and recently indicated to us that they currently do not own more than 1 percent of any company. Further, a country like Kuwait has participated in our markets for years and has always been a most responsible investor . . . . I do not believe that these countries would consider investments here which would be against our national interest. I am also confident that they would consult with us before undertaking any significant investments.

Foreign portfolio investors employ the same investment channels as their American counterparts. These are, for the most part, the New York and American exchanges, the regional exchanges, and the over-the-counter market. Foreign investors depend heavily on U.S. brokers and dealers for placing orders and procuring information on U.S. securities.[21] With respect to direct investment, foreign firms utilize a variety of sources in financing their investments in the United States. Although the use of foreign sources is significant, especially in the initial stage, U.S. banks and other U.S. sources provided the bulk of capital for all foreign-owned subsidiaries in the United States in 1974.[22] Moreover, such subsidiaries generally follow management and labor practices similar to those of their U.S. counterparts. Thus, they have had "not an unfavorable impact on the U.S. economy and U.S. working conditions."[23] At any rate, this type of investment, that is, investment in foreign-owned subsidiaries in the United States, is important primarily for European, Canadian, and possibly Japanese firms and not for the Middle East oil exporters.

Tables 7.2 through 7.5 provide the most recent information available on foreign investment in the United States. The growing relative importance of the Middle East oil-producing countries is clearly visible in Table 7.4.

The most important type of foreign portfolio investment is U.S. corporate stocks. This type of foreign investment accounted for 36.7 percent and 43.3 percent of total foreign portfolio investment in the United States in 1974 and 1975, respectively. Almost all U.S. Treasury bonds and notes and some corporate bonds consist of holdings of foreign official institutions, chiefly central banks, monetary authorities, and international lending agencies. These official holdings represent mostly international reserves of the countries concerned and are "determined mainly by balance of payments factors, independently of the ability of U.S. financial markets to attract foreign capital through

TABLE 7.2

Foreign Investment Portfolio in the United States, 1974–75

Type	1974 Billions of dollars	1974 Percent	1975 Billions of dollars	1975 Percent	Change 1975 – 74 (billions of dollars)
Stocks	24.7	36.7	37.2	43.3	12.5
Corporate bonds[a]	10.4	15.5	11.1[b]	12.9	0.7
Other private debt	8.3	12.4	8.3	9.7	0.0
U.S. Treasury bonds and notes	23.8	35.4	29.4	34.1	5.6
Total	67.2	100.0	86.0	100.0	18.8

[a]Includes issues of Federal agencies and state and municipal governments.

[b]The Middle East oil-exporting countries' share was $2,179 million as of December 31, 1975. Their net purchases in 1975 amounted to $1,427 million.

Note: Percentages and changes are calculated.

Source: U.S. Department of the Treasury, statement by Gerald L. Parsky, Assistant Secretary of the Treasury, before the Subcommittee on Foreign Commerce and Tourism, Senate Committee on Commerce, May 3, 1976, pp. 5, 21.

the operation of normal market forces."[24] Official investments of the Middle East oil exporters, however, are an exception; they move primarily in response to market criteria.

The Middle East oil-exporting countries emerged in 1975 as principal buyers of U.S. securities. Their net purchases of corporate bonds of $1,427 million helped offset the sizable sales of other countries, turning the balance positive at about $0.7 billion. Their net equity investment, that is, purchases of corporate stocks, amounted to $1,441 million or about one-third of the total foreign purchase of $4,435 million in 1975. The substantial capital flows from the Middle East oil exporters into the United States in 1975 were probably to a large extent due to the shift of the investments of these countries from treasury bills and short-term bank certificates of deposit into longer-term assets. In 1974, these countries witnessed a sudden and very large accumulation of funds and could therefore not articulate a balanced investment strategy.

The recorded volume of portfolio investment of the Middle East oil-exporting countries is probably biased downward because these countries sometimes request foreign brokers and banks to hold U.S. securities on their behalf. This practice preserves the anonymity of the original owner since foreign nominees are not subject to U.S. laws and cannot therefore be required to disclose the identity of the ultimate beneficiary(ies) of the held securities.

The magnitude of this understatement is unknown, but it must be significant since in 1974 slightly more than half the total foreign holdings of U.S. stocks were held by banks, brokers, and nominees. Of the total holdings of Switzerland, for example, 88 percent were reported in the names of banks, brokers, and nominees; the comparable percentage for France wes 68 percent. With respect to other major holders of U.S. stocks —the United Kingdom, Canada, and the Netherlands—these proportions were considerably less. One should not, however, assume that the total for this category, that is, U.S. securities held by banks, brokers, and nominees, represents mostly holdings on behalf of persons residing in countries other than the countries of the nominees, with the possible exception

TABLE 7.3

Foreign Equity Investment in the United States by Major Geographical Area, 1974–75

Area	1974		1975		1975 – 74 Change[a]
	Millions of dollars	Percent	Millions of dollars	Percent	
Europe	17,562	71.2	25,796	69.3	8,234
Canada	3,580	14.5	5,103	13.7	1,523
Latin American republics	618	2.5	825	2.2	207
Other Western Hemisphere	904	3.6	1,176	3.2	272
Middle East oil-exporting countries[b]	518	2.0	2,168	5.8	1,650[c]
Other Asia	913	3.7	1,352	3.6	439
Africa	61	0.2	86	0.2	25
Other countries and unallocated	170	0.7	240	0.7	70
International organizations	348	1.4	480	1.3	132
Total	24,671	100.0	37,225	100.0	12,554

[a]Includes $8,119 million which is due to change in market value. Thus, net foreign purchases were $4,435 million only.

[b]Principally Saudi Arabia, Kuwait, and Abu Dhabi.

[c]Net foreign purchase amounted to $1,441 in 1975. The balance is due to change in market value.

Note: Entries may not add exactly to totals due to rounding. Percentages are calculated.

Source: U.S. Department of the Treasury, Statement by Gerald L. Parsky, Assistant Secretary of the Treasury, before the Subcommittee on Foreign Commerce and Tourism, Senate Committee on Commerce, May 3, 1976, pp. 11, 23.

TABLE 7.4

Foreign Portfolio Investment in Stocks and Long-Term Debt Obligations by Major Industry, 1974

Industries	Stocks Millions of dollars	Percent	Long-term Debt Millions of dollars	Percent	Total
Agriculture, forestry and fishing	23	0.1	14	0.30	37
Mining	2,284	9.3	2,185	5.20	4,469
Construction	262	1.0	61	0.14	323
Manufacturing	14,758	59.8	8,132	19.20	22,890
Transportation and public utilities	2,662	10.8	2,506	5.90	5,168
Trade	1,067	4.3	499	1.10	1,566
Finance, insurance, and real estate	3,301	13.4	2,567	6.10	5,868
Services	279	1.1	209	0.50	488
Federal government	38	0.2	25,914	61.10	25,952
State and local governments	*	—	309	0.73	309
Total	24,671	100.0	42,427	100.00	67,098

*Less than $0.5 million or 0.

Note: Entries may not add exactly to totals due to rounding. Percentages are calculated.

Source: U.S. Department of the Treasury. Statement by Gerald L. Parsky, Assistant Secretary of the Treasury, before the Subcommittee on Foreign Commerce and Tourism, Senate Committee on Commerce, May 3, 1976, pp. 13, 19.

of Switzerland for which "the bulk of nominee holdings is for the account of persons in other countries."[25]

Although the Middle East oil-exporting countries increased their share in total foreign equity investment in the United States from 2 percent in 1974 to 5.8 percent in 1975, the latter figure is still very small compared to the European share of over 69 percent in 1975, and is also less than half the Canadian share of 13.7 percent. Nevertheless, the upward trend is unmistakable, putting the Middle East oil-exporting countries in third place right after Europe and Canada in the hierarchy of foreign investors in U.S. stocks.

Foreign portfolio investment in stocks in 1974 was concentrated in manufacturing (59.8 percent of the total), and to a much smaller extent in finance, insurance, and real estate (13.4 percent), transportation and public utilities (10.8 percent), and mining (9.3 percent). Long-term U.S. debt held by foreigners, on the other hand, is concentrated in two categories: federal government debt (61.6 percent) and manufacturing (19.2 percent). This is generally due to balance-of-payments reasons and other factors relating to

> . . . the U.S. Government capital control and restraint programs during the period from the mid-1960's to the early 1970's. Under these programs, U.S. firms were encouraged to go to foreign capital markets to raise the necessary funds to finance their direct investments abroad in lieu of moving funds from the U.S. to foreign countries.[26]

Foreign direct investment in the U.S. in 1974 amounted to $26.5 billion, of which only $1.86 billion or 7 percent was due almost entirely to investment by one Middle East oil-exporting country, presumably Saudi Arabia. The Middle East share represents Saudi participation in a U.S.-incorporated petroleum company with operating assets in that country.[27]

The major countries with direct investment in the United States are the United Kingdom, Canada, and the Netherlands. The distribution of this investment shows a noticeable clustering in manufacturing, mainly chemicals, food,

TABLE 7.5

Foreign Direct Investment in the United States by Country of Foreign Parents, 1974

Country	Billions of Dollars	Percent
United Kingdom	5.56	21
Canada	5.30	20
Netherlands	4.77	18
Latin America	2.38	9
Other EEC	2.12	8
Switzerland	1.86	7
Other (mainly Saudi Arabia)	1.86	7
Germany	1.59	6
Other Europe	0.79	3
Japan	0.27	1
Total	26.50	100

Source: U.S. Department of Commerce, Statement of Milton A. Berger and George R. Kruer of the Department of Commerce before the Senate Subcommittee on Commerce, May 3, 1976.

and machinery.[28] Information on direct investment in 1975 is unavailable. But, given that the Middle East oil-exporting countries made major foreign investments in that year, it is highly probable that they also undertook significant direct investment in the United States, perhaps in land and real estate as a means of securing balanced and diversified portfolios and as a hedge against inflationary trends.

Income payments derived from foreign portfolio investment in 1974 indicate an overall yield of nearly 7 percent.[29] Clearly, this yield is substantially lower than the U.S. rate of inflation in 1974, over 12 percent. Consequently, the real rate of return on foreign portfolio investment must have been distinctly negative. However, with respect to investment in U.S. corporate stocks and bonds, it is important to ascertain the change in market values as well. In 1975, the U.S. securities market made a strong recovery. As a result, foreign portfolio investments registered substantial gains in 1975 as compared to their depressed market value in 1974. The value of U.S. stocks held by foreigners increased by $8,119 milllion, that is, about one-third of their market value, and that of corporate bonds rose by $142 million, or about 1.4 percent of their total value.[30]

Foreign investment in the United States by the Middle East oil-exporting countries may not continue at the relatively high level of 1976. These countries, for one thing, are expected to complete the process of adjustment with respect to the composition of their portfolio holdings. The future flow of capital into the United States and other OECD countries, therefore, would once more be determined by basic forces. These include the domestic capital requirements of these countries, their regional commitments and willingness to promote further regional growth and cooperation, their foreign aid programs to Third World countries, the opportunities for remunerative investment in OECD countries, and the shift and/or change in the slope of the world's demand curve for OPEC oil. If oil prices remain constant in real terms while the quantity of petroleum demanded from Middle East sources increases, the oil revenues of the respective oil-exporting countries will rise commensurately. These countries may then produce a greater volume of oil, provided they can find satisfactory allocation of the proceeds among the above mentioned competing ends. If this happens, capital flows into the West are likely to increase significantly. If, however, such a satisfactory allocation is not or can not be found, these countries may choose to supply less oil than the market can absorb, thereby putting pressure on existing prices.

Apart from applying political and military pressure, which could only be temporarily successful and might even backfire, the West, including the United States, could work cooperatively with the Middle East oil-exporting countries to alleviate the conditions rendering higher oil-production incompatiable with the basic economic interests of the oil-exporting states.

However, given the level of oil revenues accruing to the Middle East oil-exporting countries and the present structure of their priorities, a rise in their domestic capacity to absorb funds, or in their regional commitments, or in their foreign aid programs would involve a commensurate   reduction in the total capital flows for investment purposes into the West. Whether and to what extent individual Western countries would experience a diminished flow of capital from the Middle East oil exporters depends essentially on the relative strength and competitiveness of the respective Western economies, primarily reflected in the expected rate of return on foreign investment.

IMPACT ON THE U.S. ECONOMY AND BALANCE OF PAYMENTS

The impact on the U.S. economy of the projected volume of trade (imports and exports) with the Middle East and of capital flows from the Middle East is outlined below. In this connection, it must be reiterated that regional cooperation among the Middle East countries plays a key role in expanding the absorptive capacity of those countries and thus their trade with the rest of the world.

First, the projected increases in U.S. exports to the Middle East will add to the stream of aggregate demand in the United States. This should increase the overall utilization of capacity, thereby helping reduce the unemployment of both capital and labor. The beneficial effects will be greatest when the composition of foreign demand is such that those industries suffering most from underutilization of capacity experience the highest increase in demand. Unfortunately, this is not generally the case. Nevertheless, the secondary and tertiary effects of a higher demand in one industry or sector could still play a potent role in enhancing the pace and magnitude of the current economic recovery.*

Second, apart from certain problems relating to the U.S. political stand in the Arab-Israeli dispute but not to U.S. security per se, the exchange of oil for U.S. products serves the economic and other interests of the United States as well as those of the Middle East oil-producing countries. This is a direct corollary of the principle of comparative advantage. The United States imports some of its oil requirement and pays for these imports with products that can be produced most efficiently at home. The Middle East oil exporters reap similar benefits, though the transaction runs, of course, in the opposite direction. Thus, the international exchange of oil for industrial products, food, technology, and other goods and services is in the best interests of all concerned.

Third, although the projected development of petrochemicals and other energy- and capital-intensive industries in the Middle East would not diminish the volume of U.S. trade with the region, it would effect significant changes in the composition of this trade. Paramount among these changes is the increase in Middle East exports of petrochemicals, including refined petroleum products,

_____

* To the extent that foreign demand is directed toward industries operating at high capacity ratios, it will generate some inflationary pressures.

fertilizers, LNG and LPG. The increased production of mature petrochemicals in the Middle East would require, among other things, export markets which must in part be found in the United States and other highly industrialized countries. In the long run, therefore, a readjustment in the structure of production in the West to accomodate the emerging patterns of specialization in the Middle East is indicated.

Fourth, the rapid pace of development forecast for the Middle East in the next decade is predicated on continued access of these countries to the channels of trade and technology with the West, including the United States. Thus, the transfer of modern technology is a critical factor for the success of the process of economic development in the Middle East. Consequently, the demand for Western and U.S. exports, specialized services, and high technology inputs is likely to grow at rates higher than those realized by other categories of imports.

Capital flows from the Middle East into the United States have an impact on the U.S. balance of payments, international investment position, and financial markets. However, portfolio investments of Middle East countries in the United States should not be perceived as augmenting the supply of capital available for domestic investment. In fact, the direct effects of such capital flows are generally of less significance than the indirect effects, because the former usually either mirror an increase in U.S. liabilities to one foreigner, which is offset by an equivalent reduction in these liabilities to another foreigner or merely a different time profile of imports from the United States. However, the indirect effects are significant.

Under the current system of reasonably flexible exchange rates, the flow of Middle East investments into the United States would represent a demand for U.S. rather than foreign liabilities, thus tending to strengthen the value of the dollar in foreign exchange markets.[31] In the long term, a sustained flow of foreign capital into the Untied States would have obvious implications for both imports and exports, making the former cheaper to U.S. consumers and the latter more expensive for foreign customers. However, the immediate impact would probably be concentrated on other capital items in the balance of payments because significant changes in trade patterns are difficult to effect in the short run, as they require adjustments in production and distribution channels.

The increase in Middle East investments in the United States tends, ceteris paribus, to change the international investment position of the United States, increasing the ratio of foreign investment in the United States to U.S. investment abroad. Thus, the balance between the two reverse flows, namely, the flow of dividends into and out of the United States, will diminish, changing gradually the mature creditor status of the United States. However, this is unlikely to happen in the foreseeable future because foreign capital inflows are still comparatively small in relation to the net creditor position of the United States.

The effect of foreign portfolio investment on U.S. financial markets may be analyzed as follows. An increase in the demand for U.S. securities in any segment of the capital market will tend to raise stock prices and consequently diminish their yields. The effect will not be confined to the securities directly demanded, but will through arbitrage spread to other segments of the capital market, although the impact will tend to be greater in those sectors experiencing the initial injection of new funds. The ensuing lower yields on U.S. stocks and bonds will enhance the ability of domestic borrowers to raise capital, thus tending to foster greater real investment and higher output and productivity in the economy at large.[32]

Generally foreign participation in the U.S. securities market tends to add breadth and efficiency to the market and, "to some extent, bring a new dimension to the market, i.e., proclivities for some kind of issues which may not be common to U.S. investors."[33] And, as long as foreign participation is motivated by market forces, it contributes to the health and resiliency of the capital market, and by extension, the U.S. economy. There is no need to furnish special government incentives or disincentives to guide foreign investments in the United States, including investment by the Middle East oil exporters, because such incentives interfere with the natural working of market forces that direct investment into the most desirable uses. A free market is necessary for allocative efficiency. Intervention would break down the market test and there would be "no economic basis for judging that certain kinds of transactions with foreigners are 'good' for the economy and that others are 'bad,' anymore than for such judgments on particular kinds of domestic transaction."[34]

Foreign investment in U.S. stocks exhibits volatility, that is the ratio of gross transactions to total foreign holdings is greater than that for domestic holdings. Net foreign acquisitions of U.S. stocks in 1975 were $4.4 billion, whereas gross foreign transactions amounted to $25.6 billion, equivalent in value to the total foreign holdings as of the end of 1974. Thus, the greater velocity of foreign portfolio investment results in its impact being larger than that indicated by total foreign holdings or net foreign purchases.[35] Nevertheless, foreign portfolio investors appear to lag behind their U.S. counterparts in their response to the movements of the stock market.

More importantly, foreigners as a group have been net buyers of U.S. stocks in every year since 1957, exluding 1964-66. "Thus, foreigners have on balance tended to strengthen U.S. stock prices."[36]

In summary, it is evident "that foreigners add to the depth and resiliency of the market. If, in the same process they may also add somewhat to its volatility, the latter effect may be regarded as a small cost for the larger benefits resulting from foreign participation."[37]

REGIONAL COOPERATION IN THE MIDDLE EAST AND U.S. POLITICAL INTERESTS

The possible impact of regional cooperation in the Middle East on U.S. political interests cannot be analyzed without first identifying these interests.

Fundamentally, the United States has two political objectives in the Middle East: the continued existence of Israel within recognized and secured boundaries, and the diminution, if not the elimination, of Soviet influence in the area. The question then is: In what ways and to what extent does regional cooperation among the Middle East countries, in particular the Arab states, have an impact on these basic twin objectives of U.S. foreign policy?

Regional cooperation in the Middle East, if continued, will create new economic linkages among the states of the area, thus strengthening the existing bonds of language, culture, and history. In due time, it is apt to lead to a higher form of economic integration, including eventually economic union. Such a development could ultimately culminate in complete political unification of most of the Arab world. However, the latter prospect appears at present remote and improbable. Nevertheless, the political implication of a higher degree of regional economic cooperation is sufficiently clear; it increases the cohesion of the various states and consequently enhances their political strength and military prowess. Moreover, aside from greater political cohesion, economic cooperation accelerates the pace of economic development in the region, thus helping create a modern, integrated, and strong economy, capable of sustaining a more efficient and advanced military machine. Such a development, if current Arab-Israeli tension persists, is certainly inimical to the first objective of U.S. foreign policy.

On the other hand, a diminished flow of aid and investment from the oil-rich countries to the poor states of the area is likely to heighten the existing economic polarization, thus increasing ideological bifurcation and instability in the whole region. Similarly, unrestrained rivalry among the oil exporters themselves would produce further tension and encourage adventurism. A state of little or no significant cooperation among the Arab countries perpetruates and deepens the forces of division and conflict which cannot but help the Soviet Union in its quest for influence in the area. Moreover, such a state can hardly be expected to serve the genuine interests of Israel—witness the history of four Arab-Israeli wars since 1947. It appears logical that economic and political disintegration of the Arab world begets fragmented and weak governments, some of which may easily fall into the Soviet orbit, thus exposing strategic Western interests to serious and acute dangers. It may, therefore, be concluded that disintegration is associated with greater regional instability and thus is detrimental to the second goal of U.S. foreign policy, namely, the appreciable reduction or possibly elimination of Soviet influence in the area. The contribution of Arab economic and political disintegration to the first goal is ambiguous at best. While it may be a necessary condition for the continued existence of Israel, if present tension persists, it is not by itself a guarantee of Israel's security, let alone her eventual acceptance as a Middle East state. The interests of the United States mirrored in the twin objectives referred to above are, indeed, best served through a policy of promoting orderly economic cooperation among the Arab states, and at the same time aggressively seeking a just and lasting peace in the Middle East. Such a U.S. policy would not only prevent the radicalization of most of the Arab world, but also help responsible Arab governments approach the thorny and intricate Arab-Israeli problem objectively, with a willingness to compromise and an emphasis on peace, justice, and prosperity for all the peoples of the Middle East.

NOTES

1. The diagrams and in part the analysis presented here are derived from: U.S. Federal Energy Administration: *Nation Energy Outlook* (Washington, D.C.: Government Printing Office, February 1976), pp. 21-24, 54, 58.

2. Ibid., p. XXIII.

3. Ibid., p. XXV. Emphasis in original save for the last statement.

4. Ibid., p. XXVI. Emphasis in original.

5. Ibid., p. XXIV.

6. These views are aired persuasively in Denis Hayes, *Nuclear Power: The Fifth Horseman* (Washington, D.C.: Worldwatch Institute, 1976).

7. "Uncertainty Clouds the Optimism on Oil," New York *Times*, May 28, 1976, p. D2.

8. FEA, *National Energy Outlook*, op. cit., p. 101.

9. A recent conservation bill which stands a good chance of being enacted gives numerous and generous subsidies to energy consumers—both large and small— "to back up all the talk about saving energy." See "Conserving Energy," New York *Times*, June 23, 1976, p. 36M.

10. New York *Times*, May 28, 1976, p. D2.

11. "In the second week of March imports rose to a record 8.2 million barrels a day, exceeding for the first time output from wells in the United States. Analysts believe that imports may provide as much as 44 percent of American demand this year." New York *Times*, May 28, 1976, p. D2.

12. See "Canada Energy Policy Draws Doubts," *Oil & Gas Journal*, May 24, 1976, p. 38.

13. See Frank Zarb's statement in *Federal Energy News*, June 10, 1976, p. 2. The autarkic leaning of Zarb's statement is obvious; autarky, however, runs counter to economic principles, and is generally inappropriate as a policy for a superpower.

14. In 1972, Canada's share in total U.S. exports was 25 percent and that of industrial Europe (Austria, Belgium-Luxembourg, Denmark, France, Germany, Italy, Netherlands, Norway, Sweden and Switzerland) was 21 percent. Latin America accounted for 13 percent and Japan for 9.9 percent. See Hal R. Mason et al. *The Economics of International Business* (New York: Wiley, 1975), p. 5.

15. U.S. Department of State, Office of Media Services, Bureau of Public Affairs News Release, "*American Business in the Middle East and North Africa*," Washington, D.C., May 14, 1976. Deputy advantages as follows: "We enjoy a number of commercial advantages in the Middle East. English is widely accepted as the second language; and we Americans—surprising as it may be to some—enjoy a comfortable cultural rapport with Middle Easterners. More directly, we can build on the high acceptability of U.S. goods, a strong desire for U.S. technology, and a political disposition to trade with us." p. 2. note: "Large numbers of American firms which have traditionally traded with Middle Eastern countries have raised their sales sharply in the past couple of years. Many others are embarking on new voyages of discovery as they become aware of opportunities to do

business in the area. In the broadest sense, the opportunities for trade imaginatively and energetically pursued by American business—can spell a success story that will serve the interests of the United States in many ways. Not the least of these is the impetus that it can give to the development of our friendly relations with all the countries of the region and to the continuing search for peace."

16. U.S. Department of the Treasury, *Study of Foreign Portfolio Investment in the United States*, statement of Gerald L. Parsky, Assistant Secretary of the Treasury, before the Subcommittee on Foreign Commerce and Tourism, Senate Committee on Commerce, May 3, 1976 (Washington, D.C.: Government Printing Office, 1976), p. 1.

17. U.S. Department of Commerce, *Study of Foreign Direct Investment in the United States*, statement of Milton A. Berger and George R. Kruer before the Subcommittee on Foreign and Tourism, Senate Committee on Commerce, May 3, 1976 (Washington, D.C.: Government Printing Office, 1976), p. 3. Data regarding foreign ownership of agricultural land and other real estate are inadequate and incomplete. Thus, there is "much uncertainty as to the amount and nature of land owned by aliens." (p. 11).

18. U.S. Department of the Treasury, op. cit., pp. 7, 8, 25-28.

19. Ibid., p. 9.

20. Ibid., pp. 12-13.

21. Ibid., p. 8.

22. U.S. Department of Commerce, op. cit., p. 9.

23. Ibid., p. 10.

24. U.S. Department of the Treasury, op. cit., p. 5.

25. Ibid., p. 8.

26. Ibid., p. 6.

27. U.S. Department of Commerce, op. cit., p. 4.

28. Ibid.

29. U.S. Department of the Treasury, op. cit., p. 10.

30. Ibid., pp. 23-24. The U.S. Treasury Study defines the term "foreign" to include American nationals residing in other countries. This category was responsible for 9 percent of total foreign investment in U.S. stocks in 1974, and about 0.1 percent of total foreign investment in long-term debt obligations in the same year. Ibid., pp. 13-15.

31. Department of the Treasury, op. cit., p. 14.

32. Ibid., p. 36.

33. Ibid., p. 33.

34. Ibid., p. 34.

35. Ibid., p. 37.

36. Ibid.

37. Ibid., p. 38.

TABLE A.1

Area and Population of the Arab World, 1976

| Country | Area | | Popula-tion (millions) | Percent of Total Arab Popula-tion | Ra[a] (per-cent) | Density (persons per square kilo-meter) |
	Square Kilometers	Percent of Total Area				
Algeria	2,381,741	17.48	17.33	12.0	3.2	7.3
Egypt	1,001,449[b]	7.35	38.36	26.2	2.5	38.3
Iraq	434,924	3.19	11.44	7.8	3.2	26.3
Jordan	97,740	0.71	2.81	1.9	3.4	28.7
Kuwait	17,818	0.13	1.20[c]	0.8	9.8	67.3
Lebanon[d]	10,400	0.07	3.30	2.3	2.6	317.3
Libya	1,759,540	12.91	2.41	1.6	3.7	1.4
Morocco[e]	446,550	3.27	17.82	12.2	2.7	39.9
Qatar[d]	22,014	0.16	.24[c]	0.1	9.6	10.9
Saudi Arabia	2,149,690	15.77	6.37[c]	4.3	5.0	3.0
Sudan	2,505,813	18.39	18.36	12.5	2.8	7.3
Syria	185,408	1.36	7.59	5.1	3.3	40.9
Tunisia	163,610	1.20	5.86	4.0	2.1	35.8
United Arab Emirates[d]	83,600	0.61	0.42[c]	0.3	9.5	5.0
Yemen (North)	195,000	1.43	6.63	4.5	2.2	34.0
All Other Arab Countries[f]	2,169,119	15.90	6.45	4.4	2.6	3.0
Total	13,624,416	100.00	146.59	100.0	—	10.8

[a]Rate of population growth during 1965–71.

[b]Inhabited and cultivated territory accounts for 35.580 square kilometers. Corresponding population density is 1,078.

[c]Estimates from national and other sources and the I.M.F. Survey, August 1974. The rate of growth is assumed to be half that prevailing in the smaller Gulf states.

[d]Provisional or estimated figures.

[e]Excluding the Spanish Sahara.

[f]Includes Bahrain, Mauritania—excluding the Spanish Sahara—Oman, Somalia, and Yemen (South).

Sources: United Nations, *Monthly Bulletin of Statistics*, December 1974; United Nations, *Statistical Yearbook*, 1973; KFAED, *The Arab World: Key Indicators*, April 1975. Population figures for 1976 were projected using in each case the size of population in 1970 together with the indicated growth rate.

MAJOR CATEGORIES OF U.S. EXPORTS TO THE MIDDLE EAST

Transport Equipment

All railway, road and nonmotor vehicles, aircraft, ships and boats.

Machinery Other than Electric

Steam generating coilers, both electric and nonelectric; steam-house plants; steam engines and steam turbines; aircraft; internal combustion engines, jet and gas turbines for aircraft; nuclear reactors; water turbines and other water engines; agricultural machinery and implements for cultivating, harvesting, and threshing; milk machines; tractors; office machines, including typewriters, check-writing machines, calculators, and accounting machines, statistics machines—cards or tapes, duplicating, addressing machines and parts; metalworking machines including machine tools for working metals, converters, ladles, ingot molds, castings, rolling mills and tools for metalworking; gas-operated appliances for welding, cutting, and so forth; textile and leather machinery including spinning, extruding, weaving, knitting, bleaching, washing, dressing, and sewing machinery; machines for special industries such as paper and paper pulp finishing and processing, printing and bookbinding, type making and setting, food processing machinery; construction and mining machinery including road rollers and leveling, boring, mineral-crushing equipment; heating and cooling machinery including air conditioners, furnace burners, mechanical stokers, including industrial and laboratory furnaces and ovens; refrigerators; pumps and centrifuges for liquids, gases, and filtering; mechanical handling equipment such as for lifting and loading, trucks; domestic appliances including power tools and machine tools for working metals, plastics, and so forth; parts and accessories for machine tools; calendering and similar rolling machines; weighing and spraying machinery; automobile vending machinery; railway and tramway track fixtures and fittings, ball, roller, or needleroller bearings, parts and accessories for machine taps, cocks, valves, shafts, cranks, pulleys, and joints.

Electric Machinery

Apparatus for electric circuits; equipment for distributing electricity such as wire and cable and electric insulating equipment; telecommunications apparatus such as television and radio receivers, lines, microphones, telegraph, loudspeakers, amplifiers; domestic electrical equipment including refrigerators, washing machines, electrical shavers, hair dryers, space heaters, medicinal-purpose electric equipment; radiological apparatus; electromedical apparatus, that is, X-rays; batteries, accumulators, primary batteries and cells; lamps; thermionic valves, tubes, transistors; electric starting and ignition equipment; measuring and controlling instruments; electromechanical hand tools; electron and proton accelerators; electrical machinery and apparatus, that is, electromagnets, furnaces, welding and cutting apparatus, traffic control equipment, sound and visual signalling equipment, electric condensers and electric carbons.

Manufactured Goods by Material

Iron and Steel: Pig iron, spiegeleisen, sponge iron, cast iron, iron and steel powders, shot, sponge, ferro-manganese, other ferro alloys, ingots and other primary forms of iron and steel, puddled bars and pilings, blooms, billets, slabs, and those in low carbon or alloy form, coils, bars, rods, angles, shapes, sections, wires, universals, plates, sheets, heavy and medium forms of these iron and steel materials, as well as uncoated, coated, and tinned plates, hoops and strip, rails and railway construction materials, sleepers and railway track material, tubes, pipes, fittings, seamless, welded, high-pressure, hydro-electric conduits, castings and forgings.

Manufactures of Metals: Finished structural parts and structures of iron and steel, aluminum, zinc; metal containers for storage and transport, that is, tanks, vats, reservoirs, casks, drums, boxes, cans, compressed gas cylinders; wire products, that is, electrical wire, fencing gulls, cables, ropes, blaited bands, gauze, netting, expanded metal; nails, screws, nuts, bolts, rivets, and similar articles, tacks, staples, spicks; hand tools, tools for agriculture and forestry, handsaws and blades, pliers, pincers, spanners, interchangeable parts; cutlery, blades; domestic stoves, boilers, cookers, utensils, locksmith wares, fittings and mountings of base metals, safes, chains, anchors, springs, and so on.

Nonmetallic Mineral Manufactures: Lime, cement, fabricated building material, glass, clay, building and monumental stone, refractory bricks, nonrefractory materials, ceramic blocks, tiles, pipes, grinding and polishing wheels and stones, abrasive cloths and papers, mica, mineral insulating materials, asbestos and other friction materials, articles of ceramic material; glass products, that is, rods, tubes, waste glass, optical glass, drawn or blown, unworked, in rectangles either surface-ground or polished, cast or rolled, bricks, tiles, and other construction materials of glass, safety glass toughened or laminated, sheet or plate glass, mirrors, glassware, glass carboys, bottles, jars, stoppers, tableware for household or hotel, articles made of glass, pottery, porcelain or china household wares, ornaments of ceramics, pearls and precious stones, pearls and diamonds not set or strung.

Textile Yarn, Fabrics, Made-Up Articles, not Included Elsewhere: Silk, wool, lambswool, cotton, synthetics, bleached, dyed, mercerized and nonmercerized, flax, regenerated fibers, wovens, all other fabrics, knits, crochets, linen, ramie, hemp, tulle, lace, embroidery, ribbons, trimmings, felt, elastic, coated or impregnated fabric, glass fiber, jute, special fabrics.

Textile Fibers, not Manufactured and Waste: Synthetic and regenerated fibers suitable for spinning, not carded or combed.

Rubber Manufactures, not Included Elsewhere: Tires and tubes for vehicles and aircraft, hygienic and pharmaceutical articles, transmission, conveyor, and elevator belts.

Food

Cereals and Cereal Preparations: Wheat, rice, barley, maize, rye, oats, in unmilled, flour, and bakery forms.

Oilseeds, Oil Nuts and Oil Kernels: Groundnuts, peanuts, copra, palm-nuts, and kernels, soya beans, linseed, cottonseed, castor-oil-seed, and so forth.

Miscellaneous Manufactures

Scientific and Control Equipment, Photographic Apparatus, Clocks: Spectacles, binoculars, microscopes, refracting telescopes, photographic cameras and flashlight apparatus, cinema, cameras, projectors, sound recorders, image projectors, photographic equipment; medical instruments, such as measuring, controlling, surveying, drawing, and calculating instruments for liquids and chemicals; watches and clocks; and parts for listed items.

Miscellaneous Manufactures, not Included Elsewhere: Musical instruments, sound recorders and parts, printed matter, articles of artificial plastic materials, perambulators, toys, games, sporting goods, office and stationery supplies, works of art, collectors' pieces and antiques.

Tobacco and Tobacco Manufactures: Cigars, cheroots, cigarettes, and unmanufactured tobacco.

Specialized Goods not Classified According to Kind: Armaments and other military equipment.

PERIODICALS

Middle East Economic Digest (MEED)

Middle East Economic Survey (MEES)

Petroleum Intelligence Weekly

Platt's Oilgram

Oil and Gas Journal

Al-Ahram

New York *Times*

London *Times*

Financial Times

BOOKS, PAMPHLETS, REPORTS, AND DOCUMENTS

Abdul-Hakim, M.S., et al. 1966. *The Economic Resources in the Arab World*. 2d ed. Cairo: Dar al-Qalam. (In Arabic.)

Abdul-Rasool, Faiq. 1974. "The Role of Arab Monetary Reserves in Arab Economic Integration." Baghdad: Central Bank of Iraq. (Memo, In Arabic.)

Adler, John H. 1965. *Absorptive Capacity: The Concept and Its Determinants*. Washington, D.C.: The Brookings Institution.

Al-Awadi, Yousef A. 1975. "OPEC Surplus Funds and the Investment Strategy of Kuwait." Ph.D. diss., University of Colorado.

Al-Hamad, A.Y. 1974. *Towards an Arab Financial Market*. Kuwait: KFAED.

———. 1975. *Towards Closer Economic Cooperation in the Middle East*. Kuwait: KFAED.

———. 1972. *Building Up Development-Oriented Institutions in the Arab Countries*. Kuwait: KFAED.

Al-Marayati, Abid A., ed. 1972. *The Middle East: Its Governments and Politics*. Belmont, Calif.: Duxbury Press.

Arodky, Yehia. 1970. *The Arab Common Market*. Damascus: Ministry of Culture Press. (In Arabic.)

Avery, Rosalie. 1973. "Saudi Arabia: A Capabilities Analysis." M.A. thesis, University of
Colorado.

Backman, Jules. 1964. *Chemicals in the National Economy*. Washington, D.C.: Manufacturing Chemist's Association, Inc.

Balassa, Bela. 1965. *Economic Development and Integration*. Mexico: Centro de Estudios
Monetarios Latinoamericanos.

———. 1961. *The Theory of Economic Integration*. Homewood, Ill.: Irwin.

Brown, Lester R. 1972. *The Interdependence of Nations*. Washington, D.C.: Overseas
Development Council.

Bryce, Murray D. 1960. *Industrial Development: A Guide for Accelerating Economic
Growth*. New York: McGraw-Hill.

CACI, Inc.-Federal. 1976. *Medium-Term Ability of Oil Producing Countries to Absorb Real
Goods and Services*. Arlington, Va.: CACI, Inc.-Federal.

Central Bank of Kuwait. 1971–74. *Annual Report*. Kuwait: Al-Assriya Printing Press.

Choucri, Nazli. 1976. *International Politics of Energy Interdependence*. Lexington, Mass.:
D.C. Heath.

Demir, Soliman. 1976. *The Kuwait Fund and the Political Economy of Arab Regional Development*. New York: Praeger.

Diab, Mohammed A. n.d. *Inter-Arab Economic Cooperation, 1951–1960*. Beirut: Economic
Research Institute, American University of Beirut.

El Jehaimi, Taher. 1975. "Absorptive Capacity and Alternative Investment Policies: The
Case of Libya." Ph.D. diss., University of Colorado.

El Mallakh, Ragaei. 1968. *Economic Development and Regional Cooperation: Kuwait*.
Chicago: University of Chicago Press.

———. 1977. "Energy and Economic Upsurge: The Arab States of the Gulf." Forthcoming.

El Mallakh, Ragaei, and McGuire, Carl, eds. 1974. *Energy and Development*. Boulder,
Colorado: The International Research Center for Energy and Economic Development.

El Sheikh, Riad. 1973. *Kuwait: Economic Growth of the Oil State, Problems and Policies*.
Kuwait: Kuwait University.

El-Wady Ramahi, Seif A. 1973. *Economics and Political Evolution in the Arabian Gulf
States*. New York: Carlton Press.

First National City Bank, Foreign Information Service. 1971–75. *Monthly Economic
Report*. New York: FNCB.

Hayes, Denis. 1976. *Nuclear Power: The Fifth Horseman*. Washington, D.C.: Worldwatch Institute.

Hirschman, Albert O. 1958. *The Strategy of Economic Development*. New Haven: Yale University Press.

——. 1945. *National Power and the Structure of Foreign Trade*. Berkeley, Calif.: University of California Press.

International Bank for Reconstruction and Development. 1974. *The World Bank Atlas, 1973*. New York: World Bank.

International Monetary Fund. 1971–75. *International Financial Statistics*. Washington, D.C.: IMF.

Kadhim, Mihssen. 1974. "The Strategy of Development Planning and the Absorptive Capacity of the Economy." Ph.D. diss., University of Colorado.

Kubbah, Abdul Amir. 1974. *OPEC: Past and Present*. Vienna: Petro-Economic Research Center.

Kuwait Fund for Arab Economic Development. 1975. *The Arab World: Key Indicators*. Kuwait: Press Advertising Agency.

Kuwait Planning Board. 1974. *Statistical Yearbook of Kuwait*. Kuwait: The Planning Board.

Lenczowski, George. 1976. *Middle East Oil In A Revolutionary Age*. Washington, D.C.: American Enterprise Institute.

Little, Arthur D., Inc. 1956. *A Plan for Industrial Development of Iraq*. Cambridge, Mass.: Arthur D. Little, Inc.

Little, I.M.D., and Clifford, J.M. 1966. *International Aid: An Introduction to the Problem of the Flow of Public Resources from Rich to Poor Countries*. Chicago, Ill.: Aldine.

Mason, Hal R. et al. 1975. *The Economics of International Business*. New York: Wiley.

Mercier, Claude. 1966. *Petrochemical Industry and the Possibilities of Its Establishment in the Developing Countries*. Paris: Editions Technip.

Mikesell, Raymond F. 1965. *Foreign Investment in Latin America*. Washington, D.C.: I.A.-ECOSOC, Pan American Union.

Mitchell, Hutchins, Inc., 1975. *OPEC Expenditures: Size, Timing, Nature, and Beneficiaries*. New York: Mitchell, Hutchins, Inc.

Mohamad, Fadhil Z. 1956. "Prospects for Arab Federation." Ph.D. diss., University of Colorado.

Morgan Guaranty Trust Company of New York. 1971–74. *World Financial Markets*. New York: MGTC.

Musrey, Alfred G. 1969. *An Arab Common Market: A Study in Inter-Arab Trade Relations, 1920-1967*. New York: Praeger.

Organization for Economic Cooperation and Development. 1974. *Flow of Resources from OPEC Members to Developing Countries*. Paris: OECD.

———. 1975. *Flow of Resources from OPEC Members to Developing Countries, Addendum*. Paris: OECD.

———. 1974. *Development Cooperation, 1974 Review*. Paris: OECD Publications.

Organization of Arab Petroleum Exporting Countries. 1974. *A Report on the Energy Crisis and the Development of Alternatives to Petroleum*. Kuwait: OAPEC. (In Arabic.)

Park, Yoon S. 1976. *Oil, Money and the World Economy*. Boulder, Colorado: Westview Press.

Republic of Iraq, Ministry of Planning. 1970. *The Preliminary Detailed Framework for the National Development Plan, 1970-1974*. Baghdad: Ministry of Planning.

Sadik, Mohammed T., and Snavely, William P. 1972. *Bahrain, Qatar, and the United Arab Emirates*. Lexington, Mass.: D.C. Heath.

Schneider, William. 1976. *Food, Foreign Policy, and Raw Materials Cartels*. New York: Crane, Russak.

Shashahani, Ahmed. 1976. "An Econometric Model of Development for an Oil-Based Economy: The Case of Iran." Ph.D. diss., University of Colorado.

Sherbiny, Naiem A., and Tessler, Mark A., eds. 1976. *Arab Oil: Impact on the Arab Countries and Global Implications*. New York: Praeger.

Stevens, Willy J. 1971. *Capital Absorptive Capacity in Developing Countries*. Leiden: A.W. Sijthaff.

Stockholm International Peace Research Institute. 1974. *Oil and Security*. Stockholm: Almquist & Wicksell International.

Tarbeen, Ahmed. 1959. *Arab Unity between 1916-1945*. Cairo: Al-Kamalia Publishing House. (In Arabic.)

United Nations. 1974. *Monthly Bulletin of Statistics*. New York: United Nations.

———. 1974. *Studies on Development Problems in Countries of Western Asia*. New York: United Nations.

———. 1973. *The Petrochemical Industry*. New York: United Nations.

———. 1973. *Statistical Yearbook, 1973*. New York: United Nations.

———. 1973. *Yearbook of National Accounts Statistics, 1973*. New York: United Nations.

United Nations, Department of Social Affairs. 1953. *The Determinants and Consequences of Population Trends*. New York: United Nations.

United Nations Economic and Social Council. 1975. *Multilateral Institutions for Providing Financial and Technical Assistance to Developing Countries*. New York: United Nations.

United Nations Economic and Social Office in Beirut. 1968. *Studies on Selected Development Problems in Various Countries in the Middle East, 1968*. New York: United Nations.

United Nations Food and Agricultural Organization. 1973. *Production Yearbook, 1973*. Rome: United Nations.

United Nations Industrial Development Organization. 1973. *Summaries of Industrial Development Plans, vol. III*. Vienna: UNIDO.

U.S. Department of Commerce, Milton A. Berger and George R. Kruer. May 3, 1976. Statement before the Subcommittee on Foreign Commerce and Tourism of the Senate Committee on Commerce, *Study of Foreign Direct Investment in the United States*. Washington, D.C.: Government Printing Office.

U.S. Department of Commerce. 1971–75. *Survey of Current Business*. Washington, D.C.: Government Printing Office.

U.S. Department of State. April 1976. *Foreign Economic Trends and Their Implications for the United States, IRAQ*. Washington, D.C.: Government Printing Office.

——. July 1975. *Toward a Strategy of Interdependence*. Washington, D.C.: Government Printing Office.

——. May 14, 1976. "American Business in the Middle East and North Africa." Washington, D.C.: Department of State.

U.S. Department of the Treasury. May 3, 1976. Statement of Gerald L. Parsky, Assistant Secretary of the Treasury, before the Subcommittee on Foreign Commerce and Tourism, Senate Committee on Commerce, *Study of Foreign Portfolio Investment in the United States*. Washington, D.C.: Government Printing Office.

U.S. Frederal Energy Administration. 1976. *National Energy Outlook*. Washington, D.C.: Government Printing Office.

Vakil, Firouz. 1974. *A Macro-Econometric Projection for Iran, 1973–1992*. Tehran, Iran: Plan and Budget Organization.

Vicker, Ray. 1974. *The Kingdom of Oil: The Middle East, Its People and Its Power*. New York: Scribners.

ARTICLES

Abdelhakim, S. 1975. "Population Trends in the Arab World." *Journal of the Middle East* 2. (In Arabic.)

Amuzegar, Jahangir. 1974. "Ideology and Economic Growth in the Middle East." *Middle East Journal* 28 (Winter).

Ayoub, Antoine. 1975. "Demand for Capital of the Non-Oil Producing Arab Countries and the Constraints of Supply." Paper presented to the Second International Conference on: Energy, Surplus Funds, and Absorptive Capacity, The International Research Center for Energy and Economic Development and the University of Colorado, November 6–7.

Badre, Albert Y. 1972. "Economic Development of Iraq." in *Economic Development and Population Growth in the Middle East*, ed. Charles A. Cooper and Sidney S. Alexander pp. 282-328. New York: American Elsevier Publishing Co., Inc.

Balbaa, A.E. 1975. "An Outline of Soil, Water and Agriculture in the Arab Countries." *Journal of the Middle East* 2.

Calvo, Guillermo, and Findlay, Ronald. 1976. "On the Optimal Acquisition of Foreign Capital through Investment of Oil Exports Revenues." Discussion paper 75–7623, Department of Economics, Columbia University.

Chenery, Hollis B. 1975. "Restructuring the World Economy." *Foreign Affairs* 53 (January).

Davis, Lance E. 1965. "The Investment Market, 1870–1914: The Evolution of a National Market." *Journal of Economic History* 15 (September 1965).

El Mallakh, Ragaei. 1976. "Oil Stockpiling: The False Hope." New York *Times*, March 27, p. 24c.

El Mallakh, Ragaei, and Mihssen Kadhim. 1976. "Arab Institutionalized Development Aid: An Evaluation." *Middle East Journal* 30 (Autumn).

———. 1977. "Capital Surpluses and Deficits in the Arab Middle East: A Regional Perspective." *International Journal of Middle East Studies* 8 (April).

———. 1977. "Absorptive Capacity, Surplus Funds, and Regional Capital Mobility in the Middle East." *Rivista Internazionale Di Scienze Economiche E Commerciali*. Forthcoming.

Ezzati, Ali. 1976. "Analysis of World Equilibrium Prices, Supply, Demand, Imports, and Exports of Crude Oil and Petroleum Products." *Journal of Energy and Development* 1 (Spring).

———. 1976. "Future OPEC Price and Production Strategies as Affected by Its capacity to Absorb Oil Revenues." *European Economic Review* 8 (August).

Fliakos, Constantine, and Lewison, Ronald D. 1975. "Prospects for International Oil Supply and Demand: 1975, 1980, 1985." *Journal of Energy and Development* 1 (Autumn).

Gebelein, Christopher A. 1975. "Effects of Conservation on Oil Prices: Analysis of Misconceptions." *Journal of Energy and Development* 1 (Autumn).

———. 1975. "Forecasting Absorptive Capacity for Oil Revenues: Practical Techniques for Policy Analysis." Paper presented at the Annual Meeting of the Western Economic Association, San Diego, California, June 25–28.

Gunning, J.S.; Osterrieth, M.; and Waelbroeck, J. 1976. "The Price of Energy and Potential Growth of Developed Countries." *European Economic Review* 7.

Hill, Peter. 1976. "Middle East Industrial Development Rests on Iron and Steel." *Middle East Economic Digest* (March 19).

Horvat, Branko. 1958. "The Optimum Rate of Investment." *Economic Journal* 68 (December).

Johns, Richard. 1974. "Arab Unity and Cooperation." *Financial Times*. November 21, p. 34.

Kadhim, Mihssen. 1976. "The 1964 Nationalization of Private Industry in Iraq." *American Journal of Arabic Studies* 4.

Kadhim, Mihssen, and Poulson, Barry. 1976. "Absorptive Capacity, Regional Cooperation and Industrialization in the Arab States of the Gulf." *Journal of Energy and Development* 2 (Spring).

Kadhim, Mihssen, and Leasure, William J. 1977. "An Econometric Analysis of the Theory of Demographic Transition: The Case of Iraq." *Journal of the Middle East* 4, forthcoming.

Kindleberger, Charles P. 1951. "European Economic Integration." in *Money, Trade, and Economic Growth*, ed. John Henry Williams. New York: Macmillan.

Lebanon, Alexander. 1975. "An Oligopolistic Model of the World Supply of Crude Petroleum." *Applied Economics* 7.

Lee, Dwight. 1976. "Pricing of Oil and the Immediacy of the Future." *Journal of Energy and Development* 1 (Spring).

Littell, Robert. 1963. "Our Best Investment in the Arab World." *Reader's Digest* (February), pp. 1–5.

Middle East Economic Digest. 1971. "Agriculture in the Middle East: A Special Report." *Middle East Economic Digest*, June 25.

Nashashibi, Hikmat. 1976. "The Domestication of Arab Financial Reserves: Its Necessity and Means." *Oil and Arab Cooperation* 2 (Winter). (In Arabic.)

Penrose, Edith. 1975. "International Oil Companies and Governments in the Middle East." in *The Middle East: Oil, Politics and Development*, ed. John D. Anthony. Washington, D.C.: American Enterprise Institute.

Ramazani, Rouhollah R. 1976. "Iran's Search for Regional Cooperation." *The Middle East Journal* 2 (Spring).

Schmalensee, Richard. 1976. "Resource Exploitation Theory and the Behavior of the Oil Cartel." *European Economic Review* 7.

Shashahani, Ahmed. 1976. "An Econometric Model Forecast of Iran, 1975–1985." *Journal of Energy and Development* 2 (Autumn).

Stobauch, Robert B. 1974. "The Economics of Energy vs. Non-Energy Uses of Petroleum: The Case of Petrochemicals." Paper presented to the Seminar on Administration of the Oil Resources of Arab Countries, Tripoli, Libya, April.

RAGAEI EL MALLAKH, Professor of Economics at the University of Colorado, is the Executive Director of the International Research Center for Energy and Economic Development (ICEED) at that institution and is editor of the *Journal of Energy and Development*. He is the author of or contributor to some 12 books including *Economic Development and Regional Cooperation: Kuwait* and *Energy and Development*, and his publications have appeared in the *American Economic Review, Journal of Economic Literature, Land Economics, International Development Review, Kyklos, Middle East Journal, International Journal of Middle Eastern Studies*, New York *Times*, and *Christian Science Monitor*. Dr. El Mallakh has been consultant to or a member of the World Bank, the Federal Power Commission, and the U.S. National Committee on World Petroleum Congresses. He has received research grants and fellowships from the Rockefeller Foundation, Ford Foundation, Social Science Research Council, and was the project director of the National Science Foundation study, "Implications of Regional Development in the Middle East for U.S. Trade, Capital Flows, and Balance of Payments."

MIHSSEN KADHIM holds a Ph.D. from the University of Colorado and is a Post-doctoral Fellow at the ICEED where he has been teaching and conducting research on energy and Middle East development for the past three years. Dr. Kadhim's scholarly writings have appeared in such publications as the *Middle East Journal, Journal of Energy and Development*, and the *International Journal of Middle Eastern Studies*.

BARRY W. POULSON received a B.A. from Ohio Wesleyan University, M.A. and Ph.D. degrees from Ohio State University, and is Professor of Economics at the University of Colorado. His past appointments include a Fulbright Professorship to the Universidad Autonoma de Guadalajara, economic consultant to the National Bureau of Standards of the U.S. Department of Commerce, and consultancies with Shell Oil Corporation and World Book Encyclopedia. In the past year he was co-investigator for the National Science Foundation research project "Implications of Regional Development in the Middle East for U.S. Trade, Capital Flows, and Balance of Payments." Professor Poulson is also a Director of the ICEED. His recent publications include *Absorptive Capacity in Iraq* (co-author, 1975) and "Energy, Absorptive Capacity and Patterns of Growth" (co-author), *Journal of Energy and Development* (spring 1976).

ARAB OIL: Impact on Arab Countries and Global Implications
edited by Naiem A. Sherbiny
Mark A. Tessler

DEVELOPMENT OF THE IRANIAN OIL INDUSTRY: International and Domestic Aspects
Fereidun Fesharaki

A DEVELOPMENT STRATEGY FOR IRAN THROUGH THE 1980s
Robert E. Looney

THE KUWAIT FUND AND THE POLITICAL ECONOMY OF ARAB REGIONAL DEVELOPMENT
Soliman Demir

MIDDLE EAST ECONOMIES IN THE 1970s: A Comparative Approach
Hossein Askari
John Thomas Cummings

OPEC AND THE MIDDLE EAST: The Impact of Oil on Societal Development
edited by Russell A. Stone